c.l. chernecky

The gospel of Jesus

THE GOSPEL OF JESUS has been published in the following languages:

English
Italian
Portuguese
Spanish
Czech
Malagasy

The gospel of Jesus

EDIZIONI **ISG** ISTITUTO S. GAETANO

STRADA MORA · TELEFONO 31912 · C.C.P. 28/6534 · 36100 VICENZA

226
G 26

Edizioni: Istituto S. Gaetano - Strada Mora, 12
36100 VICENZA (Italy) - Tel. 31912/22094

Original title: IL VANGELO DI GESU'.
Copyright © 1969 by MIMEP Pessano (Milano) Italy.
Introductory and explanatory notes by Paolo Acquistapace,
Angelo Albani and Massimo Astrua under the direction
of Mgr. Enrico Galbiati, and translated by Kent White M.A.
English edition © copyright 1970 by M.I.M.E.P., Pessano.
The Bible text in this publication is from the
Revised Standard Version of the Bible - Catholic Edition,
copyrighted © 1965 and 1966 by the
Division of Christian Education of the National Council
of the Churches of Christ in the U.S.A. and used by permission.
Nihil obstat: R.C. Fuller D.D. Ph. D. L.S.S.
Imprimatur: † Charles Grant, Bishop of Northampton.
Printed in Italy by Scuola Grafica, Istituto San Gaetano, Vicenza.
SBN 85439 0367.

THE GOSPEL OF JESUS

Preface to the Italian Edition

When, forty years ago, as a child of ten I began to feel the first awakening of what was to become my vocation as a biblical scholar, I was greatly helped by a little book by Fr Marco Sales, a sort of Life of Jesus made up entirely of connected passages taken from the four gospels and conveniently arranged without paraphrasing or conflating the text. I am still grateful to Fr Sales for having by this method familiarized me with the actual words of the gospels, inspired words which have a special quality of their own brooking no change or addition, and also for having made it easy for me to follow the unfolding of the story of Jesus with eager interest.

Therefore I am delighted to introduce this volume which can rightly be called the **Gospel of Jesus** since, on my advice, those who enthusiastically planned and laboriously compiled it followed the method of Fr Sales.

It has an extremely practical aim, the encouraging of the young, the very young, and indeed everybody to read the four gospels for themselves. They are not easy to read as we know by experience: books of the gospels are widely distributed among Christian families, but they are not read. This book does not take their place, but it provides the necessary background for reading them with profit.

The unified text of the gospels is not a Harmony for it avoids the mingling of phrases belonging to different gospels. As a rule each episode is described in the words of a single evangelist. It is only when some rather complex event is being described that the story is broken up so as to include the greatest wealth of detail from parallel accounts. We say 'broken up' rather than conflated and in each case the reference to the gospel from which a section is taken is made clear. The 'Synopsis' of Lagrange which shows all the variations of the gospels is the basis of this work also. But its compilers have not tried to serve the purpose of a Synopsis by quoting in the text words that vary in parallel passages; that would increase the value of the book but also the labour of reading it, which is very far from the end in view.

What is original about this book — and I believe this is most use-ful — is the illustrative method, particularly in the use of diagrams and geographical sketches. The numerous photographs are intended not only to make the book attractive and therefore interesting, but also, and principally, to give the reader a constantly renewed feeling of being faced with concrete reality, rooted in history and accurately sited. The work of our salvation is not only a doctrine; it is also a historical reality.

Mgr ENRICO GALBIATI
Doctor in Biblical Sciences

CONTENTS

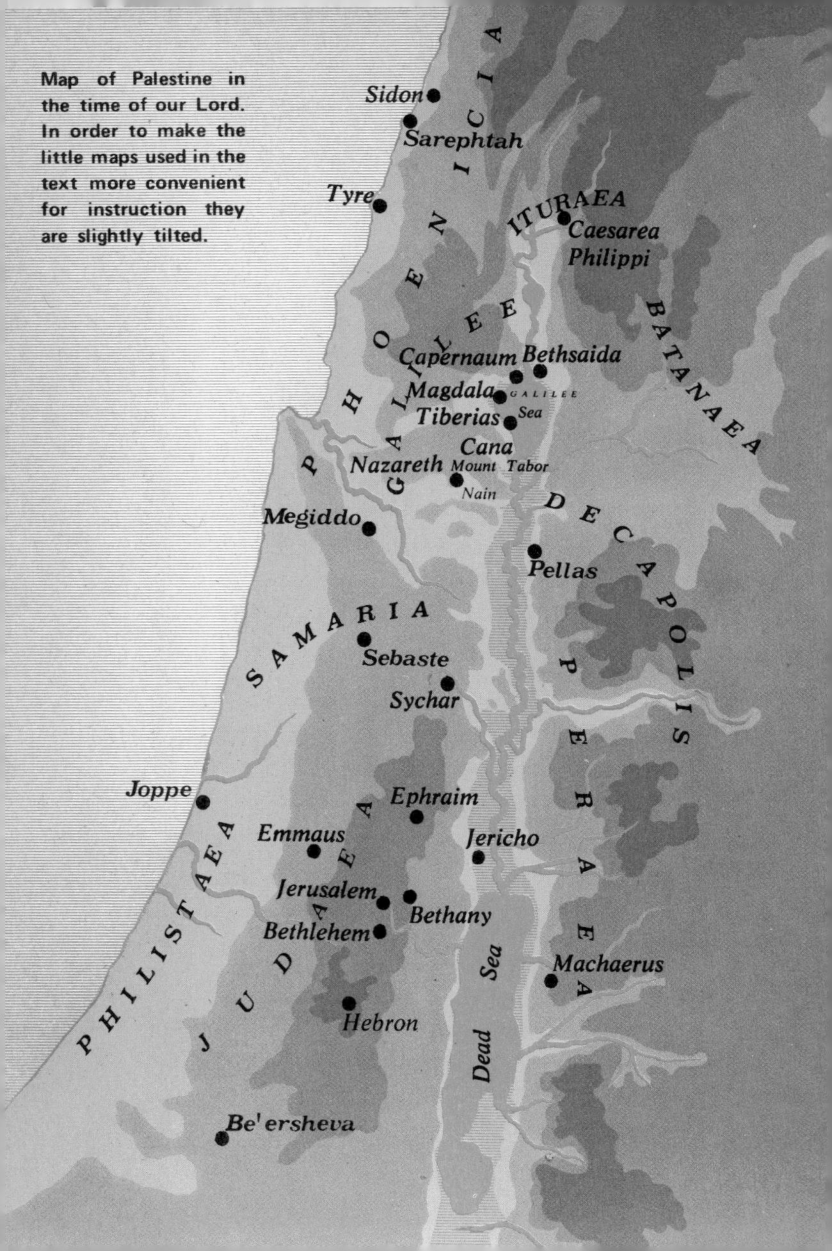

Map of Palestine in the time of our Lord. In order to make the little maps used in the text more convenient for instruction they are slightly tilted.

Sidon

Sarephtah

Tyre

PHOENICIA

ITURAEA

Caesarea Philippi

BATANAEA

GALILEE

Capernaum   Bethsaida

Magdala   GALILEE

Tiberias   Sea

Cana

Nazareth   Mount Tabor

Nain

DECAPOLIS

Megiddo

Pellas

SAMARIA

Sebaste

Sychar

P E R A E A

Joppe

Ephraim

Emmaus

Jericho

Jerusalem

Bethany

Bethlehem

Machaerus

Hebron

Dead Sea

PHILISTAEA

J U D A E A

Be'ersheva

GEOGRAPHICAL
AND HISTORICAL INTRODUCTION

I – Geography of Palestine in the time of our Lord

The ancient Orient (which we now call the Middle East) is the region in which the great events of the Bible took place. Its heart is Palestine, the land promised by God to the Hebrew people: it was here that Jesus lived.

Palestine (here shown in tilted perspective) is washed on the west by the Mediterranean Sea, and is divided throughout its length by the river Jordan, which after flowing through the Lake of Gennesaret (also called the Sea of Galilee) follows a winding course to the Dead Sea into which it empties itself. The Dead Sea has no outlet but its level is kept low by evaporation. For this reason its waters are very salty and have no fish. The Lake of Gennesaret on the other hand is full of fish.

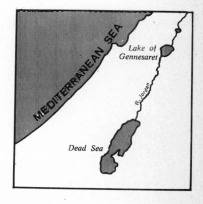

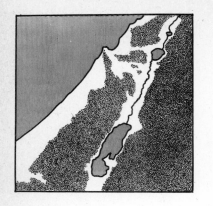

Palestine is a largely mountainous country: in the map the shaded part shows the mountainous region divided throughout its length by the deep valley of the Jordan.

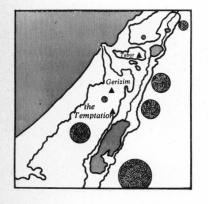

In this map the shaded circles represent districts where the mountains rise to more than 1000 metres, and the black triangles indicate certain mountains which are traditional sites of Gospel events: Mount Tabor, Mount Gerizim and the Mount of the Temptation.

The coastal strip is nearly all lowland, but the long valley of the Jordan which lies between two mountainous regions is very deep and entirely below sea-level. The Lake of Gennesaret is 212 metres below the level of the Mediterranean, and the Dead Sea no less than 392 metres.

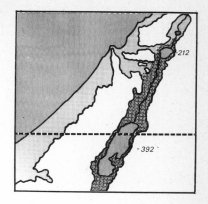

Here is a section of Palestine at the latitude of the Dead Sea, along the line marked on the last map. On the left is the Mediterranean (1), next the coastal plain (2), then the western mountain massif (3), the depression of the Dead Sea (4) and finally the eastern massif (5).

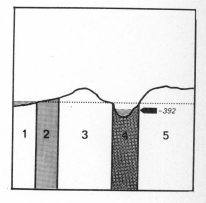

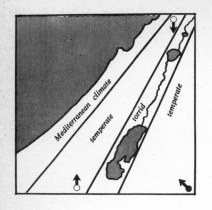

Palestine, being sub-tropical, has for all practical purposes only two seasons, the wet winter (beginning in November) and the dry summer (beginning in May.)

The temperature varies not only with the seasons but also with the altitude; the coastal plain has a Mediterranean climate, the Jordan valley a torrid one, but the two plateaux are temperate and rarely show a temperature below zero.

The favourable winds in the winter are from the south (bringing rain) and in the summer from the north (bringing coolness). Agriculture suffers from the dry wind blowing from the south-east (scirocco) at the beginning of both seasons.

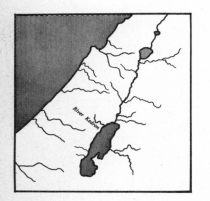

From the two mountain blocks many rivers and streams flow down to the Mediterranean or the Jordan. Among them is the brook Kedron which rises to the east of Jerusalem and will be remembered in the Gospel story of the passion of Jesus.

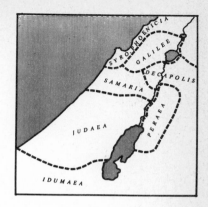

In the time of Jesus Palestine was divided into provinces, Judaea, Samaria and Galilee to the west of the Jordan (Cisjordania) and Peraea and Decapolis to the east (Transjordania).

These are the principal towns mentioned in the Gospel story:
In Judaea: Jerusalem (the holy city), Bethlehem (where Jesus was born), Ain Karim, Emmaus, Arimathaea, Ephraim, Jericho, Bethany (the home of Lazarus, Martha and Mary).
In Samaria: Samaria and Sychar.
In Galilee: Nazareth (the home of our Lady and of Jesus as a child), Cana (where Jesus wrought his first miracle), Tiberias, Magdala and Capernaum (the home of St. Peter).

Jerusalem was the Holy City **par excellence** and the Arabs still use the expression. Ancient Israel was a theocratic people, whose true Sovereign, not only in religion but also in politics, was God himself. Jerusalem, the capital, had within its walls the Temple in which God desired his mysterious presence to be honoured in the midst of his people. Because of this Jerusalem had a fundamental importance in the story of Jesus. It ought to have been the capital of the Messiah; by it Jesus ought to have been officially recognized as Messiah and Son of God. But Jerusalem was at least the first centre from which Christianity spread.

The town lies on two hills in a mountainous district about 750 metres above sea level.

Jerusalem is a very old city. It was inhabited in prehistoric times, and captured by King David in about 1000 B.C. Then it occupied only the eastern hill, on the lower slopes to the south of the great esplanade on which the Temple of Solomon was built later. In the course of centuries it spread to the west and the north, and was many times destroyed and rebuilt. In this aerial photograph the actual walls of the old city are outlined in white. Constructed

by the Turks in 1534 they correspond to the rempart of the Roman city, Aelia Capitolina (built after the Jewish revolt of 135 A.D.), and also on the northern sector to the walls built by Herod Agrippa (42 - 44 A.D.). The old city belonged to the Arab kingdom of Jordan until the war of 1967, but was then united to the rest of the city on the southern part of the western hill where stands the House of the Upper Room (now outside the walls) and incorporated in the state of Israel.

In the time of Jesus the walls of Jerusalem were further to the south, encircling the city along the line of the valley of the Kedron on the east and of the valley called Gehenna on the south. But to the north of the western hill the district now occupied by the Basilica of the Holy Sepulchre (or Calvary) was then outside the walls. Herod the Great, who died after the birth of Jesus, fortified these walls, embellished the city with great buildings among which his palace on the western hill was pre-eminent, and enlarged the Temple courts around which he built splendid colonnades. All these works were destroyed in 70 A.D. by the Roman general Titus, who later became emperor.

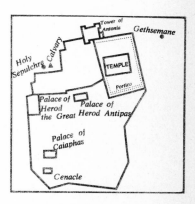

This sketch shows the plan of the walls of Jerusalem which is to be used in the text of the Gospel.

The Temple area at Jerusalem seen from the west, with the Mount of Olives in the background

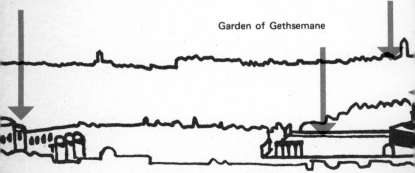

The Dome of the Rock which occupies the area of Solomon's Temple.

Site of the Tower of Antonia at the north-west corner of the esplanade.

Site of our Lord's Ascension into heaven.

Garden of Gethsemane

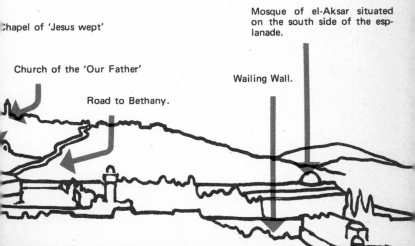

Chapel of 'Jesus wept'

Church of the 'Our Father'

Road to Bethany.

Mosque of el-Aksar situated on the south side of the esplanade.

Wailing Wall.

II – The Political and Religious Situation

When Jesus was born at Bethlehem in the year 747 from the foundation of Rome, Caesar Octavianus Augustus was Emperor of the Romans.

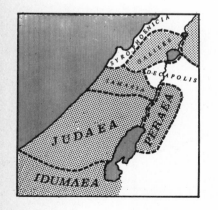

In the same year Palestine was governed by Herod, called the Great, who had been granted by the Roman senate the title King of the Jews. He was an ambitious and cruel man, but succeeded in gaining both the confidence of the Emperors and the respect of the Jews. He restored and enlarged the Temple at Jerusalem; and it was he who decreed the slaughter of the Innocents in the hope of destroying the baby Jesus.

On the death of Herod the Great (in the Roman year 750 when Jesus was three years old) the kingdom was divided between his three sons. As ruler of Judaea, Samaria and Idumea he was succeeded, with the title Ethnarch, by his son Archelaus, who was soon denounced for his cruelties to Augustus who deposed him and exiled him to Gaul (759). His ethnarchate then passed under the direct administration of Rome which governed it through Procurators. The fifth of these was Pontius Pilate who held office for ten years from 779 to 789 (26-36 A.D.).

It was he who, at the instigation of the Jewish religious leaders, had Jesus put to death.

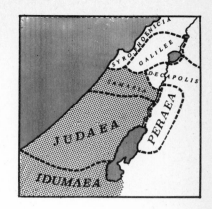

To the second son of Herod the Great, Herod Antipas, fell — with the title of Ethnarch — the government of Galilee and Peraea. It was he who had John the Baptist imprisoned and beheaded, and it was to him that Jesus was sent during his Passion.

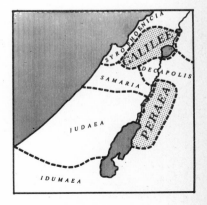

21

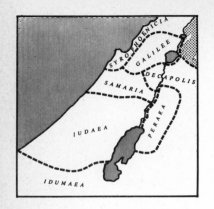

To the third son of Herod the Great, Philip, fell the government of the region to the north of the Lake of Gennesaret (Ituraea, Trachonitis, etc.) which he ruled wisely. He is mentioned in St. Luke's Gospel only.

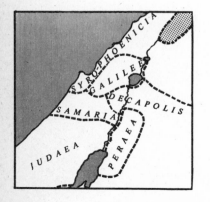

The Gospel of St. Luke (chap. 3) records that in the fifteenth year of Tiberius a certain Lysanias was tetrarch of Abilene, which had as its capital Abila, to the northwest of Damascus. An inscription of this Lysanias has been discovered. In 37 A.D. this district was allotted to Herod Agrippa I, the grandson of Herod the Great.

In 767, when Jesus was twenty years old, Augustus died and was succeeded by Tiberius. It was during his reign which lasted until 789 that Jesus suffered the death penalty, Pontius Pilate being, as we have seen, Procurator of Judaea.

In the time of Jesus two principal religious movements flourished, those of the Pharisees and Sadducees. The Pharisees accepted, in addition to the written Law given by God to Moses, the oral Law passed on by word of mouth and including many detailed precepts about exterior observances. Jesus often inveighed against their superficiality and concern with unimportant details. Among the chief of them were the Scribes (or teachers of the Law), laymen learned in the laws and traditions and very often in the Gospel associated with the Pharisees.

The Sadducees, on the other hand, did not accept any oral tradition and of the written Law they kept only the Pentateuch which, they said, allowed them to go so far as to deny the resurrection of the dead. The Sadducees were really a political party made up of the aristocracy and the priesthood.

The Romans, Herod the Great and his sons permitted these movements, but were always primarily concerned to respect the religious organisation of the Jewish people. That gave first place to the Temple and the Priesthood. The Temple of Jerusalem was the only place where the offering of sacrifice to God was permitted. It was built at God's command by Solomon in the tenth century B.C., destroyed by Nebuchadnezzar in the sixth century B.C., and rebuilt fifty years afterwards by Zerubbabel. It reached the peak of its magnificence with the works of Herod the Great inaugurated four years before Jesus was born. Its embellishment was not completed until 64 A.D., but a few years later in 70 it was razed to the ground by the armies of Titus.

The Temple of Herod was erected on a wide level space to the north-east of Jerusalem and was reached by underground stairways. Great porticoes surrounded it on all four. The south-east corner, overlooking the valley of the Kedron, was known as the Pinnacle of the Temple.

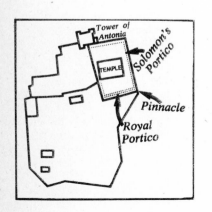

In the middle of the level space a great rectangular balustrade prevented (on pain of death) access by pagans into the Temple area. The space between the porticoes and the balustrade was called the Court of the Gentiles and was always cluttered up with the stalls of the sellers of doves, kids, and of the money-changers.

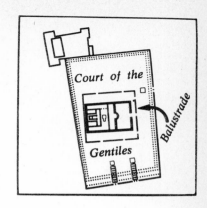

Beyond the balustrade was the imposing edifice of the Temple with the courts of women, of men and of priests, in which was set the altar of burnt offering. In the centre was the Sanctuary of the Temple, divided into two parts; the Holy Place (in which were the golden altar of incense, the table of the shew-bread and the seven-branched golden candlestick) and, shut off by a heavy curtain, the Holy of Holies (which at the time of Solomon had housed the Ark of the Covenant with the Tables of the Law) into which the High Priest alone entered once a year.

The Jewish Priesthood, to which members of the tribe of Levi only were admitted, had at its head the High Priest. The High Priests in Jesus' life time were Annas (Ananias) who reigned from 6 to 15 A.D. and continued to exercize great authority afterwards, then his five sons, unnamed in the Gospel, and finally his son-in-law, Caiaphas (18—36 A.D.), under whom Jesus was crucified.

High Priest

The High Priest was assisted in his office by Priests and Levites. The Priests who officiated in the Temple were divided into 24 courses or sections which took weekly turns in liturgical duties. The Levites for their part were allotted to humbler offices.
Note that though the Jerusalem Temple was the only place in which it was lawful to offer sacrifices to God, the Samaritans, for racial and historical reasons, had set up another temple, in opposition to the Jerusalem one, on Mount Gerizim, and there they offered their own sacrifices to God; their temple had already been reduced to ruins by the time of Jesus.

Jewish Priest

Under the High Priest the supreme authority in Judaism was exercized by the Sanhedrim. This was the assembly of the leaders of the Jews under the presidency of the reigning High Priest and was made up of 71 members divided into three groups: (a) the Chief Priests, i.e. the High Priests no longer in office and the heads of the priestly families, (b) the Elders of the People, i.e. laymen belonging to the aristocratic families. These two groups tended to be Sadducees. (c) The Scribes, or Doctors of the Law, who, as we have already said, were likely to be Pharisees. The Sanhedrim had very wide judicial and executive powers in both religious and civil affairs, to which the Romans set a limit in only a few matters as, for example, in the power of imposing the death penalty in Judaea.

In every town or village of any importance the religious life of the Jews was centred in the Synagogue, which was normally a rectangular building, with a cupboard in which were kept the scrolls of the Bible, and a pulpit from which they were read and expounded to the faithful. The reading and the common prayers were supervised by the Ruler of the Synagogue. The sermon might be given by a member of the congregation.

Synagogue at Capernaum

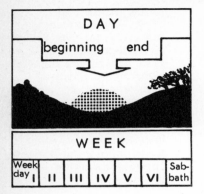

The day was considered to begin in the evening and to end at sunset. So the sabbath rest had to start on Friday evening which was called the Preparation (Greek paraskeue). The other days of the week were known by their numbers, e.g. the 'first day of the week' was that which we call the Lord's Day in honour of Christ's resurrection.

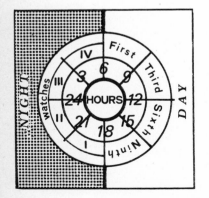

The hours between sunrise and sunset were twelve, of variable length according to the season. As a rule reference was made to the four principal hours: the first (6 a.m.), third (9), sixth (noon), and ninth (3 p.m.), the two following hours being included in each case. The night was divided into four watches (this word refers to the sentries' turn of duty) each of 3 hours.

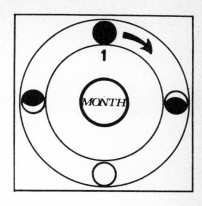

The month was calculated from the observation of the phases of the moon and contained 29 or 30 days beginning from the new moon (neomenia).

The year was made up of twelve lunar months, but every two or three years a thirteenth month was added, so as to re-establish agreement with the cycle of seasons (i.e. the solar year). That was necessary because the festivals, though fixed according to the lunar months, were also connected with the agricultural seasons. The names of the months used by the Jews after the exile in Babylon (sixth century B.C.) were of Babylonish origin. I Nisan (March—April) II Iyyar, III Sivan, IV Tamuz, V Ab, VI Elul, VII Tishri, VIII Marheshvan, IX Chislev, X Tebet, XI Shebat, XII Adar, XIII Ve-Adar.

I Nisan	March-April
II Iyyar	April-May
III Sivan	May-June
IV Tamuz	June-July
V Ab	July-August
VI Elul	August-September
VII Tishri	September-October
VIII Marheshvan	October-November
IX Chislev	November-December
X Tebet	December-January
XI Shebat	January-February
XII Adar	February-March
XIII Ve-Adar	

The Festivals were seven, of which the chief are mentioned in the Gospel.

The Passover was the first of the seven days of Unleavened Bread, from 15 to 22 Nisan (that is from the full moon in the first month); it commemorated the exodus of Israel from Egypt. On the night between 14 and 15 Nisan the paschal lamb was eaten, and on the 16th the offering of the first sheaf of barley, with which the harvest began, was made.

Seven weeks after this came Pentecost, in fact on the fiftieth day (generally 6 Sivan), on which were offered the first loaves of bread made from the corn of the new harvest. This day, called also the 'Feast of Weeks', was considered in some Jewish circles to commemorate the proclamation of the Law on Mount Sinai.

The third great festival was that of Tabernacles (or Booths) six months after the Passover, from 15 – 21 Tishri (September – October); the 22nd, called the 'last day of the Feast' (see John 7,37) was kept with special solemnity. This feast, originally called 'of the Harvest', later served as a memorial of Israel's sojourn in the desert, in tents, on the long journey to the Promised Land; so, during the eight days of the Feast, people were required to live in improvised booths of branches of trees.

The Gospel also mentions the Feast of the Dedication (Hanukka, or Feast of Lights) of the Temple (25 Chislev, November–December), which lasted eight days and had been instituted by Judas Maccabaeus in 164 B.C. to commemorate the reconsecration of the Temple after its profanation by Antiochus Epiphanes, about which we read in the first Book of Maccabees. The penitential feast of the Atonement on 10 Tishri, the only day on which the High Priest entered the Holy of Holies, is spoken of in the Epistle to the Hebrews. The other Feasts were the Civil New Year or 'Feast of Trumpets', on 1 Tishri, and the Feast of Purim (that is of Lots) on 14 and 15 Adar (February – March) to commemorate the Jews' escape from massacre in the reign of Ahasuerus (Xerxes), narrated in the Book of Esther.

The Feasts, culminating in their 'last day', and all Sabbaths in the year required the most rigorous abstention from all work and travelling.

Before the Christian era years were generally reckoned from the foundation of the city of Rome, or from the election of the Emperor. ®

With the establishment of Christianity they began to be reckoned from the birth of Christ.

An error in calculation by Dionysius the Younger (who in the sixth century introduced the present method of dating) made the birth of Christ coincide with the Roman year 754, whereas, further studies have since ascertained that Jesus was actually born in 747 or 748, that is six or seven years earlier than Dionysius supposed.

From this results the curious fact that the Christian calendar which we now use, instead of starting from the birth of Christ, actually started 6 or 7 years after it. This explains why to-day the date of the birth of Jesus is reckoned to be 6 or 7 B.C.

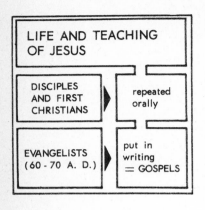

LIFE AND TEACHING
OF JESUS

DISCIPLES
AND FIRST
CHRISTIANS
▶ repeated
orally

EVANGELISTS
(60 - 70 A. D.)
▶ put in
writing
= GOSPELS

The facts of the life of Jesus, the sayings which he uttered on specific occasions and the discourses which the disciples had heard and learnt from their Master, were kept for several decades in the form of oral teaching, continually repeated and variously arranged in accordance with the needs of the first generation of Christians. No doubt some collections of this material were written down much earlier than the Gospels, but such writings, of which St. Luke and possibly another evangelist made use, have not come down to us. Between 60 and 70 A.D. all this material, both written and oral, was put together and set down in writing by three different authors, in different places and with different ends in view.

Beginning of the Gospel of St. Matthew in the Vatican Codex (Fourth Century).

St. Matthew, the apostle who had been a tax-gatherer, brought out his Gospel in Hebrew or more probably Aramaic (the language spoken at that time by the Jews in Palestine) for the Christian community of Jewish origin.

St. Mark, a disciple of St. Peter, wrote his Gospel at Rome and in Greek, bearing in mind the needs of Christians who had come from Paganism.

Beginning of the Gospel of St. Mark in the Vatican Codex (Fourth Century).

St. Luke, the disciple of St. Paul, took much from the Gospel of St. Mark, but sought out all the sources available to him, and fashioned a gospel which approaches more nearly than the others to a biography of Jesus. It was intended for Christians already familiar with the gospel teaching. He also wrote in Greek, in Greece or perhaps also in Rome, whither he followed St. Paul who was a prisoner there from 61 to 63.

Beginning of the Gospel of St. Luke in the Vatican Codex (Fourth Century).

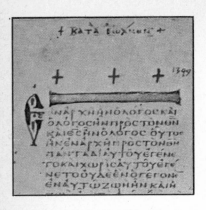

Beginning of the Gospel of St. John in the Vatican Codex (Fourth Century).

St. John wrote his Gospel in Greek at Ephesus about the year 100. He was the youngest of the apostles and, surviving till old age, wrote down, not the traditional instruction contained in the first three gospels, but his own personal teaching, repeated through long years in Asia Minor. But there are often found in this book details of chronology and of events which are of inestimable help in reconstructing the journeyings of Jesus.

The present work can rightly be called the 'Gospel of Jesus' for it takes all and only the material of the four gospels, co-ordinating it without repetition according to the real — or sometimes only the probable — sequence of events and discourses. It is no substitute for the reading of the four separate gospels, from which alone it is possible to perceive the purpose and the original plan of each evangelist, but it is hoped that it will be an easy preparation for such a reading.

Other books appeared later, claiming to complete or to rival the Gospel, but the Church did not recognize them and they are called 'apocryphal'. The word Gospel (Greek evangelion, good news) did not originally mean a book but a joyful proclamation of the salvation brought by Jesus and preached by the apostles. For this reason it is traditional to speak, not of the Gospels in the plural, but of one single Gospel, afterwards set down in writing from different points of view, that is, 'according to' Matthew, 'according to' Mark, etc.

The Gospels often refer to phrases in the Old Testament. The notes in this volume almost always quote the reference to these phrases (e.g. on page 175 there is a reference to Exodus 20,12). It is therefore necessary for readers to have a precise, even if elementary, idea of the 'Bible' and the books of which it is composed. In fact the Bible, or Holy Scripture, is not a single book, but a collection of various books written under divine inspiration and containing God's message to mankind. Some of these books had been written before the coming of Jesus, and others were written afterwards. The former make up the Old Testament and the latter the New Testament.

The books of the Old Testament are:

THE PENTATEUCH or THE LAW: Genesis, Exodus, Leviticus, Numbers, Deuteronomy.

HISTORICAL BOOKS: Joshua, Judges, Ruth, Samuel, Kings, Chronicles, Ezra, Nehemiah, Tobit, Judith, Esther, Maccabees.

WISDOM or INSTRUCTIONAL BOOKS: Job, Psalms, Proverbs, Ecclesiastes, Song of Songs, Wisdom, Ecclesiasticus.

PROPHETICAL BOOKS: The four major prophets: Isaiah, Jeremiah (with Lamentations and Baruch), Ezekiel, Daniel. The twelve minor prophets: Hosea, Joel, Amos, Obadiah, Jonah, Micah, Nahum, Habakkuk, Zephaniah, Haggai, Zechariah, Malachi.

The books of the New Testament are:

HISTORICAL BOOKS: The four Gospels and the Acts of the Apostles.

INSTRUCTIONAL BOOKS: The fourteen letters of St. Paul: Romans, I & II Corinthians, Galatians, Ephesians, Philippians, Colossians, I & II Thessalonians, I & II Timothy, Titus, Philemon, Hebrews. The seven catholic epistles: James, I & II Peter, Jude, I, II & III John.

The PROPHETIC BOOK: the Apocalypse (Revelation).
The most important of them are the four Gospels because they present to us the figure, the example and the teachings of the Son of God himself, Jesus Christ.

35

READER'S GUIDE

So as to make it easy for the reader to undestand and profit by the Gospel, care has been taken to prepare a graphic arrangement of text, notes, maps and illustrations, which, while owing much to what has been done in other books of this kind, represents on the whole something really new and original. We therefore think it essential to study this Reader's Guide with care, for it is a key to reading the 'Gospel of Jesus' with intellectual and religious profit. It is important to note that the chronology is not certain but it is adopted only as a practical framework.

Every page of the Gospel is divided into four sections:

a) The unified text of the Gospel.

b) A diagram showing the time at which the event spoken of in the text may have taken place.

c) A map of the place in which the event may have occurred. In this section are also short notes explaining the text.

d) A photograph of the said place or of objects referred to in the text.

The text of the four gospels (Matthew, Mark, Luke & John) has been arranged chronologically so as to offer a continuous narrative of the life of Jesus without repetition. It is divided into four chapters (see index) and numerous headings which facilitate reference to the various episodes. Although the chronology is not certain, it is adopted as a practical framework.

Under each heading are gathered references to the Gospel texts which speak of that episode. The reference to the text adopted is printed in heavy type. So, for example, the story of Jesus' condemnation to death, though told by all four evangelists, is quoted in the text of St. Matthew, chapter 27, verses 24 to 26 (Mt. 27, 24-26) When, under the same heading,

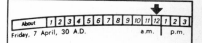

About	1	2	3	4	5	6	7	8	9	10	11	12	1	2	3

Friday, 7 April, 30 A.D.   a.m. | p.m.

The death sentence
Mt. 27, 24–26. Mk. 15, 15. Lk. 23, 25.
Jn. 19, 16–17

So when Pilate saw that he was gaining nothing, but rather that a riot was beginning, he took water and washed his hands before the crowd, saying, "I am innocent of this righteou man's blood; see to it yourselves." And all the people answered, "His blood be on us and o our children!" Then he released for them Barabbas, and having scourged Jesus, delivered him to be crucified.

texts drawn from different gospels are used, the change of evangelist is indicated to the left of the text. **Lk**

The *time* at which a biblical event may have happened is shown at the head of the page by six types of diagram.

One for the 33 years of the hidden life of Jesus:

| 7 | 6 | 5 | 4 | 3 | 2 | 1 | 1 | 2 | 3 | 4 | 5 | 6 | 7 | ● | ● | ● | ● | ● | ● | ● | ● | ● | ● | ● | ● | ● | ● | ● | ● | ● | ● | ● | ● | 27 |

Years B.C.   Years A.D.

One for the two and a half years of public life:

| X | XI | XII | I | II | III | IV | V | VI | VII | VIII | IX | X | XI | XII | I | II | III | IV | V | VI | VII | VIII | IX | X | XI | XII | I | II | III | IV |

27 A.D. **28** A.D.   **29** A.D.   **30** A.D.

One for Holy Week:

| Saturday 1 | Sunday 2 | Monday 3 | Tuesday 4 | Wednesday 5 | Thursday 6 | Friday 7 | Saturday 8 |

April, **30** A.D.

Two more detailed ones for Maundy Thursday and Good Friday:

| About | 1 | 2 | 3 | 4 | 5 | 6 | 7 | 8 | 9 | 10 | 11 | 12 | 1 | 2 | 3 | 4 | 5 | 6 | 7 | 8 | 9 | 10 | 11 | 12 | o'clock |

Thursday, **6** April, **30** A.D.   a.m.   p.m.

| About | 1 | 2 | 3 | 4 | 5 | 6 | 7 | 8 | 9 | 10 | 11 | 12 | 1 | 2 | 3 | 4 | 5 | 6 | 7 | 8 | 9 | 10 | 11 | 12 | o'clock |

Friday, **7** April, **30** A.D.   a.m.   p.m.

Lastly, one for the forty days after the Resurrection:

| Sunday 9 | ●●●●●●●●●●●●● | Sunday 16 | ●●●●●●● | ●●●●●●●●● | Thursday 18 |

April, **30** A.D.   May, **30** A.D.

Black arrowheads, moved from time to time, show in what year, month, day or hour the gospel event occured:

| X | XI | XII | I | II | III | IV | V | VI | VII | VIII | IX | X | XI | XII | I | II | III | IV | V | VI | VII | VIII | IX | X | XI | XII | I | ii | III | IV |

27 A.D. **28** A.D.   **29** A.D.   **30** A.D.

The place where the gospel event occurred is shown by a round black sign (●), or, if it was on a hill, by a triangular one (▲). Movements of people are shown by a continuous black line. Notes are preceded by an asterisk which corresponds to one beside the verse to which reference is made.

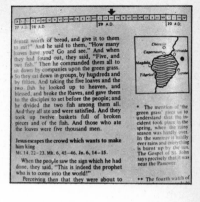

The photographic illustrations, all of which are original, are explained in short captions at the foot of the pages on which they appear and are intended to give the reader a picture of the geographical and historical environment in which Jesus lived.

39

The Gospel of Jesus

Prologue of St. John
Jn. 1, 1–18

In the beginning was the Word,
and the Word was with God,
and the Word was God.
He was in the beginning with God;
all things were made through him,
and without him was not anything made
that was made.
In him was life,
and the life was the light of men.
The light shines in the darkness,
and the darkness has not overcome it.

There was a man sent from God,
whose name was John.
He came for testimony,
to bear witness to the light,
that all might believe through him.
He was not the light,
but came to bear witness to the light.

The true light that enlightens every man
was coming into the world.
He was in the world
and the world was made through him,
yet the world knew him not.
He came to his own home,
and his own people received him not.

* St. John begins his Gospel by introducing the Son of God, whom he calls the 'Logos' or active and revealing Word of the Father (that is, the Second Person of the Holy Trinity), who is God, as the Father is, and works with him in the creation of the world. By contrast with John the Baptist (the greatest of the prophets) and Moses, the Law-giver, the incarnate Word has given us the whole truth, and grace and power to become sons of God.

But to all who received him,
who believed in his name,
he gave power to become children of God;
who were born, not of blood
nor of the will of the flesh
nor of the will of man, but of God.

And the Word became flesh and dwelt among us,
full of grace and truth;
we have beheld his glory,
glory as of the only Son from the Father.
(John bore witness to him, and cried,
"This was he of whom I said,
'He who comes after me ranks before me,
for he was before me.' ")
And from his fulness have we all received,
grace upon grace.
For the law was given through Moses;
grace and truth came through Jesus Christ.
No one has ever seen God; the only Son,
* who is in the bosom of the Father,
he has made him known.

St. Luke's Introduction
Lk. 1, 1–4

**   Inasmuch as many have undertaken to compile a narrative of the things which have been accomplished among us, just as they were delivered to us by those who from the beginning were eyewitnesses and ministers of the word, it seemed good to me also, having followed all things closely for some time past, to write an orderly account for you, most excellent Theophilus, that you may know the truth concerning the things of which you have been informed.

* 'Who is in the bosom of the Father' signifies the essential union of the Son of God with the Father. In God there are three equal Persons, but only one Nature.

** St. Luke, before writing his Gospel, questioned the surviving witnesses of the events which he had to relate. In particular we find in his work the direct or indirect reflexion of information coming from Mary, the mother of Jesus.

42

I
THE INFANCY
AND HIDDEN LIFE
OF JESUS

The Temple area at Jerusalem seen from the west, with the Mount of
Olives in the background.

The angel announces the birth of St. John
Lk. 1, 5–25

In the days of Herod, king of Judea, there was a priest named Zechariah, of the division of Abijah; and he had a wife of the daughters of Aaron, and her name was Elizabeth. And they were both righteous before God, walking in all the commandments and ordinances of the Lord blameless. But they had no child, because Elizabeth was barren, and both were advanced in years.

Now while he was serving as priest
*before God when his division was on duty, according to the custom of the priesthood, it fell to him by lot to enter the temple of the Lord and burn incense. And the whole multitude of the people were praying outside at the hour of incense. And there appeared to him an angel of the Lord standing on the right side of the altar of incense. And Zechariah was troubled when he saw him, and fear fell upon him. But the angel said to him, "Do not be afraid, Zechariah, for your prayer is heard, and your wife Elizabeth will bear you a son, and you shall call his name John.

And you will have joy and gladness, and many will rejoice at his birth; for he will be great before the Lord and he shall drink no wine nor strong drink, and he will be filled with the Holy Spirit, even from his mother's womb. And he will turn many of the sons of Israel to the Lord their God, and he will go before him in the spirit and power of Elijah, to turn the hearts of the fathers to the children, and the disobedient to the wisdom of the just, to make ready for the Lord a people prepared."

* See what has been said in the Introduction about the Jewish priesthood. Each class of priests was very numerous, so during their week of duty those who had to fulfill special functions were drawn by lot. Thus to the majority it fell to enter the Sanctuary maybe only once in their lives.

The offering of incense was made twice a day, in the morning and before sunset.

45

Nazareth seen from the north. In the centre is the Basilica built on the site of the Annunciation and in the background the Mount of the Precipice.

And Zechariah said to the angel, "How shall I know this? For I am an old man, and my wife is advanced in years." And the angel answered him, "I am Gabriel, who stand in the presence of God; and I was sent to speak to you, and to bring you this good news. And behold, you will be silent and unable to speak until the day that these things come to pass, because you did not believe my words, which will be fulfilled in their time." And the people were waiting for Zechariah, and they wondered at his delay in the temple. And when he came out, he could not speak to them, and they perceived that he had seen a vision in the temple; and he made signs to them and remained dumb. And when his time of service was ended, he went to his home.

After these days his wife Elizabeth conceived, and for five months she hid herself, saying, "Thus the Lord has done to me in the days when he looked on me, to take away my reproach among men."

The angel announces to the Virgin Mary that she will be the mother of God
Lk. 1, 26–38

In the sixth month the angel Gabriel was sent from God to a city of Galilee named Nazareth, to a virgin betrothed to a man whose name was Joseph, of the house of David; and the virgin's name was Mary. And he came to her and said, "Hail, full of grace, the Lord is with you!" But she was greatly

* 'In the sixth month' means the sixth month of St. Elizabeth's pregnancy.

47

Nazareth. Basilica of the Annunciation. The place in which the incarnation of the Word occurred.

| 7 | 6 | 5 | 4 | 3 | 2 | 1 | 1 | 2 | 3 | 4 | 5 | 6 | 7 | ● | ● | ● | ● | ● | ● | ● | ● | ● | ● | ● | ● | ● | ● | ● | ● | ● | ● | ● | 27 |

Years B.C.   Years A.D.

troubled at the saying, and considered in her mind what sort of greeting this might be. And the angel said to her, "Do not be afraid, Mary, for you have found favour with God. And behold, you will conceive in your womb and bear a son, and you shall call his name Jesus.

He will be great, and will be called the Son of the Most High; and the Lord God will give to him the throne of his father David, and he will reign over the house of Jacob for ever; and of his kingdom there will be no end."

And Mary said to the angel, "How can this be, since I have no husband?" And the angel said to her, "The Holy Spirit will come
* upon you, and the power of the Most High will overshadow you; therefore the child to be born will be called holy, the Son of God.

And behold, your kinswoman Elizabeth in her old age has also conceived a son; and this is the sixth month with her who was called barren. For with God nothing will be impossible." And Mary said, "Behold, I am the handmaid of the Lord; let it be to me according to your word." And the angel departed from her.

Mary visits Elizabeth
Lk. 1, 39–45

In those days Mary arose and went with haste into the hill country, to a city of Judah, and she entered the house of Zechariah and greeted Elizabeth. And when Elizabeth heard the greeting of Mary, the babe leaped in her womb; and Elizabeth was filled with the Holy Spirit and she exclaimed with a loud cry, "Blessed are you among women, and

* Among the Jews of this time matrimony was completed in two stages. The first was the 'betrothal' at which there was drawn up in the presence of witnesses the official marriage contract, which was considered binding from that moment; but cohabitation was not yet allowed. The second stage was the 'marriage feast' which was normally celebrated about a year afterwards with a festive rite, gathering together of relations and friends, banquet, etc. Only after this second rite did the couple enjoy the full privileges of marriage. The Annunciation took place after the first stage, the 'betrothal', but before Mary had been taken into Joseph's home.

** 'The power of the Most High will over-

49

Ain Karim. The town in the Judaean hills to which Mary went to visit her cousin Elizabeth.

| 7 | 6 | 5 | 4 | 3 | 2 | 1 | 1 | 2 | 3 | 4 | 5 | 6 | 7 | ● | ● | ● | ● | ● | ● | ● | ● | ● | ● | ● | ● | ● | ● | ● | ● | ● | ● | ● | ● | 27 |

Years B.C.   Years A.D.

blessed is the fruit of your womb! And why is this granted me, that the mother of my Lord should come to me? For behold, when the voice of your greeting came to my ears, the babe in my womb leaped for joy. And blessed is she who believed that there would be a fulfillment of what was spoken to her from the Lord."

The Magnificat
Lk. 1, 46–56

* And Mary said,
"My soul magnifies the Lord,
and my spirit rejoices in God my Saviour,
for he has regarded the low estate of his handmaiden.
For behold, henceforth all generations will call me blessed;
for he who is mighty has done great things for me,
and holy is his name.
And his mercy is on those who fear him from generation to generation.
He has shown strength with his arm, he has scattered the proud in the imagination of their hearts,
he has put down the mighty from their thrones, and exalted those of low degree;
he has filled the hungry with good things, and the rich he has sent empty away.
He has helped his servant Israel,
in remembrance of his mercy,
as he spoke to our fathers,
to Abraham and to his posterity for ever."
And Mary remained with her about three months, and returned to her home.

shadow you' means that the conception of the child, which takes place naturally in marriage, was in this case to be effected by God himself miraculously and without human intervention.

* It was fairly common practice in the Bible to express the most intense feelings towards God in the form of poetry.

51

Ain Karim. The church built over St. John the Baptist's birth-place.

The birth of John the Baptist
Lk. 1, 57–66

Now the time came for Elizabeth to be delivered, and she gave birth to a son. And her neighbours and kinfolk heard that the Lord had shown great mercy to her, and they rejoiced with her. And on the eighth day they came to circumcise the child; and they would have named him Zechariah after his father, but his mother said, "Not so; he shall be called John." And they said to her, "None of your kindred is called by this name." And they made signs to his father, inquiring what he would have him called. And he asked for a writing tablet, and wrote, "His name is John." And they all marvelled. And immediately his mouth was opened and his tongue loosed, and he spoke, blessing God. And fear came on all their neighbours. And all these things were talked about through all the hill country of Judea; and all who heard them laid them up in their hearts, saying, "What then will this child be?" For the hand of the Lord was with him.

The song of Zechariah
Lk. 1, 67 – 80

And his father Zechariah was filled with the Holy Spirit, and prophesied, saying, "Blessed be the Lord God of Israel, for he has visited and redeemed his people,
and has raised up a horn of salvation for us in the house of his servant David,
as he spoke by the mouth of his holy prophets from of old,

Ain Karim. The altar built on the spot where St. John the Baptist was born.

that we should be saved from our enemies,
and from the hand of all who hate us;
to perform the mercy promised to our fathers,
and to remember his holy convenant,
the oath which he swore to our father
Abraham, to grant us
that we, being delivered from the hand of our
enemies, might serve him without fear,
in holiness and righteousness before him all
the days of our life.
And you, child, will be called the prophet of
the Most High;
for you will go before the Lord to prepare
his ways,
to give knowledge of salvation to his people
in the forgiveness of their sins,
through the tender mercy of our God, when
the day shall dawn upon us from on high,
to give light to those who sit in darkness
and in the shadow of death,
to guide our feet into the way of peace."

And the child grew and became strong
in spirit, and he was in the wilderness till
the day of his manifestation to Israel.

* Perhaps St. Joseph
was afraid that he would
have no authority over
Mary's son since the
latter was miraculously
conceived, but the angel
reassures him and tells
him that it is for him,
Joseph, to give the name
and the legal title 'Son
of David' to the child
who is about to be born.

The angel announces the birth of Jesus to Joseph
M. 1, 18–25.

Now the birth of Jesus Christ took place
in this way. When his mother Mary had been
betrothed to Joseph, before they came
together she was found to be with child of
* the Holy Spirit; and her husband Joseph,
being a just man and unwilling to put her to
shame, resolved to send her away quietly.
But as he considered this, behold, an angel of
the Lord appeared to him in a dream,

55

| 7 | 6 | 5 | 4 | 3 | 2 | 1 | 1 | 2 | 3 | 4 | 5 | 6 | 7 | ● | ● | ● | ● | ● | ● | ● | ● | ● | ● | ● | ● | ● | ● | ● | ● | ● | 27 |

Years B.C.   Years A.D.

saying "Joseph, son of David, do not fear to take Mary your wife, for that which is conceived in her is of the Holy Spirit; she will bear a son, and you shall call his name Jesus, for he will save his people from their sins." All this took place to fulfil what the Lord had spoken by the prophet: "Behold, a virgin shall conceive and bear a son, and his name shall be called Emmanuel" (which means, God with us).

When Joseph woke from sleep, he did as the angel of the Lord commanded him; he took his wife, but knew her not until she had borne a son; and he called his name Jesus.

Genealogy of Jesus according to the royal line
Mt. 1, 1–17. Lk. 3, 23–38

* The book of the genealogy of Jesus Christ, the son of David, the son of Abraham.

Abraham was the father of Isaac, and Isaac the father of Jacob, and Jacob the father of Judah and his brothers, and Judah the father of Perez and Zerah by Tamar, and Perez the father of Hezron, and Hezron the father of Ram, and Ram the father of Amminadab and Amminadab the father of Nahson, and Nahson the Father of Salmon, and Salmon the father of Boaz by Rahab, and Boaz the father of Obed by Ruth, and Obed the father of Jesse, and Jesse the father of David the king.

And David was the father of Solomon by the wife of Uriah, and Solomon the father of Rehoboam, and Rehoboam the father of Abijah, and Abijah the father of Asa, and Asa the father of Jehoshaphat, and Jehoshaphat the father of Joram, and Joram the father of Uzziah, and Uzziah the father of Jotham,

* St. Matthew gives the royal genealogy according to which the right of succession to the throne of David was handed down

56

and Jotham the father of Ahaz, and Ahaz the father of Hezekiah, and Hezekiah the father of Manasseh, and Manasseh the father of Amos, and Amos the father of Josiah, and Josiah the father of Jechoniah and his brothers, at the time of the deportation to Babylon.

And after the deportation to Babylon: Jechoniah was the father of Shealtiel, and Shealtiel the father of Zerubbabel, and Zerubbabel the father of Abiud, and Abiud the father of Eliakim, and Eliakim the father of Azor, and Azor the father of Zadok, and Zadok the father of Achim, and Achim the father of Eliud, and Eliud the father of Eleazar, and Eleazar the father of Matthan, and Matthan the father of Jacob, and Jacob the father of Joseph the husband of Mary, of whom Jesus was born, who is called Christ.

So all the generations from Abraham to David were fourteen generations, and from David to the deportation to Babylon fourteen generations, and from the deportation to Babylon to the Christ fourteen generations.

Bethlehem. The town in Judaea where Jesus was born, seen from the Shepherd's Field.

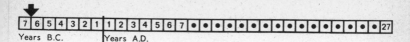
Jesus is born at Bethlehem
Lk. 2, 1–7

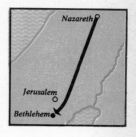

In those days a decree went out from Caesar Augustus that all the world should be enrolled. This was the first enrolment, when Quirinius was governor of Syria. And all went to be enrolled, each to his own city. And Joseph also went up from Galilee, from the city of Nazareth, to Judea, to the city of David, which is called Bethlehem, because he was of the house and lineage of David, to be enrolled with Mary, his betrothed, who was with child. And while they were there, the time came for her to be delivered. And she gave birth to her first-born son and wrapped him in swaddling cloths, and laid him in a manger, because there was no place for them in the inn.

The shepherds come to worship Jesus
Lk. 2, 8–20

And in that region there were shepherds out in the field, keeping watch over their flock by night. And an angel of the Lord appeared to them, and the glory of the Lord shone around them, and they were filled with fear. And the angel said to them, "Be not afraid; for behold, I bring you good news of a great joy which will come to all the people; for to you is born this day in the City of David a Saviour, who is Christ the Lord. And this will be a sign for you: you will find a babe wrapped in swaddling cloths and lying in a manger."

And suddenly there was with the angel a multitude of the heavenly host praising God and saying.

"Glory to God in the highest,
and on earth peace among men with whom he is pleased."

* 'First-born' in this case is not opposed to 'only - begotten'. The words 'first-born' were normally used because in Jewish law there were special rules given by God concerning the eldest son, e.g. he had to be offered at the Temple and redeemed.

In this case 'first-born' indicates the special obligations which this involved.

59

Bethlehem. The Shepherd's Field. The cave where the shepherds spent winter nights.

When the angels went away from them into heaven, the shepherds said to one another, "Let us go over to Bethlehem and see this thing that has happened, which the Lord has made known to us." And they went with haste, and found Mary and Joseph, and the babe lying in a manger. And when they, saw it they made known the saying which had been told them concerning this child; and all who heard it wondered at what the shepherds told them. But Mary kept all these things, pondering them in her heart. And the shepherds returned, glorifying and praising God for all they had heard and seen, as it had been told them.

Jesus is circumcised . . . . .
Lk. 2, 21.

And at the end of eight days, when he was circumcised, he was called Jesus, the name given by the angel before he was conceived in the womb.

* At that time there was a very lively expectation of the Messiah, and many good Jews awaited him, confident in God's promises.

. . . . . and presented in the Temple
Lk. 2, 22—40

And when the time came for their purification according to the law of Moses, they brought him up to Jerusalem to present him to the Lord (as it is written in the law of the Lord, "Every male that opens the womb shall be called holy to the Lord") and to offer a sacrifice according to what is said in the law of the Lord, "a pair of turtle-doves, or two young pigeons." Now there was a man in Jerusalem, whose name was Simeon, and this man was righteous and devout, looking for the consolation of Israel, and the Holy Spirit was upon him. And it

Bethlehem. Exterior of Constantine's Basilica of the Nativity which covers the cave in which Jesus was born.

| 7 | 6 | 5 | 4 | 3 | 2 | 1 | 1 | 2 | 3 | 4 | 5 | 6 | 7 | ● | ● | ● | ● | ● | ● | ● | ● | ● | ● | ● | ● | ● | ● | ● | ● | ● | ● | ● | 27 |

Years B.C. Years A.D.

had been revealed to him by the Holy Spirit
that he should not see death before he had
seen the Lord's Christ. And inspired by
the Spirit he came into the temple; and when
the parents brought in the child Jesus, to do
for him according to the custom of the law,
he took him up in his arms and blessed God
and said, "Lord, now lettest thou thy servant
depart in peace, according to thy word;
for mine eyes have seen thy salvation

which thou hast prepared in the presence
of all peoples,
a light for revelation to the Gentiles, and
for glory to thy people Israel."

And his father and his mother marvelled
at what was said about him; and Simeon
blessed them and said to Mary his mother,
"Behold, this child is set for the fall and
rising of many in Israel, and for a sign that
is spoken against (and a sword will pierce
through your own soul also), that thoughts
out of many hearts may be revealed."

And there was a prophetess Anna, the
daughter of Phanuel, of the tribe of Asher;
she was of a great age, having lived with her
husband seven years from her virginity,
and as a widow till she was eighty-four. She
did not depart from the temple, worshipping
with fasting and prayer night and day. And
coming up at that very hour she gave
thanks to God, and spoke of him to all who
were looking for the redemption of Jerusalem.

And when they had performed everything
according to the law of the Lord, they returned into Galilee, to their own city, Nazareth.
And the child grew and became strong, filled
with wisdom; and the favour of God was
upon him.

Bethlehem. Grotto of the Nativity. The silver star is fixed on the spot where the Saviour was born.

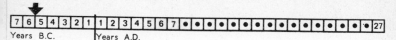
The Magi come to worship Jesus
Mt. 2, 1—12

Now when Jesus was born in Bethlehem of Judea in the days of Herod the king, behold, wise men from the East came to Jerusalem, saying, "Where is he who has been born king of the Jews? For we have seen his star in the East, and have come to worship him." When Herod the king heard this, he was troubled, and all Jerusalem with him; and assembling all the chief priests and scribes of the people, he inquired of them where the Christ was to be born. They told him, "In Bethlehem of Judea; for so it is written by the prophet:

'And you, O Bethlehem, in the land of Judah, are by no means least among the rulers of Judah;
for from you shall come a ruler
who will govern my people Israel." '

* The prophet Micah (5, 2) wrote this prophecy about 700 years before the birth of Jesus.

Then Herod summoned the wise men secretly and ascertained from them what time the star appeared; and he sent them to Bethlehem, saying, "Go and search diligently for the child, and when you have found him bring me word, that I too may come and worship him." When they had heard the king they went their way; and lo, the star which they had seen in the East went before them, till it came to rest over the place where the child was. When they saw the star, they rejoiced exceedingly with great joy; and going into the house they saw the child with Mary his mother, and they fell down and worshipped him. Then, opening their treasures, they offered him gifts, gold and frankincense and myrrh. And being warned in a dream not to return to Herod, they departed to their own country by another way.

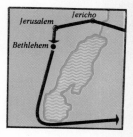

65

The Pyramid of Gizeh near Matariyeh. According to tradition it was in this village, where there was a flourishing Jewish community in Jesus' time, that the Holy Family took refuge.

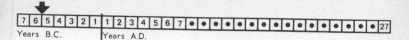
The flight of the holy family into Egypt
Mt. 2, 13–15

Now when they had departed, behold,
an angel of the Lord appeared to Joseph
in a dream and said, "Rise, take the child
and his mother, and flee to Egypt, and remain
there till I tell you; for Herod is about to
search for the child, to destroy him." And
he rose and took the child and his mother
by night, and departed to Egypt, and remained there until the death of Herod. This
was to fulfil what the Lord had spoken by
the prophet, " Out of Egypt have I called my
son."

Herod orders the slaughter of the innocents
Mt. 2, 16–18

Then Herod, when he saw that he had been
tricked by the wise men, was in a furious
rage, and he sent and killed all the male
children in Bethlehem and in all that region
who were two years old or under, according
to the time which he had ascertained from
the wise men.

Then was fulfilled what was spoken by
the prophet Jeremiah:

"A voice was heard in Ramah,
wailing and loud lamentation,
Rachel weeping for her children;
she refused to be consoled,
because they were no more."

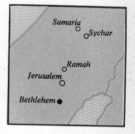

The holy family returns from Egypt
Mt. 2, 19–23

But when Herod died, behold, an angel
of the Lord appeared in a dream to Joseph in
Egypt, saying, "Rise, take the child and his
mother, and go to the land of Israel, for
those who sought the child's life are dead."

67

Beeroth, on the caravan route from Judaea to Galilee. The fountain near which the caravans used to halt.

And he rose and took the child and his mother, and went to the land of Israel. But when he heard that Archelaus reigned over Judea in place of his father Herod, he was afraid to go there, and being warned in a dream he withdrew to the district of Galilee. And he went and dwelt in a city called Nazareth, that what was spoken by the prophets might be fulfilled, "He shall be called a Nazarene."

* St. Matthew seems to refer to the prophet Isaiah (11,1) who lived about 700 years before Jesus. He called the Messiah who was to come 'a shoot' which is in Hebrew 'Nezer'; perhaps Nazareth is derived from the same word.

Jesus at the age of 12 among the doctors
Lk. 2, 41–50

Now his parents went to Jerusalem every year at the feast of the Passover. And when he was twelve years old, they went up according to custom: and when the feast was ended, as they were returning, the boy Jesus stayed behind in Jerusalem. His parents did not know it, but supposing him to be in the company they went a day's journey, and they sought him among their kinsfolk and acquaintances; and when they did not find him, they returned to Jerusalem, seeking him. After three days they found him in the temple, sitting among the teachers, listening to them and asking them questions; and all who heard him were amazed at his understanding and his answers. And when they saw him they were astonished; and his mother said to him, "Son, why have you treated us so? Behold, your father and I have been looking for you anxiously." And he said to them, "How is it that you sought me? Did you not know that I must be in my Father's house?" And they did not understand the saying which he spoke to them.

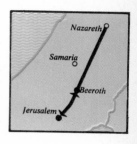

** The Temple at Jerusalem was the house in which God wished his presence to be worshipped, and was the only place where sacrifices were allowed; therefore good Jews made their way there at least once a year on the occasion of some feast, specially the Passover, so as to pray and offer their sacrifices to God.

69

| 7 | 6 | 5 | 4 | 3 | 2 | 1 | 1 | 2 | 3 | 4 | 5 | 6 | 7 | | | | | | | | | | | | | | | | | | | | 27 |

Years B.C.   Years A.D.

Jesus at Nazareth
Lk. 2, 51–52

And he went down with them and came to Nazareth, and was obedient to them; and his mother kept all these things in her heart.

And Jesus increased in wisdom and in stature, and in favour with God and man.

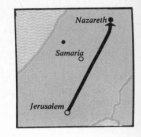

II
THE PUBLIC MINISTRY
OF JESUS

| X | XI | XII | I | II | III | IV | V | VI | VII | VIII | IX | X | XI | XII | I | II | III | IV | V | VI | VII | VIII | IX | X | XI | XII | I | II | III | IV |

27 A.D. | **28** A.D. | **29** A.D. | **30** A.D.

John the Baptist starts his mission
Mt. 3, 1–6. Mk. 1, 1–6. Lk. 3, 1–6

In the fifteenth year of the reign of Tiberius Caesar, Pontius Pilate being governor of Judea, and Herod being tetrarch of Galilee, and his brother Philip tetrarch of the region of Ituraea and Trachonitis, and Lysanias tetrarch of Abilene, in the high-priesthood of Annas and Caiaphas, the word of God came to John the son of Zechariah in the wilderness; and he went into all the region about the Jordan, preaching a baptism of repentance for the forgiveness of sins. As it is written in the book of the words of * Isaiah the prophet,
"The voice of one crying in the wilderness:
Prepare the way of the Lord,
make his paths straight.
Every valley shall be filled,
and every mountain and hill shall be brought low,
and the crooked shall be made straight,
and the rough ways shall be made smooth;
And all flesh shall see the salvation of God."

John the Baptist preaches repentance
Mt. 3, 7–10. Lk. 3, 7–9

** He said therefore to the multitudes that came out to be baptized by him, "You brood of vipers! Who warned you to flee from the wrath to come? Bear fruits that befit repentance, and do not begin to say to yourselves, 'We have Abraham as our father'; for I tell you. God is able from these stones to raise up children to Abraham. Even now the axe is laid to the root of the trees; every tree therefore that does not bear good fruit is cut down and thrown into the fire."

* The prophecy of Isaiah takes its illustration from the practice of ancient eastern kings who, when they visited their provinces were, preceded by a herald so that their subjects might prepare the roads for the passage of the royal cortege. So God is preceded by his herald who prepared a friendly welcome for the Messiah.

** Note the difference between John's Baptism and our own. John's was a symbol of penitence and God's pardon, whereas our Baptism is a sacrament instituted by Jesus, which by the merits of Jesus Christ himself truly removes all sin from the soul.

X	XI	XII	I	II	III	IV	V	VI	VII	VIII	IX	X	XI	XII	I	II	III	IV	V	VI	VII	VIII	IX	X	XI	XII	I	II	III	IV

27 A.D. | **28 A.D.** | **29 A.D.** | **30 A.D.**

John exhorts people to do their duty
Lk. 3, 10–14

And the multitudes asked him, "What then shall we do?" And he answered them, "He who has two coats, let him share with him who has none; and he who has food, let him do likewise." Tax collectors also came to be baptized, and said to him, "Teacher, what shall we do?" And he said to them, "Collect no more than is appointed you." Soldiers also asked him, "And we, what shall we do?" And he said to them, "Rob no one by violence or by false accusation, and be content with your wages."

* The tax collectors were regarded as public sinners for, as they collected taxes in the name of the oppressor, they were his collaborators, and also because they themselves were often hard to the point of injustice.

John announces that the Messiah is near
Mt. 3, 11–12. Mk. 1, 7–8. Lk. 3, 15–18

As the people were in expectation, and all men questioned in their hearts concerning John, whether perhaps he were the Christ, John answered them all, "I baptize you with water; but he who is mightier than I is coming, the thong of whose sandals I am not worthy to untie; he will baptize you with the Holy Spirit and with fire. His winnowing fork is in his hand, to clear his threshing floor, and to gather the wheat into his granary, but the chaff he will burn with unquenchable fire."

So, with many other exhortations, he preached good news to the people.

John baptizes Jesus
Mt. 3, 13–17. Mk. 1, 9–11. Lk. 3, 21–23

Then Jesus came from Galilee to the Jordan to John, to be baptized by him. John would have prevented him, saying, "I need to be baptized by you, and do you come to me?"

73

The river Jordan in the neighbourhood of Bethany beyond Jordan where
John the Baptist baptized Jesus with his baptism of repentance.

| X | XI | XII | I | II | III | IV | V | VI | VII | VIII | IX | X | XI | XII | I | II | III | IV | V | VI | VII | VIII | IX | X | XI | XII | I | II | III | IV |

27 A.D.   28 A.D.   29 A.D.   30 A.D.

But Jesus answered him. "Let it be so now; for thus it is fitting for us to fulfil all righteousness." Then he consented. And when Jesus was baptized, he went up immediately * from the water, and behold, the heavens were opened and he saw the Spirit of God descending like a dove, and alighting on him; and lo, a voice from heaven, saying, "This is my beloved Son, with whom I am well pleased."

* This is the second Epiphany (i.e. public manifestation) of Jesus. The first was that to the Magi Kings, and the third the first miracle, at Cana in Galilee.

Jesus goes into the wilderness and is tempted by the devil
Mt. 4, 1–11. Mk. 1, 12–13. Lk. 4, 1–13

Then Jesus was led up by the Spirit into the wilderness to be tempted by the devil. And he fasted forty days and forty nights, and afterward he was hungry. And the tempter came and said to him, "If you are the Son of God, command these stones to become loaves of bread." But he answered, "It is written,

* 'Man shall not live by bread alone,
but by every word that proceeds from the mouth of God."
Then the devil took him to the holy city, and set him on the pinnacle of the temple, and said to him. "If you are the Son of God, throw yourself down; for it is written,
'He will give his angels charge of you', and,
'On their hands they will bear you up, lest you strike your foot against a stone.' "
Jesus said to him, "Again it is written, 'You shall not tempt the Lord your God.' "
Again, the devil took him to a very high mountain, and showed him all the kingdoms

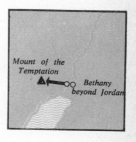

Mount of the Temptation ▲ ○○ Bethany beyond Jordan

** This is a phrase from Psalm 91, 12 in which David sings of the protection which God gives to the man who confidently commits himself to him.

The first temptation is to establish an earthly, materialistic Messianic kingdom. The second is the temptation of pride. The third is the temptation to make for himself a great human power. But Jesus remains faithful to the mission given to him by his Father. In three replies the Lord quotes

75

The Mount of the Temptation, about 10 miles from Jericho, to which Jesus withdrew so as to pray and fast before starting to preach the Good News.

of the world and the glory of them; and he said to him, "All these I will give you, if you will fall down and worship me." Then Jesus said to him, "Begone, Satan! for it is written, 'You shall worship the Lord your God and him only shall you serve.'"

Then the devil left him, and behold, angels came and ministered to him.

from Moses' book of the law, Deuteronomy; the first from 8, 3; the second from 6, 15; the third from 6, 13.

John the Baptist speaks of himself
Jn. 1, 19–28

And this is the testimony of John, when the Jews sent priests and Levites from Jerusalem to ask him, "Who are you?" He confessed, he did not deny, but confessed, "I am not the Christ." And they asked him,
* "What then? Are you Elijah?" He said, "I am not." "Are you the prophet?" And he answered, "No." They said to him then, "Who are you? Let us have an answer for those who sent us. What do you say about yourself?" He said, "I am the voice of one crying in the wilderness, 'Make straight the way of the Lord,' as the prophet Isaiah said."

Now they had been sent from the Pharisees. They asked him, "Then why are you baptizing, if you are neither the Christ, nor Elijah, nor the prophet?" John answered them, "I baptize with water; but among you stands one whom you do not know, even he who comes after me, the thong of whose sandal I am not worthy to untie." This took place in Bethany beyond the Jordan, where John was baptizing.

* The Bible says that Elijah was taken up into heaven in a chariot of fire (II Kings, 2, 11). Therefore the Jews believed that he would return to earth when the Messiah was about to appear.

77

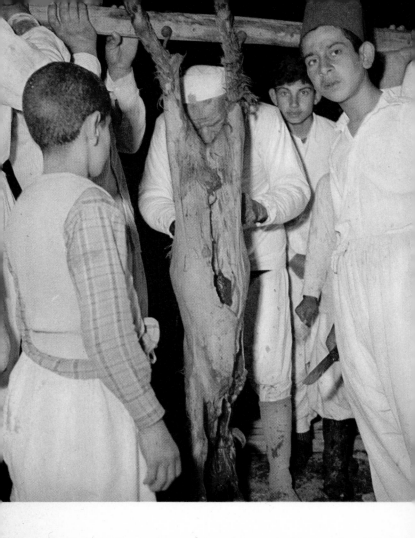

On Mount Gerizim the Samaritan High Priest makes the sacrifice of the paschal lamb. John the Baptist was alluding to a similar scene when he presented Jesus to the crowds as the Lamb of God sacrificed for our sins.

John, pointing to Jesus, says: 'Behold the Lamb of God'
Jn. 1, 29–34

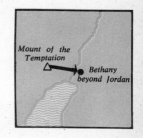

Mount of the Temptation

Bethany beyond Jordan

The next day he saw Jesus coming towards him, and said, "Behold, the Lamb of God, who takes away the sin of the world! This is he of whom I said, 'After me comes a man who ranks before me, for he was before me.' I myself did not know him; but for this I came baptizing with water, that he might be revealed to Israel." And John bore witness, "I saw the Spirit descend as a dove from heaven, and It remained on him. I myself did not know him; but he who sent me to baptize with water said to me, 'he on whom you see the Spirit descend and remain, this is he who baptizes with the Holy Spirit.' And I have seen and have borne witness that this is the Son of God."

Jesus meets his first disciples
Jn. 1, 35–51

The next day again John was standing with two of his disciples; and he looked at Jesus as he walked, and said, "Behold, the Lamb of God!" The two disciples heard him say this, and they followed Jesus. Jesus turned, and saw them following, and said to them, "What do you seek?" And they said to him, "Rabbi" (which means Teacher), "where are you staying?" He said to them, "Come and see." They came and saw where he was staying; and they stayed with him that day, for it was about the tenth hour. One of the two who heard John speak, and followed him, was Andrew, Simon Peter's brother. He first

* Jesus returns from the wilderness where he has been tempted; he is on his way back to Galilee. The image of the 'Lamb of God' was suggested to John by the prophecy of Isaiah who compares the Messiah to the lamb suffering in silence (Isa. 53,12) and to the paschal lamb, the symbol of Jesus the Redeemer.

Cana in Galilee, the village to the north of Nazareth, where Jesus worked
his first miracle, of which the church is a memorial.

| X | XI | XII | I | II | III | IV | V | VI | VII | VIII | IX | X | XI | XII | I | II | III | IV | V | VI | VII | VIII | IX | X | XI | XII | I | II | III | IV |

27 A.D. **28** A.D. **29** A.D. **30** A.D.

found his brother Simon, and said to him, "We have found the Messiah" (which means Christ.) He brought him to Jesus. Jesus looked at him, and said, "So you are Simon the son of John? You shall be called Cephas" (which means Peter).

The next day Jesus decided to go to Galilee. And he found Philip and said to him, "Follow me." Now Philip was from Bethsaida, the city of Andrew and Peter. Philip found Nathanael, and said to him, "We have found him of whom Moses in the law and also the prophets wrote, Jesus of Nazareth, the son of Joseph." Nathanael said to him, "Can anything good come out of * Nazareth?" Philip said to him, "Come and see." Jesus saw Nathanael coming to him, and said of him, "Behold, an Israelite indeed, in whom is no guile!" Nathanael said to him, "How do you know me?" Jesus answered him, "Before Philip called you, when you were under the fig tree, I saw you." Nathanael answered him, "Rabbi, you are the Son of God! You are the King of Israel!" Jesus answered him, "Because I said to you, I saw you under the fig tree, do you believe? You shall see greater things than these." And he said to him, "Truly, truly, I say to you, you will see heaven opened, and the angels of God ascending and descending upon the Son of Man."

* The town of Nazareth had played no part at all in the history of the Jewish people, and from Nathaniel's expression it seems that it did not enjoy a good reputation even as a town.

At Cana Jesus works his first miracle
Jn. 2, 1–12

On the third day there was a marriage at Cana in Galilee, and the mother of Jesus was there; Jesus also was invited to the marriage, with his disciples. When the wine

81

Cana in Galilee. Stone jar for ritual washing in the time of Jesus, kept in the Orthodox Church.

failed, the mother of Jesus said to him, "They have no wine." And Jesus said to her, "O woman, what have you to do with me? My hour has not yet come." His mother said to the servants, "Do whatever he tells you." Now six stone jars were standing there, for the Jewish rites of purification, each holding twenty or thirty gallons. Jesus said to them, "Fill the jars with water." And they filled them up to the brim. He said to them, "Now draw some out, and take it to the steward of the feast." So they took it. When the steward of the feast tasted the water now become wine, and did not know where it came from (though the servants who had drawn the water knew), the steward of the feast called the bridegroom and said to him, "Every man serves the good wine first; and when men have drunk freely, then the poor wine; but you have kept the good wine until now." This, the first of his signs, Jesus did at Cana in Galilee, and manifested his glory; and his disciples believed in him.

After this he went down to Capernaum, with his mother and his brethren and his disciples; and there they stayed for a few days.

Being in Jerusalem for the Passover, Jesus expels the merchants from the Temple
Jn. 2, 13–25. Mt. 21, 12–13. Mk. 11, 15–19. Lk. 19, 45–48

The Passover of the Jews was at hand, and Jesus went up to Jerusalem. In the temple he found those who were selling oxen and sheep and pigeons, and the money-changers at their business. And making a whip of cords, he drove them all, with the sheep and oxen, out of the temple; and he

* It is pleasant to notice that Jesus worked his first miracle after the intervention of our Lady.

** The Greek text says 'containing two or three 'metretas' apiece.' The 'metretes' was a measure of about 45 litres. The law obliged the Jews to wash before meals, not only their hands, but also crockery, plates, etc. That explains the presence of these jars at the wedding feast.

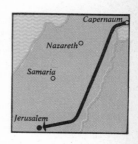

Jerusalem. The present-day appearance of the Esplanade of the Temple, the place whence Jesus expelled the merchants and money-changers.

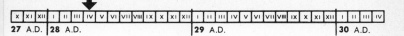
poured out the coins of the money-changers and over-turned their tables. And he told those who sold the pigeons, "Take these things away; you shall not make my Father's house a house of trade." His disciples remembered that it was written, "Zeal for thy house will consume me." The Jews then said to him, "What sign have you to show us for doing
* this?" Jesus answered them, "Destroy this temple, and in three days I will raise it up." The Jews then said, "It has taken forty-six years to build this temple, and will you raise it up in three days?" But he spoke of the temple of his body. When therefore he was raised from the dead, his disciples remembered that he had said this; and they believed the scripture and the word which Jesus had spoken.

Now when he was in Jerusalem at the Passover feast, many believed in his name when they saw the signs which he did; but Jesus did not trust himself to them, because he knew all men and needed no one to bear witness of man; for he himself knew what was in man.

Jesus and Nicodemus

Jn. 3, 1–21

Now there was a man of the Pharisees, named Nicodemus, a ruler of the Jews. This man came to Jesus by night and said to him, "Rabbi, we know that you are a teacher come from God; for no one can do these signs that you do, unless God is with him."
**Jesus answered him, "Truly, truly, I say to you, unless one is born anew, he cannot see the kingdom of God." Nicodemus said to him, "How can a man be born when he is old? Can he enter a second time into his mother's womb and be born?" Jesus answered, "Truly,

* The quotation if taken from Psalm 69, 9.

** Jesus is referring to his Body which is the true Temple of God since it is personally united to the Godhead. This is the first prophecy of his Passion and Resurrection.

***In this and the following verses Jesus affirms the necessity of baptism which is truly a new birth into the life of Grace.

85

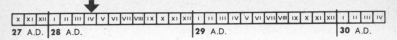

| X | XI | XII | I | II | III | IV | V | VI | VII | VIII | IX | X | XI | XII | I | II | III | IV | V | V | VI | VII | VIII | IX | X | XI | XII | I | II | III | IV |

27 A.D.   **28** A.D.   **29** A.D.   **30** A.D.

truly, I say to you, unless one is born of water and the Spirit, he cannot enter the kingdom of God. That which is born of the flesh is flesh, and that which is born of the Spirit is spirit. Do not marvel that I said to you, 'You must be born anew.' The wind blows where it wills, and you hear the sound of it, but you do not know whence it comes or whither it goes; so it is with every one who is born of the Spirit." Nicodemus said to him, "How can this be?" Jesus answered him, "Are you a teacher of Israel, and yet you do not understand this? Truly, truly, I say to you, we speak of what we know, and bear witness to what we have seen but you do not receive our testimony. If I have told you earthly things and you do not believe, how can you believe if I tell you heavenly things? No one has ascended into heaven but he who descended from he-

* aven, the Son of man. And as Moses lifted up the serpent in the wilderness, so must the Son of man be lifted up, that whoever believes in him may have eternal life."

For God so loved the world that he gave his only Son, that whoever believes in him should not perish but have eternal life. For God sent the Son into the world, not to condemn the world, but that the world might be saved through him. He who believes in him is not condemned; he who does not believe is condemned already, because he has not believed in the name of the only Son of God. And this is the judgment, that the light has come into the world, and men, loved darkness rather than light, because their deeds were evil. For every one who does evil hates the light, and does not come to the light, lest his deeds should be exposed. But he who does what is true comes to the

* In Holy Scripture (Num. 21, 8-9) it is recorded that when the Hebrews rebelled against God in the wilderness, he, as a punishment, sent poisonous snakes into their camp. Then Moses interceded for the people and, at God's request, made a brazen serpent and set it up in the middle of the camp. Anyone who had been bitten by the snakes and looked at that made by Moses, would then be cured. So, says Jesus, he too, when crucified, will bring salvation to anyone who believes in him.

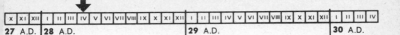

| X | XI | XII | I | II | III | IV | V | VI | VII | VIII | IX | X | XI | XII | I | II | III | IV | V | VI | VII | VIII | IX | X | XI | XII | I | II | III | IV |

27 A.D.   **28** A.D.   **29** A.D.   **30** A.D.

light, that it may be clearly seen that his deeds have been wrought in God.

Jesus is the revelation of God
Jn. 3, 31–36

He who comes from above is above all; he who is of the earth belongs to the earth, and of the earth he speaks; he who comes from heaven is above all. He bears witness to what he has seen and heard, yet no one receives his testimony; he who receives his testimony sets his seal to this, that God is true. For he whom God has sent utters the words of God, for it is not by measure that he gives the Spirit; the Father loves the Son, and has given all things into his hand. He who believes in the Son has eternal life; he who does not obey the Son shall not see life, but the wrath of God rests upon him.

John the Baptist again declares that Jesus is the Messiah
Jn. 3, 22–30

After this Jesus and his disciples went into the land of Judea; there he remained with them and baptized. John also was baptizing at Aenon near Salim, because there was much water there; and people came and were baptized. For John had not yet been put in prison.

Now a discussion arose between John's disciples and a Jew over purifying. And they came to John, and said to him, "Rabbi, he who was with you beyond the Jordan, to whom you bore witness, here he is, baptizing, and all are going to him." John answered, "No one can receive anything except what

* Jesus takes his stand in the centre of God's judgment and divides men into two categories: those who believe in him will be saved, and those who do not believe in him cannot be saved.

Another vivid picture of the river Jordan in whose waters John (at Aenon) and the disciples of Jesus (at Bethany beyond the Jordan) gave the batism of repentance.

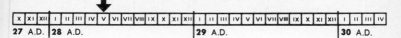

| X | XI | XII | I | II | III | IV | V | VI | VII | VIII | IX | X | XI | XII | I | II | III | IV | V | VI | VII | VIII | IX | X | XI | XII | I | II | III | IV |

27 A.D. | 28 A.D. | 29 A.D. | 30 A.D.

is given him from heaven. You yourselves
bear me witness, that I said, I am not the
Christ, but I have been sent before him.
He who has the bride is the bridegroom; the
friend of the bridegroom who stands and hears
him, rejoices greatly at the bridegroom's voice;
therefore this joy of mine is now full. He must
increase, but I must decrease."

The Baptist in prison, Jesus leaves Judaea
Mt. 4, 12. Mk. 4, 17. Lk. 3, 19–20. Jn. 4, 1–3

But Herod the tetrarch, who had been
reproved by him for Herodias, his brother's
wife, and for all the evil things that Herod
had done, added this to them all, that he
shut up John in prison.

Now when the Lord knew that the
Pharisees had heard that Jesus was making
and baptizing more disciples than John (although Jesus himself did not baptize, but
only his disciples), he left Judaea and departed
again to Galilee.

Jesus passes through Samaria. His talk with the Samaritan woman
Jn. 4, 4–42

He had to pass through Samaria. So he
came to a city of Samaria, called Sychar,
near the field that Jacob gave to his son
Joseph. Jacob's well was there, and so Jesus,
wearied as he was with his journey, sat
down beside the well. It was about the sixth
hour.

There came a woman of Samaria to
draw water. Jesus said to her, "Give me
a drink." For his disciples had gone away
into the city to buy food. The Samaritan
woman said to him, "How is it that you,
a Jew, ask a drink of me, a woman of

* This expression holds
all the greatness of the
moral character of John.
Never has he worked
for his own glory but
only for the glory of
Another (The Messiah).

89

Samaria. Mount Gerizim seen from Jacob's Well. This is what Jesus and the Samaritan woman saw during the conversation.

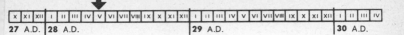

| X | XI | XII | I | II | III | IV | V | VI | VII | VIII | IX | X | XI | XII | I | II | III | IV | V | VI | VII | VIII | IX | X | XI | XII | I | II | III | IV |

27 A.D.   **28** A.D.   **29** A.D.   **30** A.D.

Samaria?" For Jews have no dealings with Samaritans. Jesus answered her. "If you knew the gift of God, and who it is that is saying to you, 'Give me a drink,' you would have asked him, and he would have given you living water." The woman said to him, "Sir, you have nothing to draw with, and the well is deep; where do you get that living water? Are you greater than our father, Jacob, who gave us the well, and drank from it himself, and his sons, and his cattle?" Jesus said to her, "Every one who drinks of this water will thirst again, but whoever drinks of the water that I shall give him will never thirst; the water that I shall give him will become in him a spring of water welling up to eternal life." The woman said to him, "Sir, give me this water, that I may not thirst, nor come here to draw."

Jesus said to her, "Go, call your husband, and come here." The woman answered him, "I have no husband." Jesus said to her, "You are right in saying, 'I have no husband'; for you have had five husbands, and he whom you now have is not your husband; this you said truly." The woman said to him, "Sir, I perceive that you are a prophet. Our fathers worshipped on this mountain; and you say that in Jerusalem is the place where men ought to worship." Jesus said to her, "Woman, believe me, the hour is coming when neither on this mountain nor in Jerusalem will you worship the Father. You worship what you do not know; we worship what we know, for salvation is from the Jews. But the hour is coming, and now is, when the true worshippers will worship the Father in spirit and truth, for such the Father seeks to worship him. God is spirit, and those

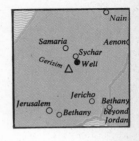

* Jesus uses the symbol of living water to mean Grace, for the reception of which we need humble recognition of our sins.

** This is the affirmation of the new religious spirit brought by Jesus. God must be recognized and worshipped primarily in the inner consciousness.

91

**Mount Gerizim. The Samaritan High Priest with the Scroll of the
Pentateuch.**

| X | XI | XII | I | II | III | IV | V | VI | VII | VIII | IX | X | XI | XII | I | II | III | IV | V | VI | VII | VIII | IX | X | XI | XII | I | II | III | IV |

27 A.D. | **28** A.D. | **29** A.D. | **30** A.D.

who worship him must worship in spirit and truth." The woman said to him, "I know that Messiah is coming (he who is called Christ); when he comes, he will show us all things." Jesus said to her, "I who speak to you am he."

Just then his disciples came. They marvelled that he was talking with a woman, but none said, "What do you wish?" or, "Why are you talking with her?" So the woman left her water jar, and went away into the city, and said to the people, "Come, see a man who told me all that I ever did. Can this be the Christ?" They went out of the city and were coming to him.

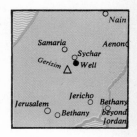

Meanwhile the disciples besought him, saying, "Rabbi, eat." But he said to them, "I have food to eat of which you do not know." So the disciples said to one another, "Has any one brought him food?" Jesus said to them, "My food is to do the will of him who sent me, and to accomplish his work. Do you not say, 'There are yet four months, then comes the harvest'? I tell you, lift up your eyes, and see how the fields are already white for harvest. He who reaps receives wages, and gathers fruit for eternal life, so that sower and reaper may rejoice together. For here the saying holds true. 'One sows and another reaps.' I sent you to reap that for which you did not labour; others have laboured, and you have entered into their labour."

Many Samaritans from that city believed in him because of the woman's testimony, "He told me all that I ever did." So when the Samaritans came to him, they asked him to stay with them; and he stayed there

93

| X | XI | XII | I | II | III | IV | V | VI | VII | VIII | IX | X | XI | XII | I | II | III | IV | V | VI | VII | VIII | IX | X | XI | XII | I | II | III | IV |

27 A.D. | **28** A.D. | **29** A.D. | **30** A.D.

two days. And many more believed because of his word. They said to the woman, "It is no longer because of your words that we believe, for we have heard for ourselves, and we know that this is indeed the Saviour of the world."

Reaching Cana, Jesus cures the nobleman's son
Jn. 4, 43–54

After the two days he departed to Galilee. For Jesus himself testified that a prophet has no honour in his own country. So when he came to Galilee, the Galileans welcomed him, having seen all that he had done in Jerusalem at the feast, for they too had gone to the feast.

So he came again to Cana in Galilee, where he had made the water wine. And at Capernaum there was an official whose son was ill. When he heard that Jesus had come from Judea to Galilee, he went and begged him to come down and heal his son, for he was at the point of death. Jesus therefore said to him, "Unless you see signs and wonders you will not believe." The official said to him, "Sir, come down before my child dies." Jesus said to him, "Go; your son will live." The man believed the word that Jesus spoke to him and went his way. As he was going down, his servants met him and told him that his son was living. So he asked them the hour when he began to mend, and they said to him, "Yesterday at the seventh hour the fever left him." The father knew that was the hour when Jesus had said to him, "Your son will live"; and he himself believed, and all his household. This was now the second sign that Jesus did when he had come from Judea to Galilee.

| | | | | | | | | | | | | | | | | | | | | | | | | | | | | | | | | |
27 A.D. | 28 A.D. | 29 A.D. | 30 A.D.

Jesus begins to preach the kingdom of God
Mt. 4, 13–17. Mk. 1, 14–15. Lk. 4, 14–15

And leaving Nazareth he went and dwelt in Capernaum by the sea, in the, territory of Zebulun and Naphtali, that what was spoken by the prophet Isaiah might be fulfilled:
"The land of Zebulun and the land of Naphtali, toward the sea, across the Jordan, Galilee of the Gentiles—the people who sat in the region and shadow of death light has dawned."
From that time Jesus began to preach, saying, "Repe it, for the kingdom of heaven is at hand."

* It is the prophecy in which Isaiah (8, 29 & 9, 1) foretells the glorious appearing of the Messiah.

Jesus calls the first disciples
Mt. 4, 18–22. Lk. 5, 1–11. Mk. 1, 19–20

While the people pressed upon him to hear the word of God, he was standing by the lake of Gennesaret. And he saw two boats by the lake; but the fishermen had gone out of them and were washing their nets. Getting into one of the boats, which was Simon's, he asked him to put out a little from the land. And he sat down and taught the people from the boat. And when he had ceased speaking, he said to Simon, "Put out into the deep and let down your nets for a catch." And Simon answered, "Master, we toiled all night and took nothing! But at your word I will let down the nets." And when they had done this, they enclosed a great shoal of fish; and as their nets were breaking, they beckoned to their partners in the other boats to come and help them. And they came and filled both the boats, so

Capernaum. Remains of the second century synagogue built on the site of that of Jesus' time.

| X | XI | XII | I | II | III | IV | V | VI | VII | VIII | IX | X | XI | XII | I | II | III | IV | V | VI | VII | VIII | IX | X | XI | XII | I | II | III | IV |

27 A.D.   **28** A.D.   **29** A.D.   **30** A.D.

that they began to sink. But when Simon Peter saw it, he fell down at Jesus' knees, saying, "Depart from me, for I am a sinful man, O Lord." For he was astonished, and all that were with him, at the catch of fish which they had taken; and so also were James and John, sons of Zebedee, who were partners with Simon. And Jesus said to Simon, "Do not be afraid; henceforth you will be catching men." And when they had brought their boats to land, they left everything and followed him.

And going on a little farther, he saw James the son of Zebedee and John his brother, who were in their boat mending the nets. And immediately he called them; and they left their father Zebedee in the boat with the hired servants, and followed him.

Jesus teaches in the synagogue at Capernaum
Mk. 1, 21–28. Lk. 4, 31–37

And they went into Capernaum; and immediately on the sabbath he entered the synagogue and taught. And they were astonished at his teaching, for he taught them as one who had authority, and not as the scribes. And immediately there was in their synagogue a man with an unclean spirit; and he cried out, "What have you to do with us, Jesus of Nazareth? Have you come to destroy us? I know who you are, the Holy One of God." But Jesus rebuked him saying, "Be silent, and come out of him!" And the unclean spirit, convulsing him and crying with a loud voice, came out of him. And they were all amazed, so that they questioned among themselves, saying, "What is this? A new teaching! With authority he commands even the unclean spirits, and they obey him."

97

| X | XI | XII | I | II | III | IV | V | VI | VII | VIII | IX | X | XI | XII | I | II | III | IV | V | VI | VII | VIII | IX | X | XI | XII | I | II | III | IV |

27 A.D. | 28 A.D. | 29 A.D. | 30 A.D.

And at once his name spread everywhere throughout all the surrounding region of Galilee.

Jesus cures Peter's mother-in-law
Mt. 8, 16–17. Mk. 1, 29–31, Lk. 4, 38–39.

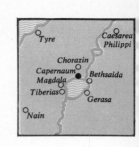

And immediately he left the synagogue, and entered the house of Simon and Andrew, with James and John.

Now Simon's mother-in-law lay sick with a fever, and immediately they told him of her. And he came and took her by the hand and lifted her up, and the fever left her; and she served them.

In the evening, Jesus cures other people at Capernaum
Mt. 8, 16–17. Mk. 1, 32–34. Lk. 4, 40–41.

Now when the sun was setting, all those who had any that were sick with various diseases brought them to him; and he laid his hands on every one of them and healed them. And demons also came out of many, crying, "You are the Son of God!" But he rebuked them, and would not allow them to speak, because they knew that he was the Christ.

Leaving Capernaum Jesus goes away to pray
Mk. 1, 35–38. Lk. 4, 42–43

And in the morning, a great while before day, he rose and went out to a lonely place, and there he prayed. And Simon and those who were with him followed him, and they found him and said to him, "Every one is searching for you." And he said to them, "Let us go on to the next towns, that I may preach there also; for that is why I came out."

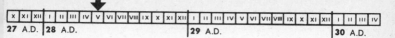
Jesus moves about in Galilee

Mt. 4, 23—25. Mk. 1, 39. Lk. 4, 44

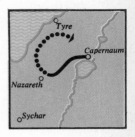

And he went about all Galilee, teaching in their synagogues and preaching the gospel of the kingdom and healing every disease and every infirmity among the people. So his fame spread throughout all Syria, and they brought him all the sick, those afflicted with various diseases and pains, demoniacs, epileptics, and paralytics, and he healed them. And great crowds followed him from Galilee and the Decapolis and Jerusalem and Judea and from beyond the Jordan.

Jesus cures a leper

Mt. 18, 2—4. Mk. 1, 40—45. Lk. 5, 12—16

And a leper came to him beseeching him, and kneeling said to him, "If you will, you can make me clean." Moved with pity, he stretched out his hand and touched him, and said to him ,"I will; be clean." And immediately the leprosy left him, and he was made clean. And he sternly charged him, and sent him away at once, and said to him, "See that you say nothing to any one; but go, show yourself to the priest, and offer for your cleansing what Moses commanded, for a proof to the people." But he went out and began to talk freely about it, and to spread the news, so that Jesus could no longer openly enter a town, but was out in the country; and people came to him from every quarter.

* Lepers were obliged by the Mosaic law to live at a distance from other people for reasons of hygiene. When they were cured their cure had to be certified by a Priest.

Jesus cures a paralytic

Mt. 9, 1—8. Mk. 2, 1—12. Lk. 5, 17—26

And when he returned to Capernaum after some days, it was reported that he was at home. And many were gathered together, so that there was no longer room for them, not even about the door; and he was preaching the word to them. And they came,

99

Lake of Gennesaret. Site of Capernaum seen from the ground behind it. The bushes conceal the remains of the synagogue.

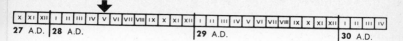

X	XI	XII	I	II	III	IV	V	VI	VII	VIII	IX	X	XI	XII	I	II	III	IV	V	VI	VII	VIII	IX	X	XI	XII	I	II	III	IV

27 A.D. **28** A.D. **29** A.D. **30** A.D.

bringing to him a paralytic carried by four men. And when they could not get near him because of the crowd, they removed the roof above him; and when they had made an opening, they let down the pallet on which the paralytic lay. And when Jesus saw their faith, he said to the paralytic, "My son, your sins are forgiven." Now some of the scribes were sitting there, questioning in their hearts, "Why does this man speak thus? It is blasphemy! Who can forgive sins but God alone?" And immediately Jesus, perceiving in his spirit that they thus questioned within themselves, said to them, "Why do you question thus in your hearts? Which is easier, to say to the paralytic. 'Your sins are forgiven.' or to say, 'Rise, take up your pallet and walk?' But that you may know that the Son of man has authority on earth to forgive sins"— he said to the paralytic— "I say to you, rise, take up your pallet and go home." And he rose, and immediately took up the pallet and went out before them all; so that they were all amazed and glorified God, saying, "We never saw anything like this!"

Jesus calls Matthew to be an apostle
Mt. 9, 9–13. Mk. 2, 13–17. Lk. 5, 27–32

He went out again beside the sea; and all the crowd gathered about him, and he taught them. And as he passed on, he saw Levi the son of Alphaeus sitting at the tax office, and he said to him, "Follow me." And he rose and followed him.

And as he sat at table in his house, many tax collectors and sinners were sitting with Jesus and his disciples; for there were many who followed him. And the scribes of the

* In the book of the prophet Daniel (chap. 7) the Messiah who comes from heaven to judge and to take possession of the eternal Kingdom is called 'Son of Man'. Jesus, applying this title to himself, affirms his own messianic dignity and at the same time avoids being taken for a political Messiah. In this episode he confirms his power to forgive sins (which is a power belonging to God only) by a miracle.

** Matthew was a 'publican' (that is, a tax collector): and, before following our Lord, he invited him to dinner in his house. Later he became an Apostle and wrote the first Gospel.

101

| X | XI | XII | I | II | III | IV | V | VI | VII | VIII | IX | X | XI | XII | I | II | III | IV | V | VI | VII | VIII | IX | X | XI | XII | I | II | III | IV |

27 A.D. **28** A.D. **29** A.D. **30** A.D.

Pharisees, when they saw that he was eating with sinners and tax collectors, said to his disciples, "Why does he eat with tax collectors and sinners?" And when Jesus heard it, he said to them, "Those who are well have no need of a physician, but those who are sick; I came not to call the righteous, but sinners."

Jesus deals with the question of fasting
Mt. 9, 14–17. **Mk. 2, 18–22.** Lk. 5, 33–39

Now John's disciples and the Pharisees were fasting; and the people came and said to him."Why do John's disciples and the disciples of the Pharisees fast, but your disciples do not fast?" And Jesus said to them, "Can the wedding guests fast while the bridegroom is with them? As long as they have the bridegroom with them, they cannot fast. The days will come, when the bridegroom is taken away from them, and then they will fast in that day. No one sews a piece of unshrunk cloth on an old garment; if he does, the patch tears away from it, the new from the old, and a worse tear is made. And no one puts new wine into old wine-skins; if he does the wine will burst the skins, and the wine is lost, and so are the skins; but new wine is for fresh skins."

'The sabbath was made for man, not man for the sabbath'
Mt. 12, 1–8. **Mk. 2, 23–28.** Lk. 6, 1–5

One sabbath he was going through the grainfields; and as they made their way his disciples began to pluck ears of grain. And the Pharisees said to him, "Look, why are they doing what is not lawful on the sabbath?" And he said to them, "Have you

102

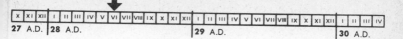
never read what David did, when he was in need and was hungry, he and those who were with him: how he entered the house of God, when Abiathar was high priest, and ate the bread of the Presence, which it is not lawful for any but the priests to eat, and also gave it to those who were with him?" And he said to them, "The sabbath was made for man, not man for the sabbath; so the Son of man is lord even of the Sabbath."

Jesus cures a man with a withered hand
Mt. 12, 9–13. Mk. 3, 1–5. Lk. 6, 6–11.

On another sabbath, when he entered the synagogue and taught, a man was there whose right hand was withered. And the scribes and the Pharisees watched him, to see whether he would heal on the sabbath, so that they might find an accusation against him. But he knew their thoughts, and he said to the man who had the withered hand, "Come and stand here." And he rose and stood there. And Jesus said to them, "I ask you, is it lawful on the sabbath to do good or to do harm, to save life or to destroy it?" And he looked around on them all, and said to him, "Stretch out your hand." And he did so, and his hand was restored. But they were filled with fury and discussed with one another what they might do to Jesus.

Jesus continues the work of healing
Mt. 4, 24–25. Mk. 3, 7–12. Lk. 6, 17–19.
Mt. 12, 17–21.

Jesus withdrew with his disciples to the sea, and a great multitude from Galilee followed; also from Judea and Jerusalem and Idumea and from beyond the Jordan and

* While David was fleeing from Saul who was trying to kill him, he betook himself to the Sanctuary (the Temple was not yet built) and asked for bread for himself and his companions. The Priest Abiathar, having no other, gave him the bread which had just been offered to God and which he found on the sacred table (see 1 Samuel, chapter 21).

** In our Lord's time the Sabbath was treated with very great respect, particularly for the rest which God had ordered. The statement that he was superior to the Sabbath enters into his plan of a progressive revelation of his Godhead, and at the same time – see the following incident – of opposing the purely formal observance of the law.

103

The western shore of the Lake of Gennesaret, near to which Jesus worked so many miracles.

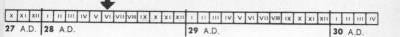

| X | XI | XII | I | II | III | IV | V | VI | VII | VIII | IX | X | XI | XII | I | II | III | IV | V | VI | VII | VIII | IX | X | XI | XII | I | II | III | IV |

27 A.D.   **28** A.D.   **29** A.D.   **30** A.D.

from about Tyre and Sidon a great multitude, hearing all that he did, came to him. And he told his disciples to have a boat ready for him because of the crowd, lest they should crush him; for he had healed many, so that all who had diseases pressed upon him to touch him. And whenever the unclean spirits beheld him, they fell down before him and cried out, "You are the Son of God." And he strictly ordered them not to make him known. This was to fulfil what was spoken by the prophet Isaiah:

"Behold my servant whom I have chosen, my beloved with whom my soul is well pleased.
I will put my Spirit upon him,
and he shall proclaim justice to the Gentiles.
He will not wrangle or cry aloud,
nor will any one hear his voice in the streets:
he will not break a bruised reed
or quench a smouldering wick,
till he brings justice to victory;
and in his name will the Gentiles hope."

* Isaiah (42,1) speaks of the future Messiah as the 'Servant of the Lord' whose mission was to bring to the people God's law, that is, what God wants of men. And the 'Servant of the Lord' was to carry out his mission firmly but also very gently.

Jesus chooses the Twelve
Mt. 5, 1; 10, 1–4. Mk. 3, 13–19. Lk. 6, 12–16

In these days he went out into the hills to pray; and all night he continued in prayer to God. And when it was day, he called his disciples, and chose from them twelve, whom he named apostles: Simon whom he named, Peter, and Andrew his brother, and James and John, and Philip, and Bartholomew, and Matthew, and Thomas, and James the son of Alphaeus, and Simon who was called the Zealot, and Judas the son of James, and Judas Iscariot, who became a traitor.

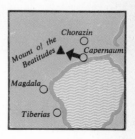

105

On top of the Mount of the Beatitudes is built this Shrine as a memorial of the Sermon on the Mount.

| X | XI | XII | I | II | III | IV | V | VI | VII | VIII | IX | X | XI | XII | I | II | III | IV | V | VI | VII | VIII | IX | X | XI | XII | I | II | III | IV |

27 A.D.　　**28** A.D.　　　　　　　　　**29** A.D.　　　　　　　　　**30** A.D.

Jesus proclaims the beatitudes
Lk. 6, 17–20. Mt. 5, 3–12. Lk. 6, 21–26

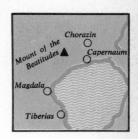

And he came down with them and stood on a level place, with a great crowd of his disciples and a great multitude of people from all Judea and Jerusalem and the sea coast of Tyre and Sidon, who came to hear him and to be healed of their diseases; and those who were troubled with unclean spirits were cured. And all the crowd sought to touch him, for power came forth from him and healed them all.

And he lifted up his eyes on his disciples, and said:

"Blessed are the poor in spirit, for theirs is the kingdom of heaven.

"Blessed are those who mourn, for they shall be comforted.

"Blessed are the meek, for they shall inherit the earth.

"Blessed are those who hunger and thirst for righteousness, for they shall be satisfied.

"Blessed are the merciful, for they shall obtain mercy.

"Blessed are the pure in heart, for they shall see God.

"Blessed are the peacemakers, for they shall be called sons of God.

"Blessed are those who are persecuted for righteousness' sake, for theirs is the kingdom of heaven.

"Blessed are you when men revile you and persecute you and utter all kinds of evil against you falsely on my account. Rejoice and be glad, for your reward is great in heaven, for so men persecuted the prophets who were before you.

107

Safed, 12 miles north of Capernaum. In all probability it was to this city that Jesus referred when he spoke of 'a city set on a hill'.

X	XI	XII	I	II	III	IV	V	VI	VII	VIII	IX	X	XI	XII	I	II	III	IV	V	VI	VII	VIII	IX	X	XI	XII	I	II	III	IV

27 A.D. **28** A.D. **29** A.D. **30** A.D.

'You are the salt of the earth and the light of the world'
Mt. 5, 13–16

"You are the salt of the earth; but if salt has lost its taste, how shall its saltness be restored? It is no longer good for anything except to be thrown out and trodden under foot by men.

"You are the light of the world. A city set on a hill cannot be hid. Nor do men light a lamp and put it under a bushel, but on a stand, and it gives light to all in the house. Let your light so shine before men, that they may see your good works and give glory to your Father who is in heaven.

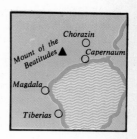

'I have not come to abolish but to fulfil'
Mt. 5, 17–20

"Think not that I have come to abolish the law and the prophets; I have come not to abolish them but to fulfil them. For truly, I say to you, till heaven and earth pass away, not an iota, not a dot, will pass from the law until all is accomplished. Whoever then relaxes one of the least of these commandments and teaches men so, shall be called least in the kingdom of heaven; but he who does them and teaches them shall be called great in the kingdom of heaven. For I tell you, unless your righteousness exceeds that of the scribes and Pharisees, you will never enter the kingdom of heaven.

'First be reconciled to your brother'
Mt. 5, 21–26

"You have heard that it was said to the men of old, 'You shall not kill; and whoever kills shall be liable to judgment.' But I say

* This is the fifth commandment of the Decalogue (see Exod. 20,13); whereas injustice was condemned in the Mosaic law. Jesus condemns lack of love for one's neighbour.

109

| X | XI | XII | I | II | III | IV | V | VI | VII | VIII | IX | X | XI | XII | I | II | III | IV | V | VI | VII | VIII | IX | X | XI | XII | I | II | III | IV |

27 A.D. 28 A.D. 29 A.D. 30 A.D.

to you that every one who is angry with his brother shall be liable to judgment; whoever insults his brother shall be liable to the council, and whoever says, 'You fool!' shall be

* liable to the hell of fire. So if you are offering your gift at the alter, and there remember that your brother has something against you, leave your gift there before the altar and go; first be reconciled to your brother, and then come and offer your gift. Make friends quickly with your accuser, while you are going with him to court, lest your accuser hand you over to the judge, and the judge to the guard, and you be put in prison; truly, I say to you, you will never get out till you have paid the last penny.

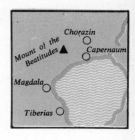

Jesus condemns evil thoughts
Mt. 5, 27–30

** "You have heard that it was said, 'You shall not commit adultery.' But I say to you that every one who looks at a woman lustfully has already committed adultery with her in his heart. If your right eye causes you to sin, pluck it out and throw it away; it is better that you lose one of your members than that your whole body be thrown into hell. And if your right hand causes you to sin, cut it off and throw it away; it is better that you lose one of your members than that your whole body go into hell.

Jesus declares that marriage is indissoluble
Mt. 5, 31–32

*** "It was also said, 'Whoever divorces his wife, let him give her a certificate of divorce.' But I say to you that every one who divorces his wife, except on the ground of unchasitiy,

* Gehenna or the Valley of Hinnom, which is synonymous with Hell in the Gospel, was situated under the southwest wall of Jerusalem; it had a sad notoriety, for in ancient times human sacrifices to the god Moloch had been carried out there.

** This is the 6th commandment (Exod. 20, 14). The Mosaic law condemns the outward act, but Jesus declares that sin is primarily in the act of the will rebelling against the will of God.

*** See Deut. 24, 1. Jesus rejects divorce.

110

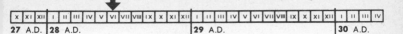

| X | XI | XII | I | II | III | IV | V | VI | VII | VIII | IX | X | XI | XII | I | II | III | IV | V | VI | VII | VIII | IX | X | XI | XII | I | II | III | IV |

27 A.D. **28** A.D. **29** A.D. **30** A.D.

makes her an adulteress; and whoever marries a divorced woman commits adultery.

'Do not swear'
Mt. 5, 33–37

"Again you have heard that it was said to the men of old, 'You shall not swear falsely, but shall perform to the Lord what you have sworn.' But I say to you, Do not swear at all, either by heaven, for it is the throne of God, or by the earth, for it is his footstool, or by Jerusalem, for it is the city of the great King. And do not swear by your head, for you cannot make one hair white or black. Let what you say be simply 'Yes' or 'No'; anything more than this comes from evil.

'Love your enemies and pray for them'
Mt. 5, 38–48. Lk. 6, 27–36

* "You have heard that it was said, 'An eye for an eye and a tooth for a tooth.' But I say to you, Do not resist one who is evil. But if any one strikes you on the right cheek, turn to him the other also; and if any one would sue you and take your coat, let him have your cloak as well, and if any one forces you to go one mile, go with him two miles. Give to him who begs from you, and do not refuse him who would borrow from you.

** "You have heard that it was said, 'You shall love your neighbour and hate your enemy.' But I say to you, Love your enemies and pray for those who persecute you, so that you may be sons of your Father who is in heaven; for he makes his sun rise on the evil and on the good, and sends rain on the just and on the unjust. For if you love those who

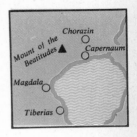

* See Levit. 19, 12. Swearing is calling upon God to witness to the truth of what is said. Here Jesus does not condemn all kinds of oaths, but desires of his faithful such loyalty to the truth that they can always be believed without useless recourse to swearing.

** The Law in Exod. 21, 24 does not intend to encourage private vendettas, but to avoid their abuses. Jesus sets against this the charity and love which must rule relations between neighbours. The true follower of Jesus must not only refrain from vengeance, but must treat others primarily with love.

***Actually the Law of Moses (Levit. 19, 18) says simply: 'Love your neighbour' but the usual

111

View of the Lake of Gennesaret from the Mount of the Beatitudes.

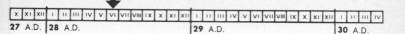

| X | XI | XII | I | II | III | IV | V | VI | VII | VIII | IX | X | XI | XII | I | II | III | IV | V | VI | VII | VIII | IX | X | XI | XII | I | II | III | IV |

27 A.D.   **28** A.D.   **29** A.D.   **30** A.D.

love you, what reward have you? Do not even the tax collectors do the same? And if you salute only your brethren, what more are you doing than others? Do not even the gentiles do the same? You, therefore, must be perfect, as your heavenly Father is perfect.

'Do not let your left hand know what your right hand is doing'
Mt. 6, 1–4

"Beware of practising your piety before men in order to be seen by them; for then you will have no reward from your Father who is in heaven.

"Thus, when you give alms, sound no trumpet before you, as the hypocrites do in the synagogues and in the streets, that they may be praised by men. Truly, I say to you, they have their reward. But when you give alms, do not let your left hand know what your right hand is doing, so that your alms may be in secret; and your Father who sees in secret will reward you.

'Pray to your Father . . . . . .in secret'
Mt. 6, 5–6; 6, 7–15

"And when you pray, you must not be like the hypocrites; for they love to stand and pray in the synagogues and at the street corners, that they may be seen by men. Truly, I say to you, they have their reward. But when you pray, go into your room and shut the door and pray to your Father who is in secret; and your Father who sees in secret will reward you.

'Fast. . . . so that no one will know that you are fasting'
Mt. 6, 16–18

"And when you fast, do not look dismal,

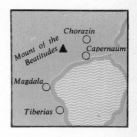

interpretation had added to this: 'Hate your enemy.' Jesus declares the greatest law to be love for all.

113

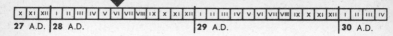

| X | XI | XII | I | II | III | IV | V | VI | VII | VIII | IX | X | XI | XII | I | II | III | IV | V | VI | VII | VIII | IX | X | XI | XII | I | II | III | IV |
27 A.D. 28 A.D.   29 A.D.   30 A.D.

like the hypocrites, for they disfigure their faces that their fasting may be seen by men. Truly, I say to you, they have their reward. But when you fast, anoint your head and wash your face, that your fasting may not be seen by men but by your Father who is in secret; and your Father who sees in secret will reward you.

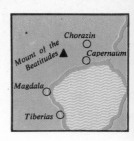

'Lay up for yourselves treasure in heaven'
Mt. 6, 19–21

"Do not lay up for yourselves treasures on earth, where moth and rust consume and where thieves break in and steal, but lay up for yourselves treasures in heaven, where neither moth nor rust consumes and thieves do not break in and steal. For where your treasure is, there will your heart be also.

The need for inner light
Mt. 6, 22–23

"The eye is the lamp of the body. So, if your eye is sound, your whole body will be full of light; but if your eye is not sound, your whole body will be full of darkness. If then the light in you is darkness, how great is the darkness!

'No one can serve two masters'
Mt. 6, 24

"No one can serve two masters; for either he will hate the one and love the other, or he will be devoted to the one and despise the other. You cannot serve
* God and mammon.

'Seek first his kingdom'
Mt. 6, 25–34

"Therefore I tell you, do not be anxious

* The word 'mammon' comes from Aramaic and means 'money'. Here it is personified as the god Mammon in contrast to God the Father.

114

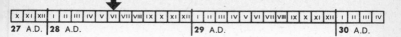
about your life, what you shall eat or what you shall drink, nor about your body, what you shall put on. Is not life more than food, and the body more than clothing? Look at the birds of the air; they neither sow nor reap nor gather into barns, and yet your heavenly Father feeds them. Are you not of more value than they? And which of you by being anxious can add one cubit to his span of life? And why are you anxious about clothing? Consider the lilies of the field, how they grow; they neither toil nor spin? yet I tell you, even Solomon in all his glory was not arrayed like one of these. But if God so clothes the grass of the field, which today is alive and tomorrow is thrown into the oven, will he not much more clothe you, O men of little faith? Therefore do not be anxious, saying, 'What shall we eat?' or 'What shall we drink?' or 'What shall we wear?' For the Gentiles seek all these things; and your heavenly Father knows that you need them all. But seek first his kingdom and his righteousness, and all these things shall be yours as well.

"Therefore do not be anxious about tomorrow, for tomorrow will be anxious for itself. Let the day's own trouble be sufficient for the day.

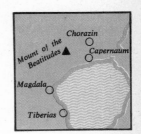

'Why do you see the speck that is in your brother's eye?'

Mt. 7, 1–6. Lk. 6, 37–42

Judge not, that you be not judged, with the judgement you pronounce you will be judged, and the measure you give will be the measure you get. Why do you see the speck that is in your brother's eye, but do not notice the log that is in your own eye?

115

Or how can you say to your brother,
'Let me take the speck out of your eye,'
when there is the log in your own eye?
You hypocrite, first take the log out of
your own eye, and then you will see clearly
to take the speck out of your brother's eye.

"Do not give dogs what is holy; and do
not throw your pearls before swine, lest
they trample them under foot and turn to
attack you.

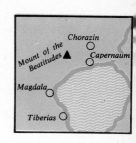

Jesus gives the rule of loving one's neighbour
Mt. 7,12

So whatever you wish that men would
do to you, do so to them; for this is the law
and the prophets.

'Enter by the narrow gate'
Mt. 7, 13–14

"Enter by the narrow gate; for the
gate is wide and the way is easy, that
leads to destruction, and those who enter
by it are many. For the gate is narrow and
the way is hard, that leads to life, and
those who find it are few.

'Beware of false prophets'
Mt. 7, 15–20. Lk. 6, 43–45

"Beware of false prophets, who come to
you in sheep's clothing but inwardly are
ravenous wolves. You will know them by
their fruits. Are grapes gathered from thorns,
or figs from thistles? So, every sound tree
bears good fruit, but the bad tree bears evil
fruit. A sound tree cannot bear evil fruit,
nor can a bad tree bear good fruit. Every tree
that does not bear good fruit is cut down
and thrown into the fire. Thus you will know
them by their fruits.

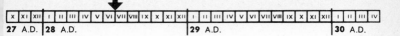

| X | XI | XII | I | II | III | IV | V | VI | VII | VIII | IX | X | XI | XII | I | II | III | IV | V | VI | VII | VIII | IX | X | XI | XII | I | II | III | IV |

27 A.D.   **28** A.D.   **29** A.D.   **30** A.D.

'Do the will of God'
Mt. 7, 21–23. Lk. 6, 46

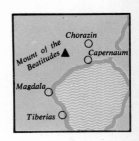

"Not every one who says to me, 'Lord, Lord,' shall enter the kingdom of heaven, but he who does the will of my Father who is in heaven. On that day many will say to me, 'Lord, Lord, did we not prophesy in your name, and cast out demons in your name, and do many mighty works in your name?' And then will I declare to them, 'I never knew you; depart from me, you evildoers.'

The parable of the house built on a rock
Mt. 7, 24–29. Lk. 6, 47–49; 7, 1

"Everyone then who hears these words of mine and does them will be like a wise man who built his house upon the rock; and the rain fell, and the floods came, and the winds blew and beat upon that house, but it did not fall, because it had been founded on the rock. And every one who hears these words of mine and does not do them will be like a foolish man who built his house upon the sand; and the rain fell, and the floods came, and the winds blew and beat against that house, and it fell; and great was the fall of it."

And when Jesus finished these sayings, the crowds were astonished at his teaching, for he taught them as one who had authority, and not as their scribes.

Jesus is astonished by the faith of the centurion
Mt. 8,1; 8, 5–13. Lk. 7, 1–10

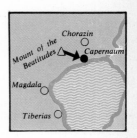

After he had ended all his sayings in the hearing of the people he entered Capernaum. Now a centurion had a slave who was

117

Capernaum. The left side of the synagogue. After his baptism Jesus left Nazareth and went to live at Capernaum. This explains the large number of miracles worked in that town.

| X | XI | XII | I | II | III | IV | V | VI | VII | VIII | IX | X | XI | XII | I | II | III | IV | V | VI | VII | VIII | IX | X | XI | XII | I | II | III | IV |

27 A.D.   **28** A.D.   **29** A.D.   **30** A.D.

dear to him, who was sick and at the point of death. When he heard of Jesus, he sent to
* him elders of the Jews, asking him to come and heal his slave. And when they came to Jesus, they besought him earnestly, saying, "He is worthy to have you do this for him, for he loves our nation, and he built us our synagogue." And Jesus went with them. When he was not far from the house, the centurion sent friends to him, saying to him, "Lord, do not trouble yourself, for I am not worthy to have you come under my roof; therefore I did not presume to come to you. But say the word, and let my servant be healed. For I am a man set under authority, with soldiers under me: and I say to one, 'Go', and he goes; and to another, 'Come', and he comes; and to my slave, 'Do this,' and he does it." When Jesus heard this he marvelled at him, and turned and said to the multitude that followed him, "I tell you, not even in Israel have I found such faith." And when those who had been sent returned to the house, they found the slave well.

* It is probable that he was an officer in the service of Herod Antipas, the tetrarch.

At Nain, Jesus restores to life a widow's son
Lk. 7, 11–17

Soon afterward he went to a city called Nain, and his disciples and a great crowd went with him. As he drew near to the gate of the city, behold, a man who had died was being carried out, the only son of his mother, and she was a widow; and a large crowd from the city was with her. And when the Lord saw her, he had compassion on her and said to her, "Do not weep." And he came and touched the bier, and the bearers stood still. And he said, "Young man, I say to

119

Nain in Galilee. The site of the ancient gate where Jesus restored to life the widow's son. The church was built as a memorial of the miracle.

| X | XI | XII | I | II | III | IV | V | VI | VII | VIII | IX | X | XI | XII | I | II | III | IV | V | VI | VII | VIII | IX | X | XI | XII | I | II | III | IV |

27 A.D. | 28 A.D. | 29 A.D. | 30 A.D.

you, arise." And the dead man sat up, and began to speak. And he gave him to his mother. Fear seized them all; and they glorified God, saying, "A great prophet has arisen among us!" and "God has visited his people!" And this report concerning him spread through the whole of Judea and all the surrounding country.

Jesus and the messengers of the Baptist
Mt. 11, 2–6. Lk. 7, 18–23

The disciples of John told him of all these things. And John, calling to him two of his disciples, sent them to the Lord, saying, "Are you he who is to come, or shall we look for another?" And when the men had come to him, they said, "John the Baptist has sent us to you, saying, 'Are you he who is to come, or shall we look for another?' " In that hour he cured many of diseases and plagues and evil spirits, and on many that were blind he bestowed sight. And he answered them, "Go and tell John what you have seen and heard: the blind receive their sight, the lame walk, lepers are cleansed, and the deaf hear, the dead are raised up, the poor have good news preached to them. And blessed is he who takes no offence at me."

Jesus commends John
Mt. 11, 7–19. Lk. 7, 24–35.

When the messengers of John had gone, he began to speak to the crowds concerning John: 'What did you go out into the wilderness to behold? A reed shaken by the wind? What then did you go out to see? A man clothed in soft raiment? Behold, those

* John the Baptist's concern is above all for his disciples. In this way he hopes to provoke Jesus into a precise definition of his Person.

** Jesus repeats the prophecy of Isaiah (35, 5) which presents the Messiah as a saviour, so as to oppose the idea of the people of his time who expected instead a Messiah who would be a glorious and invincible warrior. It was for this reason that he added: 'Blessed is he who takes no offence in me.'

121

Ruins of Magdala, on the western shore of the Lake of Gennesaret, south of Capernaum at the point where the lake is at its widest.

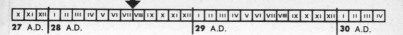

| X | XI | XII | I | II | III | IV | V | VI | VII | VIII | IX | X | XI | XII | I | II | III | IV | V | VI | VII | VIII | IX | X | XI | XII | I | II | III | IV |

27 A.D. | **28** A.D. | **29** A.D. | **30** A.D.

who are gorgeously apparelled and live in luxury are in kings' courts. What then did you go out to see? A prophet? Yes, I tell you, and more than a prophet. This is he of whom it is written,

'Behold, I send my messenger before thy face,
who shall prepare the way before thee.'

I tell you, among those born of women * none is greater than John; yet he who is least in the kingdom of God is greater than he." (When they heard this all the people and the tax collectors justified God, having been baptized with the baptism of John; but the Pharisees and the lawyers rejected the purpose of God for themselves, not having been baptized by him.)

"To what then shall I compare the men of this generation, and what are then like? They are like children sitting in the market place and calling to one another,
'We piped to you, and you did not dance; we wailed, and you did not weep.'
For John the Baptist has come eating no bread and drinking no wine; and you say, 'He has a demon.' The Son of man has come eating and drinking; and you say, 'Behold, a glutton and a drunkard, a friend of tax collectors and sinners! Yet wisdom is justified by all her children."

Jesus pardons the sinful woman
Lk. 7, 36–50

One of the Pharisees asked him to eat with him, and he went into the Pharisee's *house, and sat at table. And behold, a woman of the city, who was a sinner, when she

* The quotation is from the prophet Malachi (3, 1) who, about 500 years before Christ's coming, prophesied the coming of his messenger who was to prepare the people for the coming of the Lord.

** The reason is that John was unable to enter into the spiritual riches of the New Covenant; he was in fact the last of the Hebrew prophets.

***This woman cannot be identified either with Mary the sister of Lazarus, or with any great probability with Mary Magdalen, but was another woman whom our Lord had helped, and who perhaps came from the neighbouring town of Tiberias.

123

| X | XI | XII | I | II | III | IV | V | VI | VII | VIII | IX | X | XI | XII | I | II | III | IV | V | VI | VII | VIII | IX | X | XI | XII | I | II | III | IV |

27 A.D.   28 A.D.   29 A.D.   30 A.D.

learned that he was sitting at table in the Pharisee's house, brought an alabaster flask of ointment, and standing behind him at his feet, weeping, she began to wet his feet with her tears, and wiped them with the hair of her head, and kissed his feet, and anointed them with the ointment.

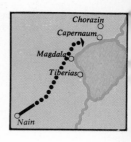

Now when the Pharisee who had invited him saw it, he said to himself, "If this man were a prophet, he would have known who and what sort of woman this is who is touching him, for she is a sinner." And Jesus answering said to him, "Simon, I have something to say to you." And he answered, "What is it, Teacher?" "A certain creditor had two debtors; one owed five hundred denarii, and the other fifty. When they could not pay, he forgave them both. Now which of them will love him more?" Simon answered, "The one, I suppose, to whom he forgave more." And he said to him, "You have judged rightly." Then turning toward the woman he said to Simon, "Do you see this woman?
* I entered your house, you gave me no water for my feet, but she has wet my feet with her tears and wiped them with her hair. You gave me no kiss, but from the time I came in she has not ceased to kiss my feet. You did not anoint my head with oil, but she has anointed my feet with ointment. Therefore I tell you, her sins, which are many, are forgiven, for she loved much; but he who is forgiven little, loves little." And he said to her, "Your sins are forgiven." Then those who were at table with him began to say among themselves, "Who is this, who even forgives sins?" And he said to the woman, "Your faith has saved you; go in peace."

* The reference is to the polite customs then in use, which were intended to express the greatest possible respect and affection with which a guest should be welcomed into one's home.

| X | XI | XII | I | II | III | IV | V | VI | VII | VIII | IX | X | XI | XII | I | II | III | IV | V | VI | VII | VIII | IX | X | XI | XII | I | II | III | IV |

27 A.D. | **28** A.D. | **29** A.D. | **30** A.D.

Jesus and his relations
Mk. 3, 20–21

Then he went home; and the crowd came together again, so that they could not even eat. And when his friends heard it, they went out to seize him, for they said, "He is beside himself."

'He who is not with me is against me'
Mt. 12, 22–30. Mk. 3, 22–27. Lk. 11, 14–23

Now he was casting out a demon that was dumb; when the demon had gone out, the dumb man spoke, and the people marvelled. But some of them said, "He casts out demons by Beelzebul, the prince of demons"; while others, to test him, sought from him a sign from heaven. But he, knowing their thoughts, said to them, "Every kingdom divided against itself is laid waste, and house falls upon house. And if Satan also is divided against himself how will his kingdom stand? For you say that I cast out demons by Beelzebul. And if I cast out demons by Beelzebul, by whom do your sons cast them out? Therefore they shall be your judges. But if it is by the finger of God that I cast out demons, then the kingdom of God has come upon you. When a strong man, fully armed, guards his own palace, his goods are in peace; but when one stronger than he assails him and overcomes him, he takes away his armour in which he trusted, and divides his spoil. He who is not with me is against me, and he who does not gather with me scatters.

* They must have been some of his relations who had come down from Nazareth to Capernaum and did not include our Lady, for she was probably already living at Caperanum, whither she had moved so as to be nearer to her son.

** Beelzebul was an idol of Ekron, which the Jews contemptuously called Belzebub ('God of flies') and identified with the devil.

| X | XI | XII | I | II | III | IV | V | VI | VII | VIII | IX | X | XI | XII | I | II | III | IV | V | VI | VII | VIII | IX | X | XI | XII | I | II | III | IV |

27 A.D. **28** A.D. **29** A.D. **30** A.D.

The Jews' greatest sin: attributing the work of the Holy Spirit to the devil
Mt. 12, 31–37. Mk. 3, 28–30

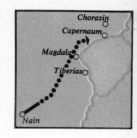

Therefore I tell you, every sin and blasphemy will be forgiven men, but the blasphemy
* against the Spirit will not be forgiven. And whoever says a word against the Son of man will be forgiven; but whoever speaks against the Holy Spirit will not be forgiven, either in this age or in the age to come.

"Either make the tree good, and its fruit good; or make the tree bad, and its fruit bad; for the tree is known by its fruit. You brood of vipers! how can you speak good, when you are evil? For out of the abundance of the heart the mouth speaks. The good man out of his good treasure brings forth good, and the evil man out of his evil treasure brings forth evil. I tell you, on the day of judgement men will render account for every careless word they utter; for by your words you will be justified, and by your words you will be condemned."

The parable of the cast-out devil
Mt. 12, 43–45. Lk. 11, 24–26

"When the unclean spirit has gone out of a man, he passes through waterless places seeking rest; and finding none he says. I will return to my house from which I came.' And when he comes he finds it swept and put in order. Then he goes and brings seven other spirits more evil than himself, and they enter and dwell there; and the last state of that man becomes worse than the first."

* By blasphemy against the Holy Spirit, Jesus meant shutting their eyes so as not to believe in what he said and did. It is therefore the sin of obstinacy in refusing to believe, for which there can be no forgiveness.

126

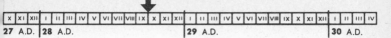

| X | XI | XII | I | II | III | IV | V | VI | VII | VIII | IX | X | XI | XII | I | II | III | IV | V | VI | VII | VIII | IX | X | XI | XII | I | II | III | IV |

27 A.D.   28 A.D.   29 A.D.   30 A.D.

'Whoever does the will of God is my brother'
Mt. 12, 46–50. Mk. 3, 31–35. Lk. 11, 27–28

And his mother and his brethren came; and standing outside they sent to him and called him. And a crowd was sitting about him; and they said to him "Your mother and brethren are outside, asking for you." And he replied, "Who are my mother and my brethren?" And looking around on those who sat about him, he said, "Here are my mother and my brethren! Whoever does the will of God is my brother, and sister, and mother."

▶ As he said this, a woman in the crowd raised her voice and said to him, "Blessed is the womb that bore you, and the breasts that you sucked!" But he said, "Blessed rather are those who hear the word of God and keep it!"

* In the manner of speech of that time this saying did not intend to suggest any lack of respect for his mother on Jesus' part; rather he intended it to show how much the will of God had always meant to her.

A few women attend to Jesus' needs
Lk. 8, 1–3

Soon afterward he went on through cities and villages, preaching and bringing the good news of the kingdom of God. And the twelve were with him, and also some women who had been healed of evil spirits and infirmities: Mary, called Magdalene, from whom seven demons had gone out, and Joanna, the wife of Chuza, Herod's steward, and Susanna, and many others, who provided for them out of their means.

The parable of the sower
Mt. 13, 1–9. Mk. 4, 1–9, Lk. 8, 4–8

That same day Jesus went out of the house and sat beside the sea. And great crowds gathered about him so that he got into a boat and sat there; and the whole

127

A piece of land in Palestine which recalls the parable of the sower. In the foreground a pathway is visible, then, above it a patch of stony ground in the middle of which can be seen a thicket of prickly thistles; higher still is a strip of good ground where seed has grown.

| X | XI | XII | I | II | III | IV | V | VI | VII | VIII | IX | X | XI | XII | I | II | III | IV | V | VI | VII | VIII | IX | X | XI | XII | I | II | III | IV |

27 A.D.   28 A.D.   29 A.D.   30 A.D.

crowd stood on the beach. And he told them many things in parables, saying: "A sower went out to sow. And as he sowed, some seeds fell along the path, and the birds came and devoured them. Other seeds fell on rocky ground, where they had not much soil, and immediately they sprang up, since they had no depth of soil, but when the sun rose they were scorched; and since they had no root they withered away. Other seeds fell upon thorns, and the thorns grew up and choked them. Other seeds fell on good soil and brought forth grain, some a hundredfold, some sixty, some thirty. He who has ears, let him hear."

Jesus explains why he teaches in parables
Mt. 13, 10–17. Mk. 4, 10–12. Lk. 8, 9–10

Then the disciples came and said to him, "Why do you speak to them in parables?" And he answered them, "To you it has been given to know the secrets of the kingdom of heaven, but to them it has not been given. For to him who has will more be given, and he will have abundance; but from him who has not, even what he has will be taken away. This is why I speak to them in parables, because seeing they do not see, and hearing they do not hear, nor do they understand. With them indeed is fulfilled the prophecy of Isaiah which says:
'You shall indeed hear but never understand,
and you shall indeed see but never perceive.
For this people's heart has grown dull,
and their ears are heavy of hearing,
and their eyes they have closed,
lest they should perceive with their eyes,
and hear with their ears,

* This saying makes our Lord's thought very clear. A person who believes will receive more and more light so as increasingly to enlarge and improve his knowledge, but one who does not respond to faith will find his faith becoming weaker and weaker until it disappears. That is why Jesus speaks in parables.

** Isa. 6, 9-10. 'You have been unwilling to listen to the Lord, and will end by understanding his words less and less. You have shut your eyes and ears, and so your heart will become ever less sensitive to the voice of God. So your sin itself will become your punishment.'

129

| X | XI | XII | I | II | III | IV | V | VI | VII | VIII | IX | X | XI | XII | I | II | III | IV | V | VI | VII | VIII | IX | X | XI | XII | I | II | III | IV |

27 A.D. **28** A.D. **29** A.D. **30** A.D.

and understand with their heart,
and turn for me to heal them.'

But blessed are your eyes, for they see.
and your ears, for they hear. Truly, I say to
you, many prophets and righteous men longed
to see what you see, and did not see it, and
to hear what you hear, and did not hear it.

Jesus explains the parable of the sower
Mt. 13, 18–23. Mk. 4, 13–20. Lk. 8, 11–15

"Hear then the parable of the sower.
When any one hears the word of the kingdom
and does not understand it, the evil one comes
and snatches away what is sown in his
heart; this is what was sown along the path.
As for what was sown on rocky ground, this
is he who hears the word and immediately
receives it with joy; yet he has no root in
himself, but endures for a while, and when
tribulation or persecution arises on account of
the word, immediately he falls away. As for
what was sown among thorns, this is he who
hears the word, but the cares of the world
and the delight in riches choke the word, and
it proves unfruitful. As for what was sown
on good soil, this is he who hears the word
and understands it; he indeed bears fruit,
in one case a hundredfold, in another sixty,
and in another thirty."

The parables of the lamp and the measure
Mk. 4, 21–25. Lk. 8, 16–18

And he said to them, "Is a lamp brought
in to be put under a bushel, or under a bed,
and not on a stand? For there is nothing hid,
except to be made manifest; nor is anything
secret, except to come to light. If any man
has ears to hear, let him hear." And he

130

| X | XI | XII | I | II | III | IV | V | VI | VII | VIII | IX | X | XI | XII | I | II | III | IV | V | VI | VII | VIII | IX | X | XI | XII | I | II | III | IV |

27 A.D. | 28 A.D. | 29 A.D. | 30 A.D.

said to them, "Take heed what you hear; the measure you give will be the measure you get, and still more will be given you. For to him who has will more be given; and from him who has not, even what he has will be taken away."

The parable of the seed growing by itself
Mk. 4, 26–29

* And he said, "The kingdom of God is as if a man should scatter seed upon the ground, and should sleep and rise night and day, and the seed should sprout and grow, he knows not how. The earth produces of itself, first the blade, then the ear, then the full grain in the ear. But when the grain is ripe, at once he puts in the sickle, because the harvest has come."

The parable of the weeds
Mt. 13, 24–30

Another parable he put before them, saying, "The kingdom of heaven may be compared to a man who sowed good seed in his field; but while men were sleeping, his enemy came and sowed weeds among the wheat, and went away. So when the plants came up and bore grain, then the weeds appeared also. And the servants of the house-holder came and said to him, Sir, did you not sow good seed in your field? How then has it weeds?' He said to them, 'An enemy has done this.' The servants said to him, 'Then do you want us to go and gather them?' But he said, 'No; lest in gathering the weeds you root up the wheat along with them. Let both grow together until the

* The phrase 'The kingdom of God, or of heaven, is like. . .' with which various parables begin, means that something like what the parable as a whole tries to express happens in the kingdom of heaven.

131

Grains of mustard 'the smallest of all the seeds' (Mt. 13,32). Even in the most minute details the Gospel shows itself extraordinarily true to reality.

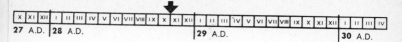

| X | XI | XII | I | II | III | IV | V | VI | VII | VIII | IX | X | XI | XII | I | II | III | IV | V | VI | VII | VIII | IX | X | XI | XII | I | II | III | IV |
27 A.D. 28 A.D. 29 A.D. 30 A.D.

harvest; and at harvest time I will tell the reapers, Gather the weeds first and bind them in bundles to be burned, but gather the wheat into my barn." '

The parable of the mustard seed
Mt. 13, 31–32. Mk. 4, 30–32. Lk. 13, 18–19

Another parable he put before them, saying, "The kingdom of heaven is like a grain of mustard seed which a man took and sowed in his field; it is the smallest of all seeds, but when it has grown it is the greatest of shrubs and becomes a tree, so that the birds of the air come and make nests in its branches."

The parable of the leaven
Mt. 13, 33. Lk. 13, 20–21

He told them another parable, "The kingdom of heaven is like leaven which a woman took and hid in three measures of meal, till it was all leavened."

Jesus teaches the crowds in parables
Mt. 13, 34–35. Mk. 4, 33–34

All this Jesus said to the crowds in parables; indeed he said nothing to them without a parable. This was to fulfil what was spoken by the prophet:
"I will open my mouth in parables,
I will utter what has been hidden since the foundation of the world."

Jesus explains the parable of the weeds
Mt. 13, 36–43

Then he left the crowds and went into the house. And his disciples came to him, saying, "Explain to us the parable of the weeds of the field." He answered, "He who sows the good seed is the Son of man; the field is the

* It is the Psalmist (Ps. 78, 2) who says, as did Jesus, that he intends to reveal the mysteries of God by means of illustrations and parables.

133

| X | XI | XII | I | II | III | IV | V | VI | VII | VIII | IX | X | XI | XII | I | II | III | IV | V | VI | VII | VIII | IX | X | XI | XII | I | II | III | IV |

27 A.D. | 28 A.D. | 29 A.D. | 30 A.D.

world, and the good seed means the sons of the kingdom; the weeds are the sons of the evil one, and the enemy who sowed them is the devil; the harvest is the close of the age, and the reapers are angels. Just as the weeds are gathered and burned with fire, so will it be at the close of the age. The Son of man will send his angels, and they will gather out of his kingdom all causes of sin and all evildoers, and throw them into the furnace of fire; there men will weep and gnash their teeth. The righteous will shine like the sun in the kingdom of their Father. He who has ears, let him hear.

The parables of the treasure and of the pearl of great value
Mt. 13, 44–46

"The kingdom of heaven is like treasure hidden in a field, which a man found and covered up; then in his joy he goes and sells all that he has and buys that field.

"Again, the kingdom of heaven is like a merchant in search of fine pearls, who, on finding one pearl of great value, went and sold all that he had and bought it.

The parable of the net
Mt. 13, 47–50

"Again, the kingdom of heaven is like a net which was thrown into the sea and gathered fish of every kind; when it was full, men drew it ashore and sat down and sorted the good into vessels but threw away the bad. So it will be at the close of the age. The angels will come out and separate the evil from the righteous, and throw them into the furnace of fire; there men will weep and gnash their teeth.

134

Jesus ends his talk about parables
Mt. 13, 51–52

"Have you understood all this?" They said to him, "Yes." And he said to them, "Therefore every scribe who has been trained for the kingdom of heaven is like a householder who brings out of his treasure what is new and what is old."

Jesus stills the storm
Mt. 8, 18; 8, 23–27. Mk. 4, 35–41. Lk. 8, 22–25

On that day, when evening had come, he said to them, "Let us go across to the other side." And leaving the crowd, they took him with them just as he was, in the boat. And other boats were with him. And a great storm of wind arose, and the waves beat into the boat, so that the boat was already filling. But he was in the stern, asleep on the cushion; and they woke him and said to him, "Teacher, do you not care if we perish?" And he woke and rebuked the wind, and said to the sea, "Peace! Be still!" And the wind ceased, and there was a great calm. He said to them, "Why are you afraid? Have you no faith?" and they, were filled with awe, and said to one another, "who then is this, that even wind and sea obey him?"

Jesus frees a demoniac at Gerasa (Gadara)
Mt. 8, 28–34. Mk. 5, 1–20. Lk. 8, 26–39

They came to the other side of the sea, to the country of the Gerasenes. And when he had come out of the boat, there met him out of the tombs a man with an unclean spirit, who lived among the tombs; and no one could bind him any more, even with a chain; for he had often been bound with fetters and chains, but the chains he wrenched apart, and the fetters he broke in pieces; and

* 'Every scribe', that is every doctor of the law who enters the kingdom of God, knowing well the Old Testament ('things old') and the New Law ('things new'), becomes a teacher of others.

The 'coasts of Decapolis' photographed from Magdala with a telephoto lens. It was from these heights that the herd of pigs charged into the waters of the lake.

| X | XI | XII | I | II | III | IV | V | VI | VII | VIII | IX | X | XI | XII | I | II | III | IV | V | VI | VII | VIII | IX | X | XI | XII | I | II | III | IV |

27 A.D. | **28 A.D.** | **29 A.D.** | **30 A.D.**

no one had the strength to subdue him. Night and day among the tombs and on the mountains he was always crying out, and bruising himself with stones. And when he saw Jesus from afar, he ran and worshipped him; and crying out with a loud voice, he said, "What have you to do with me, Jesus, Son of the Most High God? I adjure you by God, do not torment me." For he had said to him, "Come out of the man, you unclean spirit!" And Jesus asked him, "What is your name?" He replied, "My name is Legion; for we are many." And he begged him eagerly not to send them out of the country. Now a great herd of swine was feeding there on the hillside; and they begged him, "Send us to the swine, let us enter them." So he gave them leave. And the unclean spirits came out, and entered the swine; and the herd, numbering about two thousand, rushed down the steep bank into the sea, and were drowned in the sea.

The herdsmen fled, and told it in the city and in the country. And people came to see what it was that had happened. And they came to Jesus, and saw the demoniac sitting there, clothed and in his right mind, the man who had had the legion; and they were afraid. And those who had seen it told what had happened to the demoniac and to the swine. And they began to beg Jesus to depart from their neighbourhood. And as he was getting into the boat, the man who had been possessed with demons begged him that he might be with him. But he refused, and said to him, "Go home to your friends, and tell them how much the Lord has done for you, and how he has had mercy on you." And he went away and began to proclaim

137

in the Decapolis how much Jesus had done for him, and all men marvelled.

Jairus pleads with Jesus for his dying daughter
Mt. 9, 18–19. Mk. 5, 21–24. Lk. 8, 40–42

And when Jesus had crossed again in the boat to the other side, a great crowd gathered about him; and he was beside the sea. Then came one of the rulers of the synagogue, Jairus by name, and seeing him, he fell at his feet, and besought him, saying, "My little daughter is at the point of death. Come and lay your hands on her, so that she may be made well, and live." And he went with him.

And a great crowd followed him and thronged about him.

Jesus rewards the faith of the woman with a haemorrhage
Mt. 9, 20–22. Mk. 5, 25–34. Lk. 8, 43–48

And there was a woman who had had a flow of blood for twelve years, and who had suffered much under many physicians, and had spent all that she had, and was no better but rather grew worse. She had heard the reports about Jesus, and came up behind him in the crowd and touched his garment. For she said, "If I touch even his garments, I shall be made well." And immediately the hemorrhage ceased; and she felt in her body that she was healed of her disease. And Jesus, perceiving in himself that power had gone forth from him immediately turned in the crowd, and said, "Who touched my garments?" And his disciples said to him, "You see the crowd pressing around you, and yet you say, 'Who touched me?' " And he looked around to see who had done it. But the woman, knowing what had been

X	XI	XII	I	II	III	IV	V	VI	VII	VIII	IX	X	XI	XII	I	II	III	IV	V	VI	VII	VIII	IX	X	XI	XII	I	II	III	IV

27 A.D. | **28** A.D. | **29** A.D. | **30** A.D.

done to her, came in fear and trembling and fell down before him, and told him the whole truth. And he said to her, "Daughter, your faith has made you well; go in peace, and be healed of your disease."

Jesus restores Jairus's daughter to life
Mt. 9, 23–26. Mk. 5, 35–43. Lk. 8, 49–56

While he was still speaking, there came from the ruler's house some who said, "Your daughter is dead. Why trouble the Teacher any further?" But ignoring what they said, Jesus said to the ruler of the synagogue, "Do not fear, only believe." And he allowed no one to follow him except Peter and James and John the brother of James. When they came to the house of the ruler of the synagogue, he saw a tumult, and people weeping and wailing loudly. And when he had entered, he said to them, "Why do you make a tumult and weep? The child is not dead but sleeping." And they laughed at him. But he put them all outside, and took the child's father and mother and those who were with him, and went in where the child was. Taking her by the hand he said to her, "Talitha cumi"; which means, "Little girl, I say to you, arise." And immediately the girl got up and walked; for she was twelve years old. And immediately they were overcome with amazement. And he strictly charged them that no one should know this, and told them to give her something to eat.

Jesus cures two blind men
Mt. 9, 27–31

And as Jesus passed on from there, two blind men followed him, crying aloud, "Have mercy on us, Son of David." When he entered the house, the blind men came to him;

* Nearly always the Lord worked his miracles because of the compassion which human suffering aroused in him. From the beginning Jesus did not desire to declare himself as Messiah for that would have caused a popular movement of a political character; later he wished little by little to reveal himself to the people as the Son of God; for this reason, he ordered them not to let this miracle, or that which followed, be known.

139

The supposed 'Synagogue' at Nazareth. It was in that synagogue that Jesus declared that the messianic prophecy of Isaiah about the preaching of Good News was fulfilled in himself.

and Jesus said to them, "Do you believe that I am able to do this?" They said to him, "Yes, Lord". Then he touched their eyes, saying, "According to your faith be it done to you." And their eyes were opened. And Jesus sternly charged them, "See that no one knows it." But they went away and spread his fame through all that district.

Jesus cures a dumb demoniac
Mt. 9, 32–34

As they were going away, behold, a dumb demoniac was brought to him. And when the demon had been cast out, the dumb man spoke; and the crowds marvelled, saying, "Never was anything like this seen in Israel." But the Pharisees said, "He casts out demons by the prince of demons."

Jesus preaches at Nazareth, but is driven away
Mt. 13, 53–58. Mk. 6, 1–6. Lk. 4, 16–30

And he came to Nazareth, where he had been brought up; and he went to the synagogue, as his custom was, on the sabbath * day. And he stood up to read; and there was given to him the book of the prophet Isaiah. He opened the book and found the place where it was written.

"The Spirit of the Lord is upon me, because he has anointed me to preach good news to the poor.
He has sent me to proclaim release to the captives
and recovering of sight to the blind,
to set at liberty those who are oppressed,
to proclaim the acceptable year of the Lord."
And he closed the book, and gave it back to the attendant, and sat down; and the eyes of all in the synagogue were fixed on him.

* In this passage the prophet Isaiah (61, 1-2) describes the mission of the Messiah. The Lord reads it in a loud voice and then asserts: Here the prophet is speaking of me.

141

Nazareth. The hill called the Mount of the Precipice seen from the north. In the valley the old road leading down to the south.

And he began to say to them, "Today this scripture has been fulfilled in your hearing." And all spoke well of him, and wondered at the gracious words which proceeded out of his mouth; and they said, "Is not this Joseph's son?" And he said to them, "Doubtless you will quote to me this proverb, 'Physician, heal yourself; what we have heard you did at Capernaum, do here also in your own country.' " And he said, "Truly, I say to you, no prophet is acceptable in his own
* country. But in truth, I tell you, there were many widows in Israel in the days of Elijah, when the heaven was shut up three years and six months, when there came a great famine over all the land; and Elijah was sent to none
* of them but only to Zarephath, in the land of Sidon, to a woman who was a widow, And there were many lepers in Israel in the time of the prophet Elisha; and none of them was cleansed, but only Naaman the Syrian." When they heard this, all in the synagogue were filled with wrath. And they rose up and put him out of the city, and led him to the brow of the hill on which their city was built, that they might throw him down headlong. But passing through the midst of them he went away.

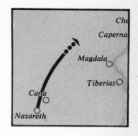

Jesus teaches the twelve apostles
Mt. 9, 35–38; 10, 1; 10, 5–15. Mk. 6, 6–11. Lk. 9, 1–5

And Jesus went about all the cities and villages, teaching in their synagogues and preaching the gospel of the kingdom, and healing every disease and every infirmity. When he saw the crowds, he had compassion for them, because they were harassed and helpless, like sheep without a shepherd. Then

* Jesus is referring to the story of Elijah (1 Kg. 17, 18-16) who, during the long famine, sought hospitality of a widow in the pagan town of Zarephath, and in return worked a miracle so that there was no lack of oil or flour in her house so long as the famine lasted.

** In the time of Elisha (disciple and successor of Elijah) there came to him Naaman, chief of the army of the King of Syria, asking to be cured of leprosy. Elisha cured him by a miracle telling him to bathe seven times in the river Jordan. The two miracles are quoted by Jesus to show how God, when he finds no response from his own people, turns his attention instead to less hostile pagans, and makes no distinction of persons.

143

X	XI	XII	I	II	III	IV	V	VI	VII	VIII	IX	X	XI	XII	I	II	III	IV	V	VI	VII	VIII	IX	X	XI	XII	I	II	III	IV

27 A.D.   **28** A.D.   **29** A.D.   **30** A.D.

he said to his disciples, "The harvest is plentiful, but the labourers are few; pray therefore the Lord of the harvest to send out labourers into his harvest."

And he called to him his twelve disciples and gave them authority over unclean spirits, to cast them out, and to heal every disease and every infirmity.

* These twelve Jesus sent out, charging them, "Go nowhere among the Gentiles, and enter no town of the Samaritans, but go rather to the lost sheep of the house of Israel. And preach as you go, saying, 'The kingdom of heaven is at hand.' Heal the sick, raise the dead, cleanse lepers, cast out demons. You received without pay, give without pay. Take no gold, nor silver, nor copper in your belts, no bag for your journey, nor two tunics, nor sandals, nor a staff; for the labourer deserves his food. And whatever town or village you enter, find out who is worthy in it, and stay with him until you depart. As you enter the house, salute it. And if the house is worthy, let your peace come upon it; but if it is not worthy, let your peace return to you. And if any one will not receive you or listen to your words, shake off the dust from your feet as you leave that house or town. Truly, I say to you, it shall be more tolerable on the day of judgement for the land of Sodom and Gomorrah than for that town.

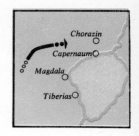

Chorazin

Capernaum

Magdala

Tiberias

Jesus gives instructions for times of persecution
Mt. 10, 16—42

"Behold, I send you out as sheep in the midst of wolves; so be wise as serpents and

* Jesus, in entrusting this first mission to his apostles, wishes to teach them not to depend on human means, but to trust in God alone. Their one concern is to be to speak of the Kingdom of Heaven.

144

| X | XI | XII | I | II | III | IV | V | VI | VII | VIII | IX | X | XI | XII | I | II | III | IV | V | VI | VII | VIII | IX | X | XI | XII | I | II | III | IV |

27 A.D.   **28** A.D.   **29** A.D.   **30** A.D.

innocent as doves. Beware of men, for they will deliver you up to councils, and flog you in their synagogues, and you will be dragged before governors and kings for my sake, to bear testimony before them and the Gentiles. When they deliver you up, do not be anxious how you are to speak or what you are to say; for what you are to say will be given to you in that hour; for it is not you who speak, but the Spirit of your Father speaking though you. Brother will deliver up brother to death, and the father his child, and children will rise against parents and have them put to death; and you will be hated by all for my name's sake. But he who endures to the end will be saved. When they persecute you in one town, flee to the next; for truly, I say to you, you will not have gone through all the towns of Israel, before the Son of man comes.

"A disciple is not above his teacher, nor a servant above his master, it is enough for the disciple to be like his teacher, and the servant like his master. If they have called the master of the house Beelzebul, how much more will they malign those of his household.

"So have no fear of them; for nothing is covered that will not be revealed, or hidden that will not be known. What I tell you in the dark, utter in the light; and what you hear whispered, proclaim upon the house-tops. And do not fear those who kill the body but cannot kill the soul; rather fear him who can destroy both soul and body in hell. Are not two sparrows sold for a penny? And not one of them will fall to the ground without your Father's will. But even the hairs of your head are all numbered. Fear

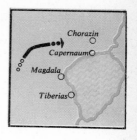

* The houses of Palestine usually had flat roofs (and this is still the case to-day) to which access was by means of an external staircase.

145

Two Palestinian sparrows, on the shore of the Lake of Gennesaret. From them, which are also objects of the fatherly care of God, Jesus takes a cue to instil in us trust in our Heavenly Father.

| X | XI | XII | I | II | III | IV | V | VI | VII | VIII | IX | X | XI | XII | I | II | III | IV | V | VI | VII | VIII | IX | X | XI | XII | I | II | III | IV |

27 A.D. **28** A.D. **29** A.D. **30** A.D.

not therefore; you are of more value than many sparrows. So every one who acknowledges me before men, I also will acknowledge before my Father who is in heaven; but whoever denies me before men, I also will deny before my Father who is in heaven.

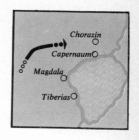

"Do not think that I have come to bring peace on earth; I have not come to bring peace, but a sword. For I have come to set a man against his father, and a daughter against her mother, and a daughter-in-law against her mother-in-law; and a man's foes will be those of his own household. He who loves father or mother more than me is not worthy of me; and he who loves son or daughter more than me is not worthy of me; and he who does not take his cross and follow me is not worthy of me. He who finds his life will lose it, and he who loses his life for my sake will find it.

"He who receives you receives me, and he who receives me receives him who sent me. He who receives a prophet because he is a prophet shall receive a prophet's reward, and he who receives a righteous man because he is a righteous man shall receive a righteous man's reward. And whoever gives to one of these little ones even a cup of cold water because he is a disciple, truly, I say to you, he shall not lose his reward."

Jesus and the twelve preach in Galilee
Mt. 11, 1. Mk. 6, 12–13. Lk. 9, 6

And when Jesus had finished instructing his twelve disciples, he went on from there to teach and preach in their cities.

147

Machaerus, on the eastern shore of the Dead Sea, where John the Baptist was imprisoned and killed by order of Herod Antipas.

| X | XI | XII | I | II | III | IV | V | VI | VII | VIII | IX | X | XI | XII | I | II | III | IV | V | V | VI | VII | VIII | IX | X | XI | XII | I | II | III | IV |

27 A.D. **28** A.D. **29** A.D. **30** A.D.

Herod Antipas is attacked by doubts
Mt. 14, 1–2. Mk. 6, 14–16. Lk. 9, 7–9

Now Herod the tetrarch heard of all that was done, and he was perplexed, because it was said by some that John had been raised from the dead, by some that Elijah had appeared, and by others that one of the old prophets had risen. Herod said, "John I beheaded; but who is this about whom I hear such things?" And he sought to see him.

How the martydom of John the Baptist came about
Mt. 14, 3–12. Mk. 6, 17–29

For Herod had sent and seized John, and bound him in prison for the sake of Herodias, his brother Philip's wife; because he had married her. For John said to Herod, "It is not lawful for you to have your brother's wife." And Herodias had a grudge against him, and wanted to kill him. But she could not, for Herod feared John, knowing that he was a righteous and holy man, and kept him safe. When he heard him, he was much perplexed; and yet he heard him gladly. But an opportunity came when Herod on his birthday gave a banquet for his courtiers and officers and the leading men of Galilee. For when Herodias's daughter came in and danced, she pleased Herod and his guests; and the king said to the girl, "Ask me for whatever you wish, and I will grant it." And he vowed to her, "What ever you ask me, I will give you, even half of my kingdom." And she went out, and said to her mother, "What shall I ask?" And she said, "The head of John the bap-

* The tetrarch (ruler of a quarter of what had been the kingdom of Herod) Herod Antipas was the son of the older Herod (he who persecuted the child Jesus) and as his inheritance from his father, had received the overlordship of Galilee and Peraea. He was the Herod who had John the Baptist imprisoned and beheaded (see the next episode.).

Sebaste. Tomb of John the Baptist, transformed into a mosque.

| X | XI | XII | I | II | III | IV | V | VI | VII | VIII | IX | X | XI | XII | I | II | III | IV | V | VI | VII | VIII | IX | X | XI | XII | I | II | III | IV |

27 A.D. | **28** A.D. | **29** A.D. | **30** A.D.

tizer." And she came in immediately with
haste to the king, and asked, saying, "I want
you to give me at once the head of John the
Baptist on a platter." And the king was exceedingly sorry; but because of his oaths and
his guests he did not want to break his word
to her. And immediately the king sent a
soldier of the guard and gave orders to bring
his head. He went and beheaded him in the
prison, and brought his head on a platter,
and gave it to the girl; and the girl gave it to
her mother. When his disciples heard of it,
they came and took his body, and laid it in a
tomb.

Jesus works the first miracle of the loaves
Mt. 14, 13–21. **Mk. 6, 30–44.** Lk. 9, 10–17
Jn. 6, 1–13.

*   The apostles returned to Jesus, and told
him all that they had done and taught. And
he said to them, "Come away by yourselves to
a lonely place, and rest a while." For many
were coming and going, and they had no
leisure even to eat. And they went away in
the boat to a lonely place by themselves.
Now many saw them going, and knew them,
and they ran there on foot from all the towns,
and got there ahead of them. As he landed
he saw a great throng, and he had compassion
on them, because they were like sheep without a shepherd; and he began to teach them
many things. And when it grew late, his
disciples came to him and said, "This is a
lonely place, and the hour is now late; send
them away, to go into the country and villages
round about and buy themselves something
to eat." But he answered them, "You give
them something to eat." And they said to
him, "Shall we go and buy two hundred

* St. Luke and St. John
tell us that they left for
Bethsaida on the other
side of the Sea of Galilee;
thence they reached the
top of a hill in the
neighbourhood.

151

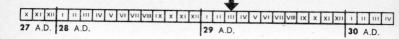
denarii worth of bread, and give it to them to eat?" And he said to them, "How many loaves have you? Go and see." And when they had found out, they said, "Five, and two fish." Then he commanded them all to
* sit down by companies upon the green grass. So they sat down in groups, by hundreds and by fifties. And taking the five loaves and the two fish he looked up to heaven, and blessed, and broke the loaves, and gave them to the disciples to set before the people; and he divided the two fish among them all. And they all ate and were satisfied. And they took up twelve baskets full of broken pieces and of the fish. And those who ate the loaves were five thousand men.

Jesus escapes the crowd which wants to make him king

Mt. 14, 22–23. Mk. 6, 45–46. Jn. 6, 14–15.

When the people saw the sign which he had done, they said, "This is indeed the prophet who is to come into the world!"

Perceiving then that they were about to come and take him by force to make him king, Jesus withdrew again to the hills by himself.

Jesus walks on the waters of the lake
Mt. 14, 22–33. Mk. 6, 47–52. Jn. 6, 16–21

Then he made the disciples get into the boat and go before him to the other side, while he dismissed the crowds. And after he had dismissed the crowds he went up into the hills by himself to pray. When evening came, he was there alone, but the boat by this time was many furlongs distant from the land, beaten by the waves; for the wind was against
** them. And in the fourth watch of the night he came to them, walking on the sea. But

* The mention of 'the green grass' gives us to understand that the incident took place in the spring, when the rainy season was hardly over. In the summer it hardly ever rains and everything is burnt up by the sun. The Gospel of St. John says precisely that it was near the Passover.

** The fourth watch of the night corresponds to the time immediately before dawn, from about 3 to 6.

when the disciples saw him walking on the sea, they were terrified, saying, "It is a ghost!" And they cried out for fear. But immediately he spoke to them, saying, "Take heart, it is I; have no fear."

And Peter answered him, "Lord, if it is you, bid me come to you on the water." He said, "Come." So Peter got out of the boat and walked on the water and came to Jesus; but when he saw the wind, he was afraid, and beginning to sink he cried out, "Lord, save me." Jesus immediately reached out his hand and caught him, saying to him, "O man of little faith, why did you doubt?" And when they got into the boat, the wind ceased. And those in the boat worshipped him, saying, "Truly you are the Son of God."

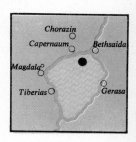

Jesus and the disciples return to the western shore of the lake
Mt. 14, 34–36. Mk. 6, 53–56

And when they had crossed over, they came to land at Gennesaret. And when the men of that place recognised him, they sent round to all that region and brought to him all that were sick, and besought him that they might only touch the fringe of his garment: and as many as touched it were made well.

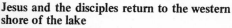

Jesus' discourse at Capernaum: 'I am the bread which came down from heaven'
Jn. 6, 22–71

On the next day the people who remained on the other side of the sea saw that there had been only one boat there, and that Jesus had not entered the boat with his disciples, but that his disciples had gone away alone. However, boats from Tiberias came

153

Yet another aspect of the synagogue at Capernaum, the city where Jesus preached the famous discourse on the Bread of Life.

| X | XI | XII | I | II | III | IV | V | VI | VII | VIII | IX | X | XI | XII | I | II | III | IV | V | VI | VII | VIII | IX | X | XI | XII | I | II | III | IV |

27 A.D. | **28** A.D. | **29** A.D. | **30** A.D.

near the place where they ate the bread after the Lord had given thanks. So when the people saw that Jesus was not there, nor his disciples, they themselves got into the boats and went to Capernaum, seeking Jesus.

When they found him on the other side of the sea, they said to him, "Rabbi, when did you come here?" Jesus answered them, "Truly, truly, I say to you, you seek me, not because you saw signs, but because you ate your fill of the loaves. Do not labour for the food which perishes, but for the food which endures to eternal life, which the Son of man will give to you; for on him has God the Father set his seal." Then they said to him, "What must we do, to be doing the works of God?" Jesus answered them, "This is the work of God, that you believe in him whom he has sent." So they said to him, "Then what sign do you do, that we may see, and believe you? What work do you perform? Our fathers ate the manna in the wilderness; as it is written, 'He gave them bread from heaven to eat.'" Jesus then said to them, "Truly, truly, I say to you, it was not Moses who gave you the bread from heaven; my Father gives the true bread from heaven. For the bread of God is that which comes down from heaven, and gives life to the world." They said to him, "Lord, give us this bread always."

Jesus said to them, "I am the bread of life; he who comes to me shall not hunger, and he who believes in me shall never thirst. But I said to you that you have seen me and yet do not believe. All that the Father gives me will come to me; and him who comes to me I will not cast out. For I have come down from heaven, not to do my own will, but

* In this chapter Jesus promises the institution of the Eucharist: to the Jews who (after the miracle of the Feeding of the 5000) are still asking for bread to eat, Jesus promises to give them His Body to eat and His Blood to drink (in the Eucharist).

155

| x | xi | xii | I | II | III | IV | V | VI | VII | VIII | IX | X | XI | XII | I | II | III | IV | V | VI | VII | VIII | IX | X | XI | XII | I | II | III | IV |

27 A.D. | 28 A.D. | 29 A.D. | 30 A.D.

the will of him who sent me; and this is the will of him who sent me, that I should lose nothing of all that he has given me, but raise it up at the last day. For this is the will of my Father, that every one who sees the Son and believes in him should have eternal life; and I will raise him up at the last day."

The Jews then murmered at him, because he said, "I am the bread which came down from heaven." They said, "Is not this Jesus the son of Joseph, whose father and mother we know? How does he now say, 'I have come down from heaven'?" Jesus answered them, "Do not murmur among yourselves. No one can come to me unless the Father who sent me draws him; and I will raise him up at the last day. It is written in the prophets, 'And they shall all be taught by God.' Every one who has heard and learned from the Father comes to me. Not that any one has seen the Father except him who is from God; he has seen the Father. Truly, truly, I say to you, he who believes has eternal life. I am the bread of life. Your

* fathers ate the manna in the wilderness, and they died. This is the bread which comes down from heaven, that a man may eat of it and not die. I am the living bread which came down from heaven; if any one eats of this bread, he will live forever; and the bread which I shall give for the life of the world is my flesh."

The Jews then disputed among themselves, saying, "How can this man give us his flesn to eat?" So Jesus said to them, "Truly, truly, I say to you, unless you eat the flesh of the Son of man and drink his blood, you have no life in you; he who eats my flesh and drinks my blood has eternal life, and I will raise

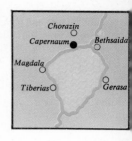

* Jesus is referring to the miraculous gift of manna (see Exod. 16, 9-36) which God rained down from heaven so as to satisfy the hungry Jews in the wilderness.

him up at the last day. For my flesh is food indeed, and by blood is drink indeed. He who eats my flesh and drinks my blood abides in me, and I in him.

As the living Father sent me, and I live because of the Father, so he who eats me will live because of me. This is the bread which came down from heaven, not such as the fathers ate and died; he who eats this bread will live for ever." This he said in the synagogue, as he taught at Capernaum.

Many of his disciples, when they heard it, said, "This is a hard saying; who can listen to it?" But Jesus, knowing in himself that his disciples murmured at it, said to them, "Do you take offence at this? Then what if you were to see the Son of man ascending where he was before? It is the spirit that gives life, the flesh is of no avail; the words that I have spoken to you are spirit and life. But there are some of you that do not believe." For Jesus knew from the first who those were that did not believe, and who it was that should betray him. And he said, "This is why I told you that no one can come to me unless it is granted him by the Father."

After this many of his disciples drew back and no longer went about with him. Jesus said to the twelve, "Will you also go away?" Simon Peter answered him, "Lord, to whom shall we go? You have the words of eternal life; and we have believed, and have come to know, that you are the Holy One of God." Jesus answered them, "Did I not choose you, the twelve, and one of you is a devil?" He spoke of Judas the son of Simon Iscariot, for he, one of the twelve, was to betray him.

Jerusalem. Excavation of the Sheep Pool or Pool of Bethesda, 'with five porticos' (Jn. 5, 2). The building in the centre of the photograph is the ruinous apse of a mediaeval church built on the site.

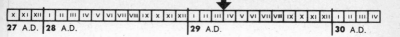

| X | XI | XII | I | II | III | IV | V | VI | VII | VIII | IX | X | XI | XII | I | II | III | IV | V | VI | VII | VIII | IX | X | XI | XII | I | II | III | IV |

27 A.D.   **28** A.D.   **29** A.D.   **30** A.D.

At Jerusalem, Jesus cures the cripple of Bethesda
Jn. 5, 1—18

After this there was a feast of the Jews, and Jesus went up to Jerusalem. Now there is in Jerusalem by the Sheep Gate a pool, in Hebrew called Bethzatha, which has five porticoes. In these lay a multitude of invalids, blind, lame, paralyzed. One man was there, who had been ill for thirty-eight years. When Jesus saw him and knew that he had been lying there a long time, he said to him, "Do you want to be healed?" The sick man answered him, "Sir, I have no man to put me into the pool when the water is troubled, and while I am going another steps down before me." Jesus said to him, "Rise, take up your pallet, and walk." And at once the man was healed, and he took up his pallet and walked.

Now that day was the sabbath. So the Jews said to the man who was cured, "It is the sabbath, it is not lawful for you to carry your pallet." But he answered them, "The man who healed me said to me, 'Take up your pallet, and walk.' " They asked him, "Who is the man who said to you, 'Take up your pallet, and walk'?" Now the man who had been healed did not know who it was, for Jesus had withdrawn, as there was a crowd in the place. Afterward, Jesus found him in the temple, and said to him, "See, you are well! Sin no more, that nothing worse befall you." The man went away and told the Jews that it was Jesus who had healed him. And this was

159

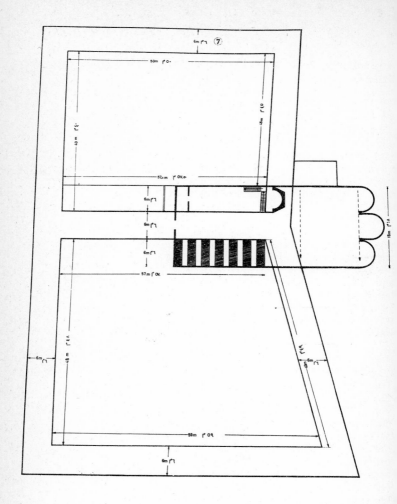

Plan of the Pool of Bethesda, reconstructed on the basis of the recent excavations. It shows the five porticos (four at the sides and one across the middle) and confirms the accuracy of the description in the Gospel.

| X | XI | XII | I | II | III | IV | V | VI | VII | VIII | IX | X | XI | XII | I | II | III | IV | V | VI | VII | VIII | IX | X | XI | XII | I | II | III | IV |

27 A.D. | **28** A.D. | **29** A.D. | **30** A.D.

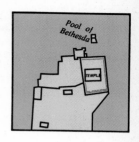

Pool of Bethesda

TEMPLE

* why the Jews persecuted Jesus, because he did this on the sabbath. But Jesus answered them, "My Father is working still, and I am working." This was why the Jews sought all the more to kill him, because he not only broke the sabbath but also called God his Father, making himself equal with God.

Jesus defends himself
Jn. 5, 19–47

Jesus said to them, "Truly, truly, I say to you, the Son can do nothing of his own accord, but only what he sees the Father doing; for whatever he does, that the Son does likewise. For the Father loves the Son, and shows him all that he himself is doing; and greater works than these will he show him, that you may marvel. For as the Father raises the dead and gives them life, so also the Son gives life to whom he will. The Father judges no one, but has given all judgement to the Son, that all may honour the Son, even as they honour the Father. He who does not honour the Son does not honour the Father who sent him. Truly, truly, I say to you, he who hears my word and believes him who sent me, has eternal life; he does not come into judgment, but has passed from death to life.

"Truly, truly, I say to you, the hour is coming, and now is, when the dead will hear the voice of the Son of God, and those who hear will live. For as the Father has life in himself, so he has granted the Son also to have life in himself, and has given him authority to execute judgement, because he

* At this stage of the Lord's preaching, the Jews have already come to understand that Jesus is proclaiming himself Son of God. From this moment they begin to accuse him of blasphemy, and consequently they start the persecution which is to bring the sentence of death upon him.

161

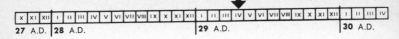

| X | XI | XII | I | II | III | IV | V | VI | VII | VIII | IX | X | XI | XII | I | II | III | IV | V | VI | VII | VIII | IX | X | XI | XII | I | II | III | IV |

27 A.D. | **28 A.D.** | **29 A.D.** | **30 A.D.**

is the Son of man. Do not marvel at this; for the hour is coming when all who are in the tombs will hear his voice and come forth, those who have done good, to the resurrection of life, and those who have done evil, to the resurrection of judgement.

"I can do nothing on my own authority; as I hear, I judge; and my judgement is just, because I seek not my own will but the will of him who sent me. If I bear witness to myself, my testimony is not true; there is another who bears witness to me, and I know that the testimony which he bears to me is true. You sent to John, and he has borne witness to the truth. Not that the testimony which I receive is from man; but I say this that you may be saved. He was a burning and shining lamp, and you were willing to rejoice for a while in his light. But the testimony which I have is greater than that of John; for the works which the Father has granted me to accomplish, these very works which I am doing, bear me witness that the Father has sent me. And that Father who sent me has himself borne witness to me. His voice you have never heard, his form you have never seen; and you do not have his word abiding in you, for you do not believe him whom he has sent. You search the scriptures, because you think that in them you have eternal life, and it is they that bear witness to me; yet you refuse to come to me that you may have life. I do not receive glory from men. But I know that you have not the love of God within you. I have come in my Father's name, and you do not receive me; if another comes in his own name, him you will receive. How can you believe, who receive glory from one another and do

| X | XI | XII | I | II | III | IV | V | VI | VII | VIII | IX | X | XI | XII | I | II | III | IV | V | VI | VII | VIII | IX | X | XI | XII | I | II | III | IV |

27 A.D.　**28** A.D.　**29** A.D.　**30** A.D.

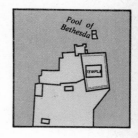

not seek the glory that comes from the only God? Do not think that I shall accuse you to the Father; it is Moses who accuses you, on whom you set your hope. If you believed Moses, you would believe me, for he wrote of me. But if you do not believe his writings, how will you believe my words?"

Jesus teaches purity of heart
Jn. 7, 1. Mk. 7, 1—16. (17—23)
Mt. 15, (1—11) 12—20.

After this Jesus went about in Galilee; he would not go about in Judea, because the Jews sought to kill him.

▶ Now when the Pharisees gathered together to him, with some of the scribes, who had come from Jerusalem, they saw that some of his disciples ate with hands defiled, that is, unwashed. (For the Pharisees, and all the Jews, do not eat unless they wash their hands, observing the tradition of the elders; and when they come from the market place, they do not eat unless they purify themselves; and there are many other traditions which they observe, the washing of cups and pots and vessels of bronze.) And the Pharisees and the scribes asked him, "Why do your disciples not live according to the tradition of the elders, but eat with hands defiled?" And he said to them, "Well did Isaiah prophesy of you hypocrites, as it is written,

'This people honours me with their lips,
but their heart is far from me;
in vain do they worship me,
teaching as docrines the precepts of men.'
You leave the commandment of God, and hold fast the tradition of men."

And he said to them, "You have a fine

* Jesus repeats and confirms the complaint already made by the prophet Isaiah (29,13) in the name of God, that the people honoured him merely outwardly while in their hearts they paid no heed to him.

163

View in Galilee, near Capernaum.

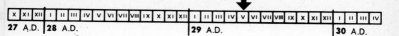

X	XI	XII	I	II	III	IV	V	VI	VII	VIII	IX	X	XI	XII	I	II	III	IV	V	VI	VII	VIII	IX	X	XI	XII	I	II	III	IV

27 A.D. 28 A.D. 29 A.D. 30 A.D.

way of rejecting the commandment of God, in order to keep your tradition! For Moses said, 'Honour your father and your mother'; and, 'He who speaks evil of father or mother, let him surely die'; but you say, 'If a man tells his father or his mother, What you would have gained from me is Corban' (that is, given to God) — then you no longer permit him to do anything for his father or mother, thus making void the word of God through your tradition which you hand on. And many such things you do."

And he called the people to him again, and said to them, "Hear me, all of you, and understand: there is nothing outside a man which by going into him can defile him; but the things which come out of a man are what defile him. "If any man has ears to hear, let him hear."

The disciples came and said to him, "Do you know that the Pharisees were offended when they heard this saying?" He answered, "Every plant which my heavenly Father has not planted will be rooted up. Let them alone; they are blind guides. And if a blind man leads a blind man, both will fall into a pit." But Peter said to him, "Explain the parable to us." And he said, "Are you also still without understanding? Do you not see that whatever goes into the mouth passes into the stomach, and so passes on? But what comes out of the mouth proceeds from the heart, and this defiles a man. For out of the heart come evil thoughts, murder, adultery, fornication, theft, false witness, slander. These are what defile a man; but to eat with unwashed hands does not defile a man."

* The Pharisees even in the face of God's command to honour their father and mother (see Exod. 20, 12 & 21, 17) had dared to admit the rite of Corban. According to this rite if the word Corban ('let it be a gift') had been pronounced over certain specified goods, such goods became holy and belonged to the Temple, so that they could not be used, even to help one's own parents.

165

Ruins of Tyre, the Phoenician city near to which occurred the moving episode of the Canaanitish woman.

| X | XI | XII | I | II | III | IV | V | VI | VII | VIII | IX | X | XI | XII | I | II | III | IV | V | VI | VII | VIII | IX | X | XI | XII | I | II | III | IV |

27 A.D.　**28** A.D.　　　　　　　　　**29** A.D.　　　　　　　　**30** A.D.

Jesus grants the request of the Canaanite woman
Mt. 15, 21–28. Mk. 7, 24–30

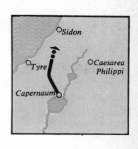

And Jesus went away from there and withdrew to the district of Tyre and Sidon. And behold, a Canaanite woman from that region came out and cried, "Have mercy on me, O Lord, Son of David; my daughter is severely possessed by a demon." But he did not answer her a word. And his disciples came and begged him, saying, "Send her away, for she is crying after us." He answered, "I was sent only to the lost sheep of the house of Israel." But she came and knelt before him, saying, "Lord, help me". And he answered, "It is not fair to take the children's bread and throw it to the dogs." She said, "Yes, Lord, yet even the dogs eat the crumbs that fall from their master's table." Then Jesus answered her, "O woman, great is your faith! Be it done for you as you desire." And her daughter was healed instantly.

Jesus cures the deaf man who stammered
Mk. 7, 31–37

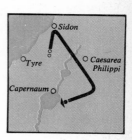

Then he returned from the region of Tyre, and went through Sidon to the Sea of Galilee, through the region of the Decapolis. And they brought to him a man who was deaf and had an impediment in his speech; and they besought him to lay his hand upon him. And taking him aside from the multitude privately, he put his fingers into his ears, and he spat and touched his tongue; and looking up to heaven, he sighed, and said to him, "Ephphatha," that is, "Be opened." And his ears were opened, his tongue was released, and he spoke plainly. And he charged them to tell no one; but the more he charged them,

167

| x | xı | xıı | ı | ıı | ııı | ıv | v | vı | vıı | vııı | ıx | x | xı | xıı | ı | ıı | ııı | ıv | v | vı | vıı | vııı | ıx | x | xı | xıı | ı | ıı | ııı | ıv |

27 A.D.   28 A.D.   29 A.D.   30 A.D.

the more zealously they proclaimed it. And they were astonished beyond measure, saying, "He has done all things well; he even makes the deaf hear and the dumb speak."

Jesus works the second miracle of the loaves
Mt. 15, 29–39. Mk. 8, 1–10

And Jesus went on from there and passed along the Sea of Galilee. And he went up into the hills, and sat down there. And great crowds came to him, bringing with them the lame, the maimed, the blind, the dumb, and many others, and they put them at his feet, and he healed them, so that the throng wondered, when they saw the dumb speaking, the maimed whole, the lame walking, and the blind seeing; and they glorified the God of Israel.

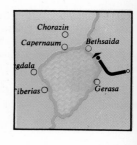

Then Jesus called his disciples to him and said, "I have compassion on the crowd, because they have been with me now three days, and have nothing to eat; and I am unwilling to send them away hungry, lest they faint on the way." And the disciples said to him, "Where are we to get bread enough in the desert to feed so great a crowd?" And Jesus said to them, "How many loaves have you?" They said, "Seven, and a few small fish." And commanding the crowd to sit down on the ground, he took the seven loaves and the fish, and having given thanks he broke them and gave them to the disciples, and the disciples gave them to the crowds. And they all ate and were satisfied; and they took up seven baskets full of the broken pieces left over. Those who ate were four thousand men, besides women and children. And sending away the crowds he got into the boat and went to the region of Magadan.

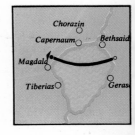

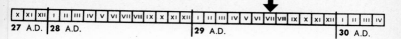
The Pharisees ask Jesus for a sign from heaven
Mt. 16, 1–4. Mk. 8, 11–13

And the Pharisees and Sadducees came, and to test him they asked him to show them a sign from heaven. He answered them, "When it is evening, you say, 'It will be fair weather; for the sky is red.' And in the morning, 'It will be stormy today, for the sky is red and threatening.' You know how to interpret the appearance of the sky, but you cannot interpret the signs of the times. An evil and adulterous generation seeks for a sign, but no sign shall be given to it except the sign of Jonah." So he left them and departed.

The sign from heaven is Jesus himself
Mt. 12, 38–42. Lk. 11, 29–36

When the crowds were increasing, he began to say, "This generation is an evil generation; it seeks a sign, but no sign shall be given to it except the sign of Jonah. For as Jonah became a sign to the men of Nineveh, so will the Son of man be to this generation. The queen of the South will arise at the judgement with the men of this generation and condemn them; for she came from the ends of the earth to hear the wisdom of Solomon, and behold, something greater than Solomon is here. The men of Nineveh will arise at the judgement with this generation and condemn it; for they repented at the preaching of Jonah, and behold, something greater than Jonah is here.

"No one after lighting a lamp puts it in a cellar or under a bushel, but on a stand, that those who enter may see the light. Your

169

| X | XI | XII | I | II | III | IV | V | VI | VII | VIII | IX | X | XI | XII | I | II | III | IV | V | VI | VII | VIII | IX | X | XI | XII | I | II | III | IV |

27 A.D. | 28 A.D. | 29 A.D. | 30 A.D.

eye is the lamp of your body; when your eye is sound, your whole body is full of light; but when it is not sound, your body is full of darkness. Therefore be careful lest the light in you be darkness. If then your whole body is full of light, having no part dark, it will be wholly bright, as when a lamp with its rays gives you light."

'Take heed and beware of the leaven of the Pharisees'
Mt. 16, 5–12. Mk. 8, 14–21

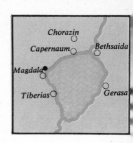

When the disciples reached the other side, they had forgotten to bring any bread. Jesus said to them, "Take heed and beware of the leaven of the Pharisees and Sadducees." And they discussed it among themselves, saying, "We brought no bread." But Jesus, aware of this, said, "O men of little faith, why do you discuss among yourselves the fact that you have no bread? Do you not yet perceive? Do you not remember the five loaves of the five thousand, and how many baskets you gathered? Or the seven loaves of the four thousand, and how many baskets you gathered? How is it that you fail to perceive that I did not speak about bread? Beware of the leaven of the Pharisees and Sadducees." Then they understood that he did not tell them to beware of the leaven of bread, but of the teaching of the Pharisees and Sadducees.

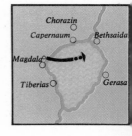

Jesus cures the blind man of Bethsaida
Mk. 8, 22–26

And they came to Bethsaida. And some people brought to him a blind man, and begged him to touch him. And he took the blind man by the hand, and led him out of the village; and when he had spit on his

| X | XI | XII | I | II | III | IV | V | VI | VII | VIII | IX | X | XI | XII | I | II | III | IV | V | VI | VII | VIII | IX | X | XI | XII | I | II | III | IV |

27 A.D. **28** A.D. **29** A.D. **30** A.D.

eyes and laid his hands upon him, he asked him, "Do you see anything?" And he looked up and said, "I see men; but they look like trees, walking." Then again he laid his hands upon his eyes; and he looked intently and was restored, and saw everything clearly. And he sent him away to his home, saying, "Do not even enter the village."

Peter confesses the divinity of Jesus and Jesus promises him the primacy
Mt. 16, 13–20. Mk. 8, 27–30. Lk. 9, 18–21

Now when Jesus came into the district of Caesarea Philippi, he asked his disciples, "Who do men say that the Son of man is?" And they said, "Some say John the Baptist, others say Elijah, and others Jeremiah or one of the prophets." He said to them, "But who do you say that I am?" Simon Peter replied, "You are the Christ, the Son of the living God." And Jesus answered him, "Blessed are you, Simon Bar-Jona! For flesh and blood has not revealed this to you, but my Father who is in heaven. And I tell you, you are Peter, and on this rock I will build my church, and the powers of death shall not prevail against it. I will give you the keys of the kingdom of heaven, and whatever you bind on earth shall be bound in heaven, and whatever you loose on earth shall be loosed in heaven." Then he strictly charged the disciples to tell no one that he was the Christ.

* Now that his disciples know clearly that he is the Messiah, Jesus begins to reveal to them the sorrowful aspect of his mission, foretelling his Passion.

Jesus begins to speak of his passion and death
Mt. 16, 21–23. Mk. 8, 31–33. Lk. 9, 22

* From that time Jesus began to show his disciples that he must go to Jerusalem and suffer many things from the elders and

171

Mount Tabor, the 'high mountain' of which the Gospel speaks, on the top of which Jesus was transfigured.

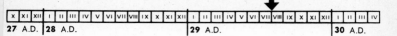

| X | XI | XII | I | II | III | IV | V | VI | VII | VIII | IX | X | XI | XII | I | II | III | IV | V | VI | VII | VIII | IX | X | XI | XII | I | II | III | IV |

27 A.D.　　　**28** A.D.　　　　　　　　**29** A.D.　　　　　　　　**30** A.D.

chief priests and scribes, and be killed, and on the third day be raised. And Peter took him and began to rebuke him, saying, "God forbid, Lord! This shall never happen to you." But he turned and said to Peter, "Get behind me, Satan! You are a hindrance to me; for you are not on the side of God, but of men."

'If any man would come after me, let him deny himself'
Mt. 16, 24–28. Mk. 8, 34–38; 9–1. Lk. 9, 23–27

Then Jesus told his disciples, "If any man would come after me, let him deny himself and take up his cross and follow me. For whoever would save his life will lose it, and whoever loses his life for my sake will find it. For what will it profit a man, if he gains the whole world and forfeits his life? Or what shall a man give in return for his life? For the Son of man is to come with his angels in the glory of his Father, and then he will repay every man for what he has done. Truly, I say to you, there are some standing here who will not taste death before they see the Son of man coming in his kingdom."

On a high mountain Jesus is transfigured
Mt. 17, 1–13. Mk. 9, 2–3. Lk. 9, 28–36

And after six days Jesus took with him Peter and James and John his brother, and led them up a high mountain apart. And he was transfigured before them, and his face shone like the sun, and his garments became white as light. And behold, there appeared to them Moses and Elijah, talking with him. And Peter said to Jesus, "Lord, it is well that we are here; if you wish, I will make three booths here, one for you and one for Moses and one for Elijah." He was still speaking,

* Christian tradition has identified this 'high mountain' with Mount Tabor. The Transfiguration had also the purpose of confirming the Apostles' faith in Jesus' Messianic dignity.

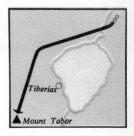

173

An ancient road leading down from Tabor towards the plain.

when lo, a bright cloud overshadowed them, and a voice from the cloud said, "This is my beloved Son, with whom I am well pleased; listen to him." When the disciples heard this, they fell on their faces, and were filled with awe. But Jesus came and touched them, saying, "Rise, and have no fear." And when they lifted up their eyes, they saw no one but Jesus only.

And as they were coming down the mountain, Jesus commanded them, "Tell no one the vision, until the Son of man is raised from the dead." And the disciples asked him, "Then why do the scribes say that first Elijah must come?" He replied, "Elijah does come, and he is to restore all things; but I
* tell you that Elijah has already come, and they did not know him, but did to him whatever they pleased. So also the Son of man will suffer at their hands." Then the disciples understood that he was speaking to them of John the Baptist.

* Elijah had already come, said Jesus, not in his own person but in that of John the Baptist.

Jesus cures an epileptic
Mt. 17, 14–21. Mk. 9, 14–29. Lk. 9, 37–42

And when they came to the disciples, they saw a great crowd about them, and scribes arguing with them. And immediately all the crowd, when they saw him were greatly amazed, and ran up to him and greeted him. And he asked them, "What are you discussing with them?" And one of the crowd answered him, "Teacher, I brought my son to you, for he has a dumb spirit; and whenever it seizes him, it dashes him down; and he foams and grinds his teeth and becomes rigid; and I asked your disciples to cast it out, and they were not able." And he answered them, "O faithless generation, how long am I to be

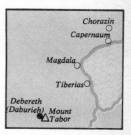

175

The village of Daburieh, at the foot of Mount Tabor, where Jesus cured the epileptic boy.

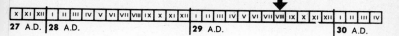

| X | XI | XII | I | II | III | IV | V | VI | VII | VIII | IX | X | XI | XII | I | II | III | IV | V | VI | VII | VIII | IX | X | XI | XII | I | II | III | IV |

27 A.D.   **28** A.D.   **29** A.D.   **30** A.D.

with you? How long am I to bear with you?
Bring him to me." And they brought the boy
to him; and when the spirit saw him, immediately it convulsed the boy, and he fell on
the ground and rolled about, foaming at
the mouth. And Jesus asked his father, "How
long has he had this?" And he said, "From
childhood. And it has often cast him into
the fire and into the water, to destroy him;
but if you can do anything, have pity on us
and help us." And Jesus said to him, "If you
can! All things are possible to him who
believes." Immediately the father of the
child cried out and said, "I believe; help my
unbelief!" And when Jesus saw that a crowd
came running together, he rebuked the unclean spirit, saying to it. "You dumb and deaf
spirit, I command you, come out of him, and
never enter him again." And after crying out
and convulsing him terribly, it came out, and
the boy was like a corpse; so that most of
them said, "He is dead". But Jesus took him
by the hand and lifted him up, and he arose.
And when he had entered the house, his
disciples asked him privately, "Why could we
not cast it out?" And he said to them, "This
kind cannot be driven out by anything but
prayer and fasting."

Jesus again predicts his death
Mt. 17, 22–23. **Mk. 9, 30–32.** Lk. 9, 43–45.

They went on from there and passed
through Galilee. And he would not have any
one know it; for he was teaching his disciples,
saying to them, "The Son of man will be
delivered into the hands of men, and they
will kill him; and when he is killed, after
three days he will rise." But they did not
understand the saying, and they were afraid
to ask him.

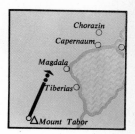

177

The so-called 'fishes of St. Peter', which abound in the Lake of Gennesaret.

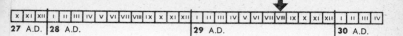
The half-shekel of the tribute
Mt. 17, 24–27

When they came to Capernaum the collectors of the half-shekel tax went up to Peter and said, "Does not your teacher pay the tax?" He said, "Yes". And when he came home, Jesus spoke to him first, saying, "What do you think, Simon? From whom do kings of the earth take toll or tribute? From their sons or from others?" And when he said, "From others," Jesus said to him, "Then the sons are free. However, not to give offence to them, go to the sea and cast a hook, and take the first fish that comes up, and when you open its mouth you will find a shekel; take that and give it to them for me and for yourself."

Jesus insists upon humility
Mt. 18, 1–5. Mk. 9, 33–37. Lk. 9, 46–48

And they came to Capernaum; and when he was in the house he asked them, "What were you discussing on the way?" But they were silent; for on the way they had discussed with one another who was the greatest. And he sat down and called the twelve; and he said to them, "If any one would be first, he must be last of all and servant of all." And he took a child, and put him in the midst of them; and taking him in his arms, he said to them, "Whoever receives one such child in my name receives me; and whoever receives me, receives not me but him who sent me."

Jesus counsels tolerance
Mk. 9, 38–41. Lk. 9, 49–50.

John said to him, "Teacher, we saw a man

*   The half-shekel was a Greek silver coin, and represented the annual tax which the Jews had to pay to the Temple at Jerusalem, that is to the 'House of God'. Therefore Jesus, being the Son of God, declared himself exempt from the tax. The half-shekel, two drachms, was the equivalent of two Roman denarii, the average pay for two day's work.

179

A mill-stone of the time of Jesus, kept at Capernaum. On the lower part, shaped like a cone, is placed the upper, a double funnel, which is then turned by a donkey. The corn is placed in the upper funnel and comes out, ground, at the bottom.

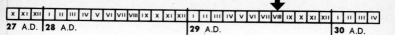

| X | XI | XII | I | II | III | IV | V | VI | VII | VIII | IX | X | XI | XII | I | II | III | IV | V | VI | VII | VIII | IX | X | XI | XII | I | II | III | IV |

27 A.D. **28** A.D. **29** A.D. **30** A.D.

casting out demons in your name, and we forbade him, because he was not following us". But Jesus said, "Do not forbid him; for no one who does a mighty work in my name will be able soon after to speak evil of me. For he that is not against us is for us. For truly, I say to you, whoever gives you a cup of water to drink because you bear the name of Christ, will by no means lose his reward.

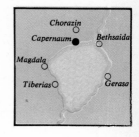

Jesus condemns those who lead others astray
Mt. 18, 6–9. Mk. 9, 42–50. Lk. 17, 1–2

Whoever causes one of these little ones who believe in me to sin, it would be better for him if a great millstone were hung round his neck and he were thrown into the sea. And if your hand causes you to sin, cut it off; it is better for you to enter life maimed, than with two hands to go to hell, to the unquenchable fire. And if your foot causes you to sin, cut it off; it is better for you to enter life lame than with two feet to be thrown into hell. And if your eye causes you to sin, pluck it out; it is better for you to enter the kingdom of God with one eye than with two eyes to be thrown into hell, where their worm does not die, and the fire is not quenched. For every one will be salted with fire. Salt is good; but if the salt has lost its saltness, how will you season it? Have salt in yourselves, and be at peace with one another."

| X | XI | XII | I | II | III | IV | V | VI | VII | VIII | IX | X | XI | XII | I | II | III | IV | V | VI | VII | VIII | IX | X | XI | XII | I | II | III | IV |

27 A.D. **28** A.D. **29** A.D. **30** A.D.

Jesus inculcates kindness to children and to those who go astray
Mt. 18, 10–14

"See that you do not despise one of these little ones; for I tell you that in heaven their angels always behold the face of my Father who is in heaven. What do you think? If a man has a hundred sheep, and one of them has gone astray, does he not leave the ninety-nine on the hills and go in search of the one that went astray? And if he finds it, truly, I say to you, he rejoices over it more than over the ninety-nine that never went astray. So it is not the will of my Father who is in heaven that one of these little ones should perish.

Jesus teaches brotherly correction
Mt. 18, 15–17. Lk. 17, 3–4

"If your brother sins against you, go and tell him his fault, between you and him alone. If he listens to you, you have gained your brother. But if he does not listen, take one or two others along with you, that every word may be confirmed by the evidence of two or three witnesses. If he refuses to listen to them, tell it to the church; and if he refuses to listen even to the church, let him be to you as a Gentile and a tax collector.

Jesus confers on the apostles the power to forgive
Mt. 18, 18–22

Truly, I say to you, whatever you bind on earth shall be bound in heaven, and whatever you loose on earth shall be loosed in heaven. Again I say to you, if two of you agree on earth about anything they ask, it

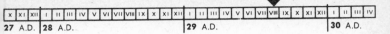

| X | X I | XII | I | II | III | IV | V | VI | VII | VIII | IX | X | X I | XII | I | II | III | IV | V | VI | VII | VIII | IX | X | X I | XII | I | II | III | IV |

| 27 A.D. | 28 A.D. | | 29 A.D. | | 30 A.D. |

will be done for them by my Father in heaven. For where two or three are gathered in my name, there am I in the midst of them."

Then Peter came up and said to him, "Lord, how often shall my brother sin against me, and I forgive him? As many as seven times?" Jesus said to him, "I do not say to you seven times, but seventy times seven.

Parable of the servants in debt
Mt. 18, 23–35

"Therefore the kingdom of heaven may be compared to a king who wished to settle accounts with his servants. When he began the reckoning, one was brought to him who owed him ten thousand talents; and as he could not pay, his lord ordered him to be sold, with his wife and children and all that he had, and payment to be made. So the servant fell on his knees, imploring him, 'Lord, have patience with me, and I will pay you everything.' And out of pity for him the lord of that servant released him and forgave him the debt. But that same servant, as he went out, came upon one of his fellow servants who owed him a hundred denarii; and seizing him by the throat he said, 'Pay what you owe.' So his fellow servant fell down and besought him, 'Have patience with me, and I will pay you.' He refused and went and put him in prison till he should pay the debt. When his fellow servants saw what had taken place, they were greatly distressed, and they went and reported to their lord all that had taken place. Then his lord summoned him and said to him, 'You wicked servant! I forgave you all that debt because you besought me; and should not you have had mercy on your

* A talent (equal to about 20 kg. of silver) was the equivalent of 6000 denarii. That is, the first servant owed about sixty million denarii, against the hundred denarii which were owed to him.

The enormous disproportion between the debts of the two servants was used by Jesus so as to bring out as far as possible the contrast between the immense mercy of God for us and the wretchedness of our petty sins.

183

The ruins of Chorazin, one of the towns in Galilee in which Jesus worked so many miracles and which were not converted.

| X | XI | XII | I | II | III | IV | V | VI | VII | VIII | IX | X | XI | XII | I | II | III | IV | V | VI | VII | VIII | IX | X | XI | XII | I | II | III | IV |

27 A.D. 28 A.D. 29 A.D. 30 A.D.

fellow servant as I had mercy on you?' And in anger his lord delivered him to the jailers, till he should pay all his debt. So also my heavenly Father will do to every one of you if you do not forgive your brother from your heart."

Jesus sets out for Jerusalem
Lk. 9, 51

When the days drew near for him to be received up, he set his face to go to Jerusalem.

Conditions for following Jesus
Mt. 8, 19–22. Lk. 9, 57–62

As they were going along the road, a man said to him, "I will follow you wherever you go." And Jesus said to him, "Foxes have holes, and birds of the air have nests; but the Son of man has nowhere to lay his head." To another he said, "Follow me." But he said, "Lord, let me first go and bury my father." But he said to him, "Leave the dead to bury their own dead; but as for you, go and proclaim the kingdom of God." Another said, "I will follow you, Lord; but let me first say farewell to those at my home." Jesus said to him, "No one who puts his hand to the plough and looks back is fit for the kingdom of God."

'Woe to you, Chorazin! Woe to you, Bethsaida!'
Mt. 11, 20–24. Lk. 10, 13–15

Then he began to upbraid the cities where most of his mighty works had been done, because they did not repent.

"Woe to you, Chorazin! woe to you, Bethsaida! for if the mighty works done in

* Of the three towns accursed by Jesus because of the pride of their inhabitants, only vestiges remain to-day, as though to witness to the fulfilment of Jesus' prophecy.

185

View of the Valley of Sichem from Mount Gerizim in the middle of
Samaria.

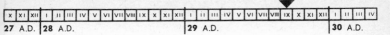

| X | XI | XII | I | II | III | IV | V | VI | VII | VIII | IX | X | XI | XII | I | II | III | IV | V | VI | VII | VIII | IX | X | XI | XII | I | II | III | IV |

27 A.D.　28 A.D.　29 A.D.　30 A.D.

you had been done in Tyre and Sidon, they would have repented long ago in sackcloth and ashes. But I tell you, it shall be more tolerable on the day of judgement for Tyre and Sidon than for you. And you, Capernaum, will you be exalted to heaven? You shall be brought down to Hades. For if the mighty works done in you had been done in Sodom, it would have remained until this day. But I tell you that it shall be more tolerable on the day of judgement for the land of Sodom than for you."

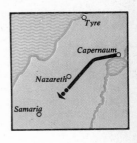

Jesus is not welcomed in Samaria
Lk. 9, 52–56

And he sent messengers ahead of him, who went and entered a village of the Samaritans, to make ready for him; but the people would not receive him, because his face was set toward Jerusalem. And when his disciples James and John saw it, they said, "Lord, do you want us to bid fire come down from heaven and consume them?" But he turned and rebuked them. And they went on to another village.

Jesus sends the 70 disciples to preach
Lk. 10, 1–12; 10, 16

After this the Lord appointed seventy others, and sent them on ahead of him, two by two, into every town and place where he himself was about to come. And he said to them, "The harvest is plentiful, but the labourers are few; pray therefore the Lord of the harvest to send out labourers into his harvest. Go your way; behold, I send you out as lambs in the midst of wolves. Carry no purse, no bag, no sandles; and salute no

* Membership in the Hebrew people, blessed by God in Abram and his descendants was primarily a matter of race. The Samaritans, descendants of the tribe of Joseph, had, during the course of centuries, been much mixed with foreigners. So the Jews looked down upon them, and the Samaritans reacted by making themselves a temple of their own on Mount Gerizim.

** 'Salute no one' means simply 'Do not waste precious time on your journey in long complimentary greetings in the eastern fashion'.

187

one on the road. Whatever house you enter, first say, 'Peace be to this house!' And if a son of peace is there, your peace shall rest upon him; but if not, it shall return to you. And remain in the same house, eating and drinking what they provide, for the labourer deserves his wages; do not go from house to house. Whenever you enter a town and they receive you, eat what is set before you; heal the sick in it and say to them, 'The kingdom of God has come near to you.' But whenever you enter a town and they do not receive you, go into its streets and say, 'Even the dust of your town that clings to our feet, we wipe off against you; nevertheless know this, that the kingdom of God has come near.' I tell you, it shall be more tolerable on that day for Sodom than for that town.

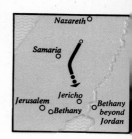

"He who hears you hears me, and he who rejects you rejects me, and he who rejects me rejects him who sent me."

The return of the disciples
Lk. 10, 17–20

The seventy returned with joy, saying, "Lord, even the demons are subject to us in your name!" And he said to them, "I saw Satan fall like lightning from heaven. Behold, I have given you authority to tread upon serpents and scorpions, and over all the power of the enemy; and nothing shall hurt you. Nevertheless do not rejoice in this, that the spirits are subject to you; but rejoice that your names are written in heaven."

'Come to me'
Mt. 11, 25–30. Lk. 10, 21–22

At that time Jesus declared, "I thank thee, Father, Lord of heaven and earth, that

188

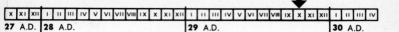

| X | XI | XII | I | II | III | IV | V | VI | VII | VIII | IX | X | XI | XII | I | II | III | IV | V | VI | VII | VIII | IX | X | XI | XII | I | II | III | IV |

27 A.D. **28** A.D. **29** A.D. **30** A.D.

thou hast hidden these things from the wise and understanding and revealed them to babes; yea, Father, for such was thy gracious will. All things have been delivered to me by my Father; and no one knows the Son except the Father, and no one knows the Father except the Son and any one to whom the Son chooses to reveal him. Come to me, all who labour and are heavy laden, and I will give you rest. Take my yoke upon you, and learn from me; for I am gentle and lowly in heart, and you will find rest for your souls. For my yoke is easy, and my burden is light."

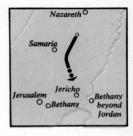

'Blessed are the eyes which see what you see'
Lk. 10, 23–24

Then turning to the disciples he said privately, "Blessed are the eyes which see what you see! For I tell you that many prophets and kings desired to see what you see, and did not see it, and to hear what you hear, and did not hear it."

The parable of the good Samaritan
Lk. 10, 25–37

And behold, a lawyer stood up to put him to the test, saying, "Teacher, what shall I do to inherit eternal life?" He said to him, "What is written in the law? How do you read?" And he answered, "You shall love the Lord your God with all your heart, and with all your soul, and will all your strength, and with all your mind: and your neighbour as yourself." And he said to him, "You have answered right; do this, and you will live."

But he, desiring to justify himself, said to Jesus, "And who is my neighbour?" Jesus replied, "A man was going down from

* The meaning of our Lord's sentence is: you have hidden what I teach from learned and clever people and have revealed it to the unlearned. God has communicated his mysteries not to the learned (scribes and pharisees) who have become proud and cunning, but to simple people who are still humble before God. In this saying Jesus clearly asserts the mystery of his divine Sonship.

** Jesus refers to the great figures of Jewish history whose greatest inspiration had been the expectation of the Messiah.

***See the two commandments as recorded respectively in Deut. 6,5 and Lv. 9, 18.

189

The desert road from Jerusalem to Jericho, the setting which Jesus used for the parable of the Good Samaritan.

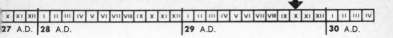
Jerusalem to Jericho, and he fell among robbers, who stripped him and beat him, and departed, leaving him half dead. Now by chance a priest was going down that road; and when he saw him he passed by on the other side. So likewise a Levite, when he came to the place and saw him, passed by on the other side. But a Samaritan, as he journeyed, came to where he was; and when he saw him, he had compassion, and went to him and bound up his wounds, pouring on oil and wine; then set him on his own beast and brought him to an inn, and took care of him. And the next day he took out two denarii and gave them to the innkeeper, saying, 'Take care of him; and whatever more you spend, I will repay you when I come back.' Which of these three, do you think, proved neighbour to the man who fell among the robbers?" He said, "The one who showed mercy on him." And Jesus said to him, "Go and do likewise."

Jesus visits Martha and Mary
Lk. 10, 38–42

Now as they went on their way, he entered a village; and a woman named Martha received him into her house. And she had a sister called Mary, who sat at the Lord's feet and listened to his teaching. But Martha was distracted with much serving; and she went to him and said, "Lord, do you not care that my sister has left me to serve alone? Tell her then to help me." But the Lord answered her, "Martha, Martha, you are anxious and troubled about many things; one thing is needful. Mary has chosen the good portion, which shall not be taken away from her."

* The one thing necessary is that which brings us nearer to eternal life at each moment. At this moment it was more important to listen to Jesus than to worry about making a good impression on the Master.

191

Bethany, the village about two miles east of Jerusalem where Jesus was often the guest of his friend Lazarus and of the latter's sisters Martha and Mary.

| X | XI | XII | I | II | III | IV | V | VI | VII | VIII | IX | X | XI | XII | I | II | III | IV | V | VI | VII | VIII | IX | X | XI | XII | I | II | III | IV |

27 A.D.   28 A.D.   29 A.D.   30 A.D.

Jesus teaches to pray: the Our Father
Lk. 11, 1–2. Mt. 6, 7–15

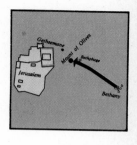

He was praying in a certain place, and when he ceased, one of his disciples said to him, "Lord, teach us to pray, as John taught his disciples." And he said to them:

▶ "In praying do not heap up empty phrases as the Gentiles do; for they think that they will be heard for their many words. Do not be like them, for your Father knows what you need before you ask him. Pray then like this:

Our Father who art in heaven,
Hallowed be thy name.
Thy kingdom come,
Thy will be done,
On earth as it is in heaven.
Give us this day our daily bread;
And forgive us our debts,
As we also have forgiven our debtors;
And lead us not into temptation,
But deliver us from evil.

For if you forgive men their trespasses, your heavenly Father also will forgive you; but if you do not forgive men their trespasses, neither will your Father forgive your trespasses.

The parable of the importunate friend
Lk. 11, 5–8

And he said to them, "Which of you who has a friend will go to him at midnight and say to him, 'Friend, lend me three loaves; for a friend of mine has arrived on a journey, and I have nothing to set before him'; and he will answer from within, 'Do not bother me; the door is now shut, and my children are with me in bed; I cannot get up and give you anything?'

* The most perfect prayer is this which was taught us by our Lord himself. First of all we need to praise and glorify God and then we may ask for whatever is necessary for our own lives.

193

x	xI	xII	I	II	III	IV	V	VI	VII	VIII	IX	x	xI	xII	I	II	III	IV	V	VI	VII	VIII	IX	x	xI	xII	I	II	III	IV

27 A.D.   **28** A.D.   **29** A.D.   **30** A.D.

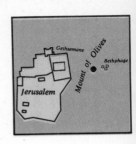

I tell you, though he will not get up and give him anything because he is his friend, yet because of his importunity he will rise and give him whatever he needs.

'Ask, and it will be given you'
Lk. 11, 9–13

And I tell you, Ask, and it will be given you; seek, and you will find; knock, and it will be opened to you. For every one who asks receives, and he who seeks finds, and to him who knocks it will be opened. What father among you, if his son asks for a fish, will instead of a fish give him a serpent; or if he asks for an egg, will give him a scorpion? If you, then, who are evil, know how to give good gifts to your children, how much more will the heavenly Father give the Holy Spirit to those who ask him!"

Jesus at Jerusalem for the feast of Tabernacles
Jn. 7, 2–13

Now the Jews' feast of Tabernacles was at hand. So his brethren said to him, "Leave here and go to Judea, that your disciples may see the works you are doing. For no man works in secret if he seeks to be known openly. If you do these things, show yourself to the world." For even his brethren did not believe in him. Jesus said to them, "My time has not yet come, but your time is always here. The world cannot hate you, but it hates me because I testify of it that its works are evil. Go to the feast yourselves; I am not going up to this feast, for my time has not yet fully come." So saying, he remained in Galilee.

But after his brethren had gone up to the feast, then he also went up, not publicly

194

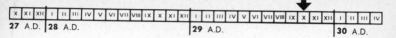

| X | XI | XII | I | II | III | IV | V | VI | VII | VIII | IX | X | XI | XII | I | II | III | IV | V | VI | VII | VIII | IX | X | XI | XII | I | II | III | IV |

27 A.D.   28 A.D.   29 A.D.   30 A.D.

but in private. The Jews were looking for him at the feast, and saying, "Where is he?" And there was much muttering about him among the people. While some said, "He is a good man," others said, "No, he is leading the people astray." Yet for fear of the Jews no-one spoke openly of him.

Jesus declares: 'It is God who has sent me' Jn. 7, 14–29

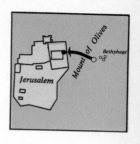

About the middle of the feast Jesus went up into the temple and taught. The Jews marvelled at it, saying, "How is it that this man has learning, when he has never studied?" So Jesus answered them, "My teaching is not mine, but his who sent me; if any man's will is to do his will, he shall know whether the teaching is from God or whether I am speaking on my own authority. He who speaks on his own authority seeks his own glory; but he who seeks the glory of him who sent him is true, and in him there is no falsehood. Did not Moses give you the law? Yet none of you keeps the law. Why do you seek to kill me?" The people answered, "You have a demon! Who is seeking to kill you?" Jesus answered them, "I did one deed, and you all marvel at it. Moses gave you circumcision (not that it is from Moses, but from the fathers), and you circumcise a man upon the sabbath. If on the sabbath a man receives circumcision, so that the law of Moses may not be broken, are you angry with me because on the sabbath I made a man's whole body well? Do not judge by appearances, but judge with right judgement."

Some of the people of Jerusalem therefore said, "Is not this the man whom they seek to kill? And here he is, speaking openly,

* Jesus here refers to the miracle which he had worked earlier, that is the curing of the cripple at the Pool of Bethesda.

195

Women at the Fountain of Elisha near Jericho, Spring water (or 'living water' in contrast to the stagnant water of a tank) is often used by Jesus as an illustration of the Divine Life which he bestows on believers.

| X | XI | XII | I | II | III | IV | V | VI | VII | VIII | IX | X | XI | XII | I | II | III | IV | V | VI | VII | VIII | IX | X | XI | XII | I | II | III | IV |
27 A.D. | 28 A.D. | 29 A.D. | 30 A.D.

nd they say nothing to him! Can it be that
he authorities really know that this is the
Christ? Yet we know where this man comes
from; and when the Christ appears, no one
will know where he comes from." So Jesus
proclaimed, as he taught in the temple, "You
know me, and you know where I come from?
But I have not come of my own accord; he
who sent me is true, and him you do not
know. I know him, for I come from him, and
he sent me."

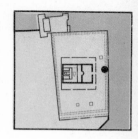

The Jews send police to arrest Jesus
n. 7, 30–36

So they sought to arrest him; but no one
laid hands on him, because his hour had not
yet come. Yet many of the people believed in
him; they said, "When the Christ appears,
will he do more signs than this man has done?"

The Pharisees heard the crowd thus muttering about him, and the chief priests and
Pharisees sent officers to arrest him. Jesus
then said, "I shall be with you a little longer,
and then I go to him who sent me; you will
seek me and you will not find me; where I
am you cannot come." The Jews said to one
another, "Where does this man intend to go
that we shall not find him? Does he intend to
go to the Dispersion among the Greeks and
teach the Greeks? What does he mean by
saying, 'You will seek me and you will not
find me.' and, 'Where I am you cannot
come'?"

Jesus promises the Holy Spirit to believers
n. 7, 37–39

On the last day of the feast, the great day,
Jesus stood up and proclaimed, "If any one
thirst, let him come to me and drink. He

* The Jews are allud-
ing to the popular belief
that the Messiah would
appear unexpectedly af-
ter spending his youth
in an unknown place.

** This is the first al-
lusion to his death made
by Jesus in Jerusalem:
'You will seek me and
will not find me.' To
look for God and not
to find him is one of
the gravest threats to
unbelievers in the Bible.

197

The southern part of the Temple esplanade. In the time of Jesus the majestic Royal Portico stood within the battlemented wall.

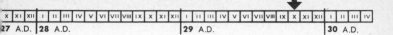

X	XI	XII	I	II	III	IV	V	VI	VII	VIII	IX	X	XI	XII	I	II	III	IV	V	VI	VII	VIII	IX	X	XI	XII	I	II	III	IV

27 A.D. | **28** A.D. | **29** A.D. | **30** A.D.

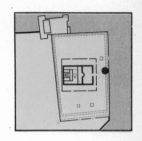

who believes in me, as the scripture has said, 'Out of his heart shall flow rivers of living water.' " Now this he said about the Spirit, which those who believed in him were to receive; for as yet the Spirit had not been given, because Jesus was not yet glorified.

The people are divided about Jesus
Jn. 7, 40–44.

When they heard these words, some of the people said, "This is really the prophet." Others said, "This is the Christ." But some said, "Is the Christ to come from Galilee? Has not the scripture said that the Christ is descended from David, and comes from Bethlehem, the village where David was?" So there was a division among the people over him. Some of them wanted to arrest him, but no one laid hands on him.

The Sanhedrim also is divided about Jesus
Jn. 7, 45–53.

The officers then went back to the chief priests and Pharisees, who said to them, "Why did you not bring him?" The officers answered, "No man ever spoke like this man!" The Pharisees answered them, "Are you led astray, you also? Have any of the authorities or of the Pharisees believed in him? But this crowd, who do not know the law, are accursed." Nicodemus, who had gone to him before, and who was one of them, said to them, "Does our law judge a man without first giving him a hearing and learning what he does?" They replied, "Are you from Galilee too? Search and you will see that no prophet is to rise from Galilee." They went each to his own house.

* Jesus was descended from David and really was born at Bethlehem while Mary and Joseph were there for the census. But this last detail about his childhood was not known by the great majority of the people.

** The judicial procedure here mentioned is that laid down by the Law of Moses in Deut. 17, 4.

199

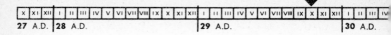

| X | XI | XII | I | II | III | IV | V | VI | VII | VIII | IX | X | XI | XII | I | II | III | IV | V | VI | VII | VIII | IX | X | XI | XII | I | II | III | IV |

27 A.D.   28 A.D.   29 A.D.   30 A.D.

Jesus absolves the woman taken in adultery
Jn. 8, 1–11

Jesus then went to the Mount of Olives. Early in the morning he came again to the temple; all the people came to him, and he sat down and taught them. The scribes and the Pharisees brought a woman who had been caught in adultery, and placing her in the midst they said to him, "Teacher, this woman has been caught in the act of adultery. Now in the law Moses commanded us to stone such. What do you say about her?" This they said to test him, that they might have some charge to bring against him. Jesus bent down and wrote with his finger on the ground. And as they continued to ask him, he stood up and said to them, "Let him who is without sin among you be the first to throw a stone at her." And once more he bent down and wrote with his finger on the ground. But when they heard it, they went away, one by one, beginning with the eldest, and Jesus was left alone with the woman standing before him, Jesus looked up and said to her, "Woman, where are they? Has no one condemned you?" She said, "No one, Lord." And Jesus said, "Neither do I condemn you; go, and do not sin again."

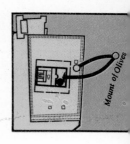

Mount of Olives

'I am the light of the world'
Jn. 8, 12–20

Again Jesus spoke to them, saying, "I * am the light of the world; he who follows me will not walk in darkness, but will have the light of life." The Pharisees then said to him, "You are bearing witness to yourself; your testimony is not true." Jesus answered, "Even if I do bear witness to myself, my testimony

* Jesus takes his start ing point from the il luminations made fo the Feast, and by this as sertion intends to poin out that he is the Mes siah. Indeed in the book of Isaiah the prophe (49,6) God says to hi Messenger (i.e. the Mess iah): 'I will give you a a light to the nations that my salvation may reach to the end of the earth.'

| X | XI | XII | I | II | III | IV | V | VI | VII | VIII | IX | X | XI | XII | I | II | III | IV | V | VI | VII | VIII | IX | X | XI | XII | I | II | III | IV |

27 A.D.   28 A.D.   29 A.D.   30 A.D.

is true, for I know whence I have come and whither I am going, but you do not know whence I come or whither I am going. You judge according to the flesh, I judge no one. Yet even if I do judge, my judgement is true, for it is not I alone that judge, but I and he who sent me. In your law it is written that the testimony of two men is true; I bear witness to myself, and the Father who sent me bears witness to me." They said to him therefore, "Where is your Father?" Jesus answered, "You know neither me nor my Father; if you knew me, you would know my Father also." These words he spoke in the treasury, as he taught in the temple; but no one arrested him, because his hour had not yet come.

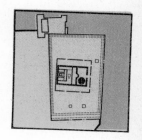

'You will die in your sins unless you believe'
Jn. 8, 21–29

Again he said to them, "I go away, and you will seek me and die in your sin; where I am going, you cannot come." Then said the Jews, "Will he kill himself, since he says, 'Where I am going, you cannot come'?" He said to them, "You are from below, I am from above; you are of this world, I am not of this world. I told you that you would die in your sins, for you will die in your sins unless you believe that I am he." They said to him, "Who are you?" Jesus said to them, "Even what I have told you from the beginning. I have much to say about you and much to judge; but he who sent me is true, and I declare to the world what I have heard from him." They did not understand that he spoke to them of the Father. So

* Jesus was in a place (aerarium) adjacent to the Hall of the Treasure, in whose walls were cut thirteen openings into which the Jews thrust the coins of the Temple offering.

** This is another allusion to his death. Now that he was in Jerusalem, Jesus made many such hints, because he wished that, when he was crucified, the Jews should have no reason for being shocked by it but should remember that he had predicted it to them.

201

Mamre. The well of Abraham. This great figure of the Old Testament was at the centre of a keen dispute between Jesus and the Jewish leaders.

| X | XI | XII | I | II | III | IV | V | VI | VII | VIII | IX | X | XI | XII | I | II | III | IV | V | VI | VII | VIII | IX | X | XI | XII | I | II | III | IV |

27 A.D.   **28** A.D.   **29** A.D.   **30** A.D.

Jesus said, "When you have lifted up the Son of man, then you will know that I am he, and that I do nothing on my own authority but speak thus as the Father taught me. And he who sent me is with me; he has not left me alone, for I always do what is pleasing to him."

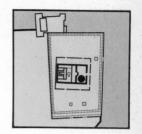

'Every one who commits sin is a slave to sin'
Jn. 8, 30–36

As he spoke thus, many believed in him. Jesus then said to the Jews who had believed in him, "If you continue in my word, you are truly my disciples, and you will know the truth, and the truth will make you free." They answered him, "We are descendants of Abraham, and have never been in bondage to any one. How is it that you say, 'You will be made free'?"

Jesus answered them, "Truly, truly, I say to you, every one who commits sin is a slave to sin. The slave does not continue in the house for ever; the son continues for ever. So if the Son makes you free, you will be free indeed.

The unbelieving Jews are not God's children
Jn. 8, 37–47

I know that you are descendants of Abraham; yet you seek to kill me, because my word finds no place in you. I speak of what I have seen with my Father, and you do what you have heard from your father."

They answered him, "Abraham is our father." Jesus said to them, "If you were Abraham's children, you would do what Abraham did, but now you seek to kill me, a man who has told you the truth which I heard from God; this is not what Abraham did.

203

A view of the Dome of the Rock, a very beautiful shrine built in the middle of the Temple esplanade.

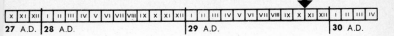

| X | XI | XII | I | II | III | IV | V | VI | VII | VIII | IX | X | XI | XII | I | II | III | IV | V | VI | VII | VIII | IX | X | XI | XII | I | II | III | IV |

27 A.D. 28 A.D. 29 A.D. 30 A.D.

You do what your father did." They said to him, "We were not born of fornication; we have one Father, even God." Jesus said to them "If God were your Father, you would love me, for I proceeded and came forth from God; I came not of my own accord, but he sent me. Why do you not understand what I say? It is because you cannot bear to hear my word. You are of your father the devil, and your will is to do your father's desires. He was a murderer from the beginning, and has nothing to do with the truth, because there is no truth in him. When he lies, he speaks according to his own nature, for he is a liar and the father of lies.

But, because I tell the truth, you do not believe me. Which of you convicts me of sin? If I tell the truth, why do you not believe me? He who is of God hears the words of God; the reason why you do not hear them is that you are not of God."

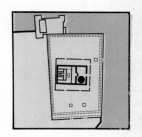

Jesus affirms his eternal existence
Jn. 8, 48–59

The Jews answered him, "Are we not right in saying that you are a Samaritan and have a demon?" Jesus answered, "I have not a demon; but I honour my Father, and you dishonour me. Yet I do not seek my own glory; there is One who seeks it and he will be the judge. Truly, truly, I say to you, if any one keeps my word, he will never see death." The Jews said to him, "Now we know that you have a demon. Abraham died, as did the prophets; and you say, 'If any one keeps my word, he will never taste death.' Are you greater than our father Abraham, who died? And the prophets died! Who do you claim to be?" Jesus answered, "If I glorify myself, my

* That is: the Jews do not understand his language because of their hostile attitude towards him.

205

Jerusalem. Entrance to the Fountain of Gihon, which by way of an underground channel cut out of the rock by Hezekiah, provides water for the Pool of Siloam. It was near this fountain that David's son, Solomon, builder of the first Temple at Jerusalem, was consecrated king.

| X | XI | XII | I | II | III | IV | V | VI | VII | VIII | IX | X | XI | XII | I | II | III | IV | V | VI | VII | VIII | IX | X | XI | XII | I | II | III | IV |

27 A.D.   28 A.D.   29 A.D.   30 A.D.

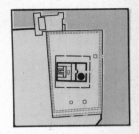

glory is nothing; it is my Father who glorifies me, of whom you say that he is your God. But you have not known him; I know him. If I said, I do not know him, I should be a liar like you; but I do know him and I keep his word. Your father Abraham rejoiced that he was to see my day; he saw it and was glad." The Jews then said to him, "You are not yet fifty years old, and have you seen Abraham?" Jesus said to them, "Truly, truly, I say to you, before Abraham was, I am". So they took up stones to throw at him; but Jesus hid himself, and went out of the temple.

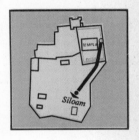

Jesus cures a man born blind
Jn. 9, 1–41

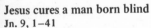

As he passed by, he saw a man blind from his birth. And his disciples asked him, "Rabbi, who sinned, this man or his parents, that he was born blind?" Jesus answered, "It was not that this man sinned, or his parents, but that the works of God might be made manifest in him. We must work the works of him who sent me, while it is day; night comes, when no one can work. As long as I am in the world, I am the light of the world." As he said this, he spat on the ground and made clay of the spittle and anointed the man's eyes with the clay, saying to him, "Go, wash in the pool of Siloam" (which means Sent). So he went and washed and came back seeing. The neighbours and those who had seen him before as a beggar, said, "Is not this the man who used to sit and beg?" Some said, "It is he"; others said, "No, but he is like him." He said, "I am the man." They said to him, "Then how were

* Jesus ends his discourses in Jerusalem with a clear affirmation of his Godhead: only God exists from all eternity (before Abraham ever was).

** Jesus corrects the thought of the Apostles. They thought that disabilities were a punishment from God, but Jesus taught that in suffering there is a mystery in which God tests or purifies men.

Jerusalem. Road leading to the Pool of Siloam. The great cliff in the middle of the photograph is the southern escarpment of Ophel, the hill on which the holy city stands.

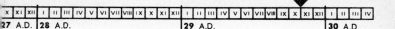

| X | XI | XII | I | II | III | IV | V | VI | VII | VIII | IX | X | XI | XII | I | II | III | IV | V | VI | VII | VIII | IX | X | XI | XII | I | II | III | IV |

27 A.D.   28 A.D.   29 A.D.   30 A.D.

your eyes opened?" He answered, "The man called Jesus made clay and anointed my eyes and said to me, 'Go to Siloam and wash'; so I went and washed and received my sight." They said to him, "Where is he?" He said, "I do not know."

They brought to the Pharisees the man who had formerly been blind. Now it was a sabbath day when Jesus made the clay and opened his eyes. The Pharisees again asked him how he had received his sight. And he said to them, "He put clay on my eyes and, washed, and I see." Some of the Pharisees said, "This man is not from God, for he does not keep the sabbath." But others said, "How can a man who is a sinner do such signs?" There was a division among them. So they again said to the blind man, "What do you say about him, since he has opened your eyes?" He said, "He is a prophet."

The Jews did not believe that he had been blind and had received his sight, until they called the parents of the man who had received his sight, and asked them, "Is this your son, who you say was born blind? How then does he now see?" His parents answered, "We know that this is our son, and that he was born blind; but how he now sees we do not know, nor do we know who opened his eyes. Ask him; he is of age, he will speak for himself." His parents said this because they feared the Jews, for the Jews had already agreed that if any one should confess him to be Christ, he was to be put out of the synagogue. Therefore his parents said, "He is of age, ask him."

So for the second time they called the man who had been blind, and said to him, "Give God the praise; we know that this man is a

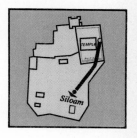

* The Jewish leaders tried to isolate Jesus with the threat of the maximum civil and religious penalty for those who became his disciples, excommunication.

209

Jerusalem. The Pool of Siloam as it is today. Water reaches it from the Fountain of Gihon. It was here that the man born blind regained his sight.

| X | XI | XII | I | II | III | IV | V | VI | VII | VIII | IX | X | XI | XII | I | II | III | IV | V | VI | VII | VIII | IX | X | XI | XII | I | II | III | IV |

27 A.D.   **28** A.D.   **29** A.D.   **30** A.D.

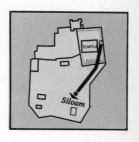

sinner." He answered, "Whether he is a sinner, I do not know; one thing I know, that though I was blind, now I see." They said to him, "What did he do to you? How did he open your eyes?" He answered them, "I have told you already, and you would not listen. Why do you want to hear it again? Do you too want to become his disciples?" And they reviled him, saying, "You are his disciple, but we are disciples of Moses. We know that God has spoken to Moses, but as for this man, we do not know where he comes from." The man answered, "Why, this is a marvel! You do not know where he comes from, and yet he opened my eyes. We know that God does not listen to sinners, but if any one is a worshipper of God and does his will, God listens to him. Never since the world began has it been heard that any one opened the eyes of a man born blind. If this man were not from God he could do nothing." They answered him, "You were born in utter sin, and would you teach us?" And they cast him out.

Jesus heard that they had cast him out, and having found him he said, "Do you believe in the Son of man?" He answered, "And who is he, sir, that I may believe in him?" Jesus said to him, "You have seen him, and it is he who speaks to you." He said, "Lord, I believe"; and he worshipped him. Jesus said, "For judgment I came into this world, that those who do not see may see, and that those who see may become blind." Some of the Pharisees near him heard this, and they said to him, "Are we also blind?" Jesus said to them, "If you were blind, you would have no guilt; but now that you say, 'We see,' your guilt remains."

211

| X | XI | XII | I | II | III | IV | V | VI | VII | VIII | IX | X | XI | XII | I | II | III | IV | V | VI | VII | VIII | IX | X | XI | XII | I | II | III | IV |

27 A.D. 28 A.D. 29 A.D. 30 A.D.

Jesus speaks of himself as 'the door of the sheep' and 'the good shepherd'
Jn. 10, 1–21

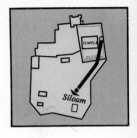

* "Truly, truly, I say to you, he who does not enter the sheepfold by the door but climbs in by another way, that man is a thief and a robber; but he who enters by the door is the shepherd of the sheep. To him the gatekeeper opens; the sheep hear his voice, and he calls his own sheep by name and leads them out. When he has brought out all his own, he goes before them, and the sheep follow him, for they know his voice. A stranger they will not follow, but they will flee from him, for they do not know the voice of strangers." This figure Jesus used with them, but they did not understand what he was saying to them.

So Jesus again said to them, "Truly, truly, I say to you, I am the door of the sheep. All who came before me are thieves and robbers; but the sheep did not heed them. I am the door; if any one enters by me, he will be saved, and will go in and out and find pasture. The thief comes only to steal and kill and destroy; I came that they may have life, and have it abundantly. I am the good shepherd. The good shepherd lays down his life for the sheep. He who is a hireling and not a shepherd, whose own the sheep are not, sees the wolf coming and leaves the sheep and flees; and the wolf snatches them and scatters them. He flees because he is a hireling and cares nothing for the sheep. I am the good shepherd; I know my own and my own know me, and the Father knows me and I know the Father; and I lay down my life for the sheep. And I have other sheep, that are not of

* For these illustrations Jesus had in mind the pastoral customs of the Jews. The flocks were usually kept all the time in the open country, where there were no sheds but only large enclosures, the sheepfolds, where all were gathered together in the evening. In the morning each shepherd went into the fold to call his flocks which, recognizing his voice, followed him. Thus he led them to pasture. Taking his inspiration from these images Jesus teaches us how great is the love with which he follows and cares for his people.

212

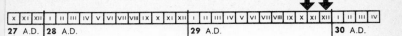

x	XI	XII	I	II	III	IV	V	VI	VII	VIII	IX	X	XI	XII	I	II	III	IV	V	VI	VII	VIII	IX	X	XI	XII	I	II	III	IV

27 A.D.   28 A.D.   29 A.D.   30 A.D.

this fold; I must bring them also, and they will heed my voice. So there shall be one flock, one shepherd. For this reason the Father loves me, because I lay down my life, that I may take it again. No one takes it from me, but I lay it down of my own accord. I have power to lay it down, and I have power to take it again; this charge I have received from my Father."

There was again a division among the Jews because of these words. Many of them said, "He has a demon, and he is mad; why listen to him?" Others said, "These are not the sayings of one who has a demon. Can a demon open the eyes of the blind?"

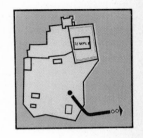

Jesus solemnly affirms his divinity
Jn. 10, 22–39

It was the feast of the Dedication at Jerusalem; it was winter, and Jesus was walking in the temple, in the portico of Solomon. So the Jews gathered round him and said to him, "How long will you keep us in suspense? If you are the Christ, tell us plainly." Jesus answered them, "I told you, and you do not believe. The works that I do in my Father's name, they bear witness to me; but you do not believe, because you do not belong to my sheep. My sheep hear my voice, and I know them, and they follow me; and I give them eternal life, and they shall never perish, and no one shall snatch them out of my hand. My Father, who has given them to me, is greater than all, and no one is able to snatch them of the Father's hand. I and the Father are one."

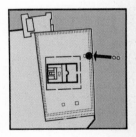

* The Feast of the Dedication (Hanukkah Feast of Lights) commemorated the reconsecration of the Temple after its profanation by King Antiochus IV.

213

Jerusalem. The south-eastern corner of the Temple court. Along the eastern side (foreshortened in the photograph) ran Solomon's Portico; along the southern (facing us), the Royal Portico. Where they met was the summit of the 'Pinnacle of the Temple', the highest point of the walls of Jerusalem.

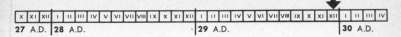

| X | XI | XII | I | II | III | IV | V | VI | VII | VIII | IX | X | XI | XII | I | II | III | IV | V | VI | VII | VIII | IX | X | XI | XII | I | II | III | IV |

27 A.D.　**28** A.D.　　　　　　　　　**29** A.D.　　　　　　　　　**30** A.D.

The Jews took up stones again to stone him. Jesus answered them, "I have shown you many good works from the Father; for which of these do you stone me?" The Jews answered him, "We stone you for no good work but for blasphemy; because you, being a man, make yourself God." Jesus answered them, "Is it not written in your law, 'I said, you are gods'? If he called them gods to whom the word of God came (and scripture cannot be broken), do you say of him whom the Father consecrated and sent into the world, 'You are blaspheming,' because I said, 'I am the Son of God'? If I am not doing the works of my Father, then do not believe me; but if I do them, even though you do not believe me, believe the works, that you may know and understand that the Father is in me and I am in the Father." Again they tried to arrest him, but he escaped from their hands.

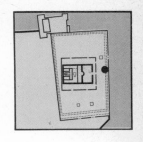

* In this place, Bethany beyond Jordan (different from Bethany where he had raised Lazarus from the dead) Jesus continued to teach those who had followed him and to work many miracles.

Jesus withdraws beyond the Jordan, into Peraea
Mt. 19, 1–2. Mk. 10, 1. Jn. 10, 40–42

* He went away again across the Jordan to the place where John at first baptized, and there he remained. And many came to him; and they said, "John did no sign, but everything that John said about this man was true." And many believed in him there.

Jesus forbids divorce
Mt. 19, 3–12. Mk. 10, 2–12

And Pharisees came up to him and tested him by asking, "Is it lawful to divorce one's wife for any cause?" He answered, "Have you not read that he who made them from the beginning made them male and female, and

215

Children at Nazareth. The children whom Jesus took up and blessed must have been like these.

said, 'For this reason a man shall leave his father and mother and be joined to his wife, and the two shall become one'? So they are no longer two but one. What therefore God has joined together, let no man put asunder." They said to him, "Why then did Moses command one to give a certificate of divorce, and to put her away?" He said to them, "For your hardness of heart Moses allowed you to divorce your wives, but from the beginning it was not so. And I say to you: whoever divorces his wife, except for unchastity, and marries another, commits adultery; and he who marries a divorced woman commits adultery."

The disciples said to him, "If such is the case of a man with his wife, it is not expedient to marry." But he said to them, "Not all men can receive this precept, but only those to whom it is given. For there are eunuchs who have been so from birth, and there are eunuchs who have been made eunuchs by men, and there are eunuchs who have made themselves eunuchs for the sake of the kingdom of heaven. He who is able to receive this, let him receive it."

Jesus blesses the children
Mt. 19, 13–15. Mk. 10, 13–16. Lk. 18, 15–17

And they were bringing children to him, that he might touch them; and the disciples rebuked them. But when Jesus saw it he was indignant, and said to them, "Let the children come to me, do not hinder them; for to such belongs the Kingdom of God. Truly, I say to you, whoever does not receive the kingdom of God like a child shall not enter it." And he took them in his arms and blessed them, laying his hands upon them.

Aenon
Sychar
Jericho
Bethany
Bethany beyond Jordan
Machaerus

* Moses tolerated divorce as a lesser evil. As it was only men who had the right of repudiating their wives(and not vice versa), he prescribed the 'writ'or certificate of divorce so as to limit abuses and restrict the practice. In essence it was a defence of the woman. See Deut. 24,1. Jesus with his authority re-establishes the law of God in its initial purity. See Gen. 2, 24.

** That is with simplicity and filial trust in God, such as a child feels for his own parents.

*** In face of these arguments based on the advantage of a more easy-going way of life. Jesus puts forward his ideal of perfection: chastity for love of the Kingdom of God.

217

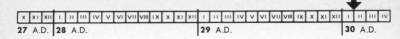

'If you would be perfect ...'

Mt. 19, 16–22. **Mk. 10, 17–22.** Lk. 18, 18–23

And as he was setting out on his journey, a man ran up and knelt before him, and asked him, "Good Teacher, what must I do to inherit eternal life?" And Jesus said to him, "Why do you call me good? No one is good * but God alone. You know the commandments: 'Do not kill, Do not commit adultery, Do not steal, Do not bear false witness, Do not defraud, Honour your father and mother." And he said to him, "Teacher, all these I have observed from my youth." And Jesus looking upon him loved him, and said to him, "You lack one thing; go, sell what you have, and give to the poor, and you will have a treasure in heaven; and come follow me." At that saying his countenance fell, and he went away sorrowful; for he had great possessions.

Jesus gives a warning against attachment to riches

Mt. 19, 23–26. **Mk. 10, 23–27.** Lk. 18,24–27.

And Jesus looked around and said to his disciples, "How hard it will be for those who have riches to enter the kingdom of God!" And the disciples were amazed at his words. But Jesus said to them again, "Children, how hard it is for those who trust in riches to enter the kingdom of God! It is ** easier for a camel to go through the eye of a needle than for a rich man to enter the kingdom of God." And they were exceedingly astonished, and said to him, "Then who can be saved?" Jesus looked at them and said, "With men it is impossible, but not with God; for all things are possible with God."

* The Lord reminds him first of the 'duty' of obeying commandments, and then puts before him his 'counsel' for an even more perfect life, that is, the actual abandonment of all material things for a greater freedom and interior disposition towards Grace.

** With an illustration natural to oriental speech Jesus warns us of the great difficulty (not impossibility of the salvation of those who possess so much material wealth that they end by being over attached to it.

218

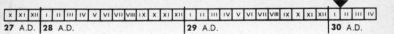
Jesus invites men to embrace poverty
Mt. 19, 27–30. Mk. 10, 28–31. Lk. 18, 28–30

Then Peter said in reply, "Lo, we have left everything and followed you. What then shall we have?" Jesus said to them, "Truly, I say to you, in the new world, when the Son of man shall sit on his glorious throne, you who have followed me will also sit on twelve thrones, judging the twelve tribes of Israel. And every one who has left houses or brothers or sisters or father or mother or children or lands, for my name's sake, will receive a hundredfold, and inherit eternal life. But many that are first will be last, and the last first."

Jesus condemns the superficiality of the Pharisees
Lk. 11, 37–44

While he was speaking, a Pharisee asked him to dine with him; so he went in and sat at table. The Pharisee was astonished to see that he did not first wash before dinner. And the Lord said to him, "Now you Pharisees cleanse the outside of the cup and of the dish, but inside you are full of extortion and wickedness. You fools! Did not he who made the outside make the inside also? But give for alms those things which are within; and behold, everything is clean for you.

"But woe to you Pharisees! for you tithe mint and rue and every herb, and neglect justice and the love of God; these you ought to have done, without neglecting the others. Woe to you Pharisees! for you love the best seat in the synagogues and salutations in the market places. Woe to you! for you are like graves which are not seen,

* Jesus omits the washings in order to protest against the formalism of the Pharisees and also to make an opportunity for explaining to them how the observance of the regulations of the law in a purely external way is blameworthy before God and shows insincerity of soul. God wishes us to draw near to him first of all inwardly and then outwardly.

Jerusalem. The Sepulchre of the prophet Zechariah, in the valley of the Kedron, past which Jesus often walked.

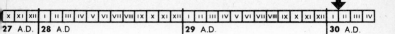

| XI | XI | XII | I | II | III | IV | V | VI | VII | VIII | IX | X | XI | XII | I | II | III | IV | V | VI | VII | VIII | IX | X | XI | XII | I | II | III | IV |

27 A.D.   28 A.D.   29 A.D.   30 A.D.

and men walk over them without knowing it."

Jesus reproves the selfishness of the doctors of the law
Lk. 11, 45−54. Mt. 23, 34−36

One of the lawyers answered him, "Teacher, in saying this you reproach us also." And he said, "Woe to you lawyers also! for you load men with burdens hard to bear, and you yourselves do not touch the burdens with one of your fingers. Woe to you! for you build the tombs of the prophets whom your fathers killed. So you are witnesses and consent to the deeds of your fathers; for they killed them, and you build their tombs. Therefore also the Wisdom of God said, 'I will send them prophets and apostles, some of whom they will kill and persecute,' that the blood of all the prophets, shed from the foundation of the world, may be required of this generation, from the blood of Abel to the blood of Zechariah, who perished between the altar and the sanctuary. Yes, I tell you, it shall be required of this generation. Woe to you lawyers! for you have taken away the key of knowledge; you did not enter yourselves, and you hindered those who were entering."

As he went away from there, the scribes and the Pharisees began to press him hard, and to provoke him to speak of many things, lying in wait for him, to catch at something he might say.

Jesus says to the crowd: 'Be on your guard against the Pharisees!'
Lk. 12, 1−3

In the meantime, when so many thousands

* In the first book of the Bible (Gen. 4, 8) is related the story of the murder of the innocent Abel by the hand of Cain; in the last book of the Hebrew Bible (II Chron. 24, 20) it is related of the High Priest Zechariah that as he was dying, murdered by order of King Joash, he cried: 'Yahweh sees and he will avenge!'. According to a Jewish tradition the stain of Zechariah's blood between the altar and the temple remained red for centuries, until the destruction of the temple itself.

** The scribes who had studied the law and therefore had to interpret it and teach it to the people ('have taken away' the key of knowledge') in reality had not understood its true meaning (in fact they

221

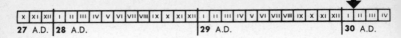

| X | XI | XII | I | II | III | IV | V | VI | VII | VIII | IX | X | XI | XII | I | II | III | IV | V | VI | VII | VIII | IX | X | XI | XII | I | II | III | IV |

27 A.D.   **28** A.D.   **29** A.D.   **30** A.D.

of the multitude had gathered together that they trod upon one another, he began to say to his disciples first, "Beware of the leaven of the Pharisees, which is hypocrisy. Nothing is covered up that will not be revealed, or hidden that will not be known. Whatever you have said in the dark shall be heard in the light, and what you have whispered in private rooms shall be proclaimed upon the housetops."

He says to his friends: 'Do not be afraid of men'
Lk. 12, 4–7

"I tell you, my friends, do not fear those who kill the body, and after that have no more that they can do. But I will warn you whom to fear: fear him who, after he has killed, has power to cast into hell; yes, I tell you, fear him! Are not five sparrows sold for two pennies? And not one of them is forgotten before God. Why, even the hairs of your head are all numbered. Fear not; you are of more value than many sparrows."

'Do not be ashamed of me'
Lk. 12, 8–12

"And I tell you, every one who acknowledges me before men, the Son of man also will acknowledge before the angels of God; but he who denies me before men will be denied before the angels of God. And everyone who speaks a word against the Son of man will be forgiven; but he who blasphemes against the Holy Spirit will not be forgiven. And when they bring you before the synagogues and the rulers and the authorities, do not be anxious how or what you are to

did not recognize the Massiah in Jesus). As a result 'they had prevented others going into' the true meaning of Holy Scripture.

222

| X | XI | XII | I | II | III | IV | V | VI | VII | VIII | IX | X | XI | XII | I | II | III | IV | V | VI | VII | VIII | IX | X | XI | XII | I | II | III | IV |

27 A.D.   **28** A.D.   **29** A.D.   **30** A.D.

answer or what you are to say; for the Holy Spirit will teach you in that very hour what you ought to say."

Jesus desires indifference to worldly goods
Lk. 12, 13–15

One of the multitude said to him, "Teacher, bid my brother divide the inheritance with me." But he said to him, "Man, who made me a judge or divider over you?" And he said to them, "Take heed, and beware of all covetousness; for a man's life does not consist in the abundance of his possessions."

Parable of the rich fool
Lk. 12, 16–21

And he told them a parable, saying, "The land of a rich man brought forth plentifully; and he thought to himself, 'What shall I do, for I have nowhere to store my crops? And he said, 'I will do this: I will pull down my barns, and build larger ones; and there I will store all my grain and my goods. And I will say to my soul, Soul, you have ample goods laid up for many years; take your ease, eat, drink, be merry.' But God said to him, 'Fool! This night your soul is required of you; and the things you have prepared, whose will they be?' So is he who lays up treasure for himself, and is not rich toward God."

'Provide yourselves with a treasure in the heavens'
Lk. 12, 32–34

"Fear not, little flock, for it is your Father's good pleasure to give you the kingdom. Sell your possessions, and give alms; provide yourselves with purses that

223

| X | XI | XII | I | II | III | IV | V | VI | VII | VIII | IX | X | XI | XII | I | II | III | IV | V | VI | VII | VIII | IX | X | XI | XII | I | II | III | IV |

27 A.D.   28 A.D.   29 A.D.   30 A.D.

do not grow old, with a treasure in the heavens that does not fail, where no thief approaches and no moth destroys. For where your treasure is, there will your heart be also."

Jesus urges watchfulness
Lk. 12, 35–40

"Let your loins be girded and your lamps burning, and be like men who are waiting for their master to come home from the marriage feast, so that they may open to him at once when he comes and knocks. Blessed are those servants whom the master finds awake when he comes; truly, I say to you, he will gird himself and have them sit at table, and he will come and serve them. If he comes in the second watch, or in the third, and finds them so, blessed are those servants! But know this, that if the householder had known at what hour the thief was coming he would have been awake and would not have left his house to be broken into. You also must be ready; for the Son of man is coming at an hour you do not expect."

Parable of the conscientious and careless servants
Lk. 12, 41–48

Peter said, "Lord, are you telling this parable for us or for all?" And the Lord said, "Who then is the faithful and wise steward, whom his master will set over his household, to give them their portion of food at the proper time? Blessed is that servant whom his master when he comes will find so doing. Truly, I tell you, he will set him over all his possessions. But if that servant says to himself, 'My master is de-

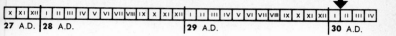

| X | XI | XII | I | II | III | IV | V | VI | VII | VIII | IX | X | XI | XII | I | II | III | IV | V | VI | VII | VIII | IX | X | XI | XII | I | II | III | IV |

27 A.D. **28** A.D. **29** A.D. **30** A.D.

layed in coming,' and begins to beat the menservants and the maidservants, and to eat and drink and get drunk, the master of that servant will come on a day when he does not expect him and at an hour he does not know, and will punish him, and put him with the unfaithful. And that servant who knew his master's will, but did not make ready or act according to his will, shall receive a severe beating. But he who did not know, and did what deserved a beating, shall receive a light beating. Every one to whom much is given, of him will much be required; and of him to whom men commit much they will demand the more.

Jesus asks for enthusiasm and heroism
Lk. 12, 49-53

"I came to cast fire upon the earth; and would that it were already kindled! I have a baptism to be baptized with; and how I am constrained until it is accomplished! Do you think that I have come to give peace on earth? No, I tell you, but rather division; for henceforth in one house there will be five divided, three against two and two against three; they will be divided, father against son and son against father, mother against daughter and daughter against her mother, mother-in-law against her daughter-in-law and daughter-in-law against her mother-in-law."

Jesus exhorts men to conversion while there is time
Lk. 12, 54-59

He also said to the multitudes, "When you see a cloud rising in the west, you say at once, 'A shower is coming'; and so it happens. And when you see the south wind blowing,

* Jesus is speaking of the spiritual renewal which he has come to bring on the earth; this is like an inner fire which comes between us and our passions, and also makes divisions between men, between those who welcome it and those who resist it.

225

Jerusalem. Round base of a tower at Siloam. Jesus spoke of the fall of a tower at Siloam causing the death of eighteen people.

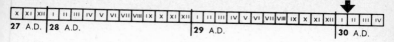

| X | XI | XII | I | II | III | IV | V | VI | VII | VIII | IX | X | XI | XII | I | II | III | IV | V | VI | VII | VIII | IX | X | XI | XII | I | II | III | IV |

27 A.D.   **28** A.D.   **29** A.D.   **30** A.D.

you say, 'There will be scorching heat'; and it happens. You hypocrites! You know how to interpret the appearance of earth and sky; but why do you not know how to interpret the present time?

"And why do you not judge for yourselves what is right? As you go with your accuser before the magistrate, make an effort to settle with him on the way, lest he drag you to the judge, and the judge hand you over to the officer, and the officer put you in prison. I tell you, you will never get out till you have paid the very last copper."

The need for a change of life
Lk. 13, 1–5

There were some present at that very time who had told him of the Galileans whose blood Pilate had mingled with their sacrifices. And he answered them, "Do you think that these Galileans were worse sinners than all the other Galileans, because they suffered thus? I tell you, No; but unless you repent you will all likewise perish. Or those eighteen upon whom the tower in Siloam fell and killed them, do you think that they were worse offenders than all the others who dwelt in Jerusalem? I tell you, No; but unless you repent you will all likewise perish."

The urgency of a change of life
Lk. 13, 6–9

And he told this parable: "A man had a fig tree planted in his vineyard; and he came seeking fruit on it and found none. And he said to the vinedresser, 'Lo, these three years I have come seeking fruit on this fig tree, and I find none. Cut it down; why should it use up the ground?' And he answered him, 'Let

* During the Jewish Festivals Pilate was always present in Jerusalem for fear of disturbances caused by the overcrowding in the city. From this reference it would seem that some Galileans, while offering sacrifice in the Temple had somehow incurred Pilate's suspicion and that he had intervened rather harshly and had some of them killed. The way in which this incident was reported to Jesus reveals the opinion usual at that time, which supposed that every misfortune was God's punishment summarily inflicted for the sins of those who experienced it.

** It seems that this refers to workmen who were employed round the tower of Siloam which for some reason unknown to us collapsed on them and killed eighteen.

227

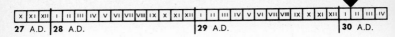

| X | XI | XII | I | II | III | IV | V | VI | VII | VIII | IX | X | XI | XII | I | II | III | IV | V | VI | VII | VIII | IX | X | XI | XII | I | II | III | IV |

27 A.D.   **28** A.D.   **29** A.D.   **30** A.D.

it alone, sir, this year also, till I dig about it and put on manure. And if it bears fruit next year, well and good; but if not, you can cut it down.' "

Jesus heals a crippled woman on the sabbath
Lk. 13, 10–17

Now he was teaching in one of the synagogues on the sabbath. And there was a woman who had had a spirit of infirmity for eighteen years; she was bent over and could not fully straighten herself. And when Jesus saw her, he called her and said to her, "Woman, you are freed from your infirmity." And he laid his hands upon her, and immediately she was made straight, and she praised God. But the ruler of the synagogue, indignant because Jesus had healed on the sabbath, said to the people, "There are six days on which work ought to be done; come on those days and be healed, and not on the sabbath day." Then the Lord answered him, "You * hypocrites! Does not each of you on the sabbath untie his ox or his ass from the manger, and lead it away to water it? And ought not this woman, a daughter of Abraham whom Satan bound for eighteen years, be loosed from this bond on the sabbath day?" As he said this, all his adversaries were put to shame; and all the people rejoiced at all the glorious things that were done by him.

'Try your best to enter by the narrow door'
Lk. 13, 22–30

He went on his way through towns and villages, teaching, and journeying toward Jerusalem. And some one said to him, "Lord, will those who are saved be few?" And he

* The rest on the sabbath day was very strictly observed among the Jews. But to God's command (the third commandment) formalistic regulations had been added. Jesus, in this and other similar incidents, opposes a way of keeping the law which had become entirely external, without any admixture of inner charity.

| X | XI | XII | I | II | III | IV | V | VI | VII | VIII | IX | X | XI | XII | I | II | III | IV | V | VI | VII | VIII | IX | X | XI | XII | I | II | III | IV |
27 A.D. 28 A.D. 29 A.D. 30 A.D.

said to them, "Strive to enter by the narrow door; for many, I tell you, will seek to enter and will not be able. When once the householder has risen up and shut the door, you will begin to stand outside and to knock at the door, saying, 'Lord, open to us.' He will answer you, 'I do not know where you come from.' Then you will begin to say, 'We ate and drank in your presence, and you taught in our streets.' But he will say, 'I tell you, I do not know where you come from; depart from me, all you workers of iniquity!' There you will weep and gnash your teeth, when you see Abraham and Isaac and Jacob and all the prophets in the kingdom of God and you yourselves thrust out. And men will come from east and west, and from north and south, and sit at table in the kingdom of God. And behold, some are last who will be first, and some are first who will be last."

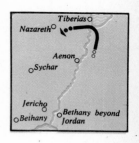

'Go and tell that fox (Herod)'
Lk. 13, 31—33

At that very hour some Pharisees came, and said to him, "Get away from here, for Herod wants to kill you." And he said to them, "Go and tell that fox, 'Behold, I cast out demons and perform cures today and tomorrow, and the third day I finish my course. Nevertheless I must go on my way today and tomorrow and the day following; for it cannot be that a prophet should perish away from Jerusalem.'

Jesus works another cure on the sabbath day
Lk. 14, 1—6

One sabbath when he went to dine at the house of a ruler who belonged to the

* The Jewish people were God's chosen people (the 'first'), but if they did not accept Jesus then they would be rejected and in their place would be called into the Kingdom of God other peoples (the 'last') from all the corners of the earth.

** Jesus was in the territory of the tetrarch, Herod Antipas who after having beheaded John the Baptist, was afraid of a popular rising in favour of Jesus. But Jesus did not fear him for he knew that his time had not yet come and that his end was to be at Jerusalem. The three days were a symbol of the short time which by them separated Jesus from his supreme sacrifice.

229

The Lake of Gennesaret with, in the background, Tiberias, the city founded by Herod Antipas in honour of Tiberius. In 18 A.D. 'that fox Herod' made it the capital of his tetrarchy and the seat of his residence. It seems that Jesus never set foot in it.

| X | XI | XII | I | II | III | IV | V | VI | VII | VIII | IX | X | XI | XII | I | II | III | IV | V | VI | VII | VIII | IX | X | XI | XII | I | II | III | IV |

27 A.D.　　**28** A.D.　　　　　　　　　**29** A.D.　　　　　　　　**30** A.D.

Pharisees, they were watching him. And behold, there was a man before him who had dropsy. And Jesus spoke to the lawyers and Pharisees, saying, "Is it lawful to heal on the sabbath, or not?" But they were silent. Then he took him and healed him, and let him go. And he said to them, "Which of you, having an ass or an ox that has fallen into a well, will not immediately pull him out on a sabbath day?" And they could not reply to this.

'The man who humbles himself will be exalted'
Lk. 14, 7–11

Now he told a parable to those who were invited, when he marked how they chose the places of honour, saying to them, "When you are invited by any one to a marriage feast, do not sit down in a place of honour, lest a more eminent man than you be invited by him; and he who invited you both will come, and say to you, 'Give place to this man,' and then you will begin with shame to take the lowest place. But when you are invited, go and sit in the lowest place, so that when your host comes he may say to you, 'Friend, go up higher'; then you will be honoured in the presence of all who sit at table with you. For every one who exalts himself will be humbled, and he who humbles himself will be exalted."

Jesus urges unselfishness
Lk. 14, 12–14

He said also to the man who had invited him, "When you give a dinner or a banquet, do not invite your friends or your brothers or your kinsmen or rich neighbours, lest they also invite you in return, and you be repaid. But when you give a feast, invite the poor, the maimed, the lame, the blind, and you

* Jesus insists on the fact that unselfishness is one of the characteristics of real charity: anyone who expects a reward for the good that he does may look for it only from God in the day of the last judgement.

231

| X | XI | XII | I | II | III | IV | V | VI | VII | VIII | IX | X | XI | XII | I | II | III | IV | V | VI | VII | VIII | IX | X | XI | XII | I | II | III | IV |

27 A.D. | **28** A.D. | **29** A.D. | **30** A.D.

will be blessed, because they cannot repay you. You will be repaid at the resurrection of the just."

The parable of those invited to dinner
Lk. 14, 15–24

When one of those who sat at table with him heard this, he said to him, "Blessed is he who shall eat bread in the kingdom of God!" But he said to him, "A man once gave a great banquet, and invited many; and at the time for the banquet he sent his servant to say to those who had been invited, 'Come: for all is now ready.' But they all alike began to make excuses. The first said to him, 'I have bought a field, and I must go out and see it; I pray you, have me excused.' And another said, 'I have bought five yoke of oxen, and I go to examine them; I pray you, have me excused.' And another said, 'I have married a wife, and therefore I cannot come.' So the servant came and reported this to his master. Then the householder in anger said to his servant, 'Go out quickly to the streets and lanes of the city, and bring in the poor and maimed and blind and lame.' And the servant said, 'Sir, what you commanded has been done, and still there is room.' And the master said to the servant, 'Go out to the highways and hedges, and compel people to come in, that my house may be filled. For I tell you, none of those men who were invited shall taste my banquet.' "

Other conditions for following Jesus
Lk. 14, 25–35

Now great multitudes accompanied him; and he turned and said to them, "If any one * comes to me and does not hate his own

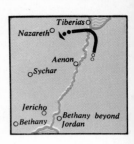

* The word 'hate' (= love less well) is opposed to 'prefer'. Jesus meant that anyone who wished to follow him must prefer him to every other person, and all worldly possessions.

232

| X | XI | XII | I | II | III | IV | V | VI | VII | VIII | IX | X | XI | XII | I | II | III | IV | V | VI | VII | VIII | IX | X | XI | XII | I | II | III | IV |

27 A.D.   28 A.D.   29 A.D.   30 A.D.

father and mother and wife and children and brothers and sisters, yes, and even his own life, he cannot be my disciple. Whoever does not bear his own cross and come after me, cannot be my disciple. For which of you, desiring to build a tower, does not first sit down and count the cost, whether he has enough to complete it? Otherwise when he has laid a foundation, and is not able to finish, all who see it begin to mock him, saying, 'This man began to build, and was not able to finish.' Or what king, going to encounter another king in war, will not sit down first and take counsel whether he is able with ten thousand to meet him who comes against him with twenty thousand? And if not, while the other is yet a great way off, he sends an embassy and asks terms of peace. So therefore, whoever of you does not renounce all that he has cannot be my disciple.

"Salt is good; but if salt has lost its taste, how shall its saltness be restored? It is fit neither for the land nor for the dunghill; men throw it away. He who has ears to hear, let him hear."

The parable of the lost sheep
Lk. 15, 1–7

Now the tax collectors and sinners were all drawing near to hear him. And the Pharisees and the scribes murmured, saying, "This man receives sinners and eats with them."

So he told them this parable: "What man of you, having a hundred sheep, if he has lost one of them, does not leave the ninety-nine in the wilderness, and go after the one which is lost, until he finds it? And when he has found it, he lays it on his shoulders,

233

| X | XI | XII | I | II | III | IV | V | VI | VII | VIII | IX | X | XI | XII | I | II | III | IV | V | VI | VII | VIII | IX | X | XI | XII | I | II | III | IV |

27 A.D. | **28** A.D. | **29** A.D. | **30** A.D.

rejoicing. And when he comes home, he calls together his friends and his neighbours, saying to them, 'Rejoice with me, for I have found my sheep which was lost.' Just so, I tell you, there will be more joy in heaven over one sinner who repents than over ninety-nine righteous persons who need no repentance."

The parable of the lost drachma
Lk. 15, 8–10

"Or what woman, having ten silver coins, if she loses one coin, does not light a lamp and sweep the house and seek diligently until she finds it? And when she has found it, she calls together her friends and neighbours, saying, 'Rejoice with me, for I have found the coin which I had lost.' Just so, I tell you, there is joy before the angels of God over one sinner who repents."

The parable of the prodigal son
Lk. 15, 11–32

And he said, "There was a man who had two sons; and the younger of them said to his father, 'Father, give me the share of property that falls to me.' And he divided his living between them. Not many days later, the younger son gathered all he had and took his journey into a far country, and there he squandered his property in loose living. And when he had spent everything, a great famine arose in that country, and he began to be in want. So he went and joined himself to one of the citizens of that * country, who sent him into his fields to feed swine. And he would gladly have fed on the pods that the swine ate; and no one gave him anything. But when he came to himself he said, 'How many of my father's hired ser-

* The Jews held these animals in horror and considered them unclean.

234

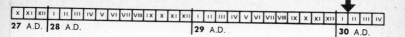

| X | XI | XII | I | II | III | IV | V | VI | VII | VIII | IX | X | XI | XII | I | II | III | IV | V | VI | VII | VIII | IX | X | XI | XII | I | II | III | IV |

27 A.D.   **28** A.D.   **29** A.D.   **30** A.D.

vants have bread enough and to spare, but I perish here with hunger! I will arise and go to my father, and I will say to him, "Father, I have sinned against heaven and before you; I am no longer worthy to be called your son; treat me as one of your hired servants." And he arose and came to his father. But while he was yet at a distance, his father saw him and had compassion, and ran and embraced him and kissed him. And the son said to him, 'Father, I have sinned against heaven and before you; I am no longer worthy to be called your son; treat me as one of your hired servants.' But the father said to his servants. 'Bring quickly the best robe, and put it on him; and put a ring on his hand, and shoes on his feet; and bring the fatted calf and kill it, and let us eat and make merry; for this my son was dead, and is alive again; he was lost, and is found.' And they began to make merry.

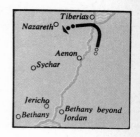

"Now his elder son was in the field; and as he came and drew near to the house, he heard music and dancing. And he called one of the servants and asked what this meant. And he said to him, 'Your brother has come, and your father has killed the fatted calf, because he has received him safe and sound.' But he was angry and refused to go in. His father came out and entreated him, but he answered his father, 'Lo, these many years I have served you, and I never disobeyed your command; yet you never gave me a kid, that I might make merry with my friends. But when this son of yours came, who has devoured your living with harlots, you killed for him the fatted calf!' And he said to him, 'Son, you are always with me, and all that is mine is yours. It was fitting to make merry

Another view of Galilee which Jesus passed through on his way back to Judaea.

| X | XI | XII | I | II | III | IV | V | VI | VII | VIII | IX | X | XI | XII | I | II | III | IV | V | VI | VII | VIII | IX | X | XI | XII | I | II | III | IV |
27 A.D.   28 A.D.   29 A.D.   30 A.D.

and be glad, for this your brother was dead, and is alive; he was lost, and is found.' "

The parable of the dishonest steward
Lk. 16, 1–13

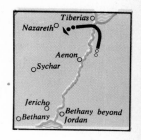

He also said to the disciples, "There was a rich man who had a steward, and charges were brought to him that this man was wasting his goods. And he called him and said to him, 'What is this that I hear about you? Turn in the account of your stewardship, for you can no longer be steward.' And the steward said to himself, 'What shall I do, since my master is taking the stewardship away from me? I am not strong enough to dig, and I am ashamed to beg. I have decided what to do, so that people may receive me into their houses when I am put out of the stewardship.' So, summoning his master's debtors one by one, he said to the first, 'How much do you owe my master?' He said, 'A hundred measures of oil.' And he said to him, 'Take your bill, and sit down quickly and write fifty.' Then he said to another, 'And how much do you owe?' He said, 'A hundred measures of wheat.' He said to him, 'Take your bill, and write eighty'. The master commended the dishonest steward for his prudence; for the sons of this world are wiser in their own generation than the sons of light. And I tell you, make friends for yourselves by means of unrighteous mammon, so that when it fails they may receive you into the eternal habitations.

"He who is faithful in a very little is faithful also in much; and he who is dishonest in a very little is dishonest also in much. If then you have not been faithful in the unrighteous mammon, who will entrust to

* The parable is obviously not intended to justify or to suggest imitation of the fraud carried out by the dishonest steward: rather Jesus means – 'as sinners are crafty in doing wrong, so you must make use of your intelligence in doing good

237

| X | XI | XII | I | II | III | IV | V | VI | VII | VIII | IX | X | XI | XII | I | II | III | IV | V | VI | VII | VIII | IX | X | XI | XII | I | II | III | IV |

27 A.D.   28 A.D.   29 A.D.   30 A.D.

you the true riches? And if you have not been faithful in that which is another's, who will give you that which is your own? No servant can serve two masters; for either he will hate the one and love the other, or he will be devoted to the one and despise the other. You cannot serve God and mammon."

Jesus requires righteousness and strength of character
Lk. 16, 14—17

*   The Pharisees, who were lovers of money, heard all this, and they scoffed at him. But he said to them, "You are those who justify yourselves before men, but God knows your hearts; for what is exalted among men is an abomination in the sight of God.

"The law and the prophets were until John; since then the good news of the Kingdom of God is preached, and every one enters it violently. But it is easier for heaven and earth to pass away, than for one dot of the law to become void."

The parable of the poor Lazarus and the wicked rich man
Lk. 16, 19—31

"There was a rich man, who was clothed in purple and fine linen and who feasted sumptuously every day. And at his gate lay a poor man named Lazarus, full of sores, who desired to be fed with what fell from the rich man's table; moreover the dogs came and licked his sores. The poor man died and was carried by the angels to Abraham's bosom. The rich man also died and was buried; and in Hades, being in torment, he lifted up his eyes, and saw Abraham far off and Lazarus

*   The Jews mistakenly thought that misfortunes were always God's punishment, and that wealth was always a sign of his blessing; the richer they were the more righteous did they think themselves. This idea made them go to all lengths to ensure that this sign of divine protection (wealth) should never fail them.

238

| X | XI | XII | I | II | III | IV | V | VI | VII | VIII | IX | X | XI | XII | I | II | III | IV | V | VI | VII | VIII | IX | X | XI | XII | I | II | III | IV |

27 A.D. **28** A.D. **29** A.D. **30** A.D.

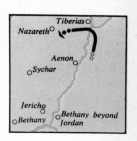

in his bosom. And he called out, 'Father Abraham, have mercy upon me, and send Lazarus to dip the end of his finger in water and cool my tongue; for I am in anguish in this flame.' But Abraham said, 'Son, remember that you in your lifetime received your good things and Lazarus in like manner evil things, but now he is comforted here, and you are in anguish. And besides all this, between us and you a great chasm has been fixed, in order that those who would pass from here to you may not be able, and none may cross from there to us.' And he said, 'Then I beg you, father, to send him to my father's house, for I have five brothers, so that he may warn them, lest they also come into this place of torment.' But Abraham said, 'They have Moses and the prophets; let them hear them.' And he said, 'No, father Abraham; but if some one goes to them from the dead, they will repent.' He said to him, 'If they do not hear Moses and the prophets, neither will they be convinced if some one should rise from the dead.' "

* This is a typical eastern expression which, translated into our manner of speaking, means that if we have a lively faith even the working of miracles is not beyond us. The lives of the Apostles and Saints are a confirmation of this.

If you had faith . . .
Lk. 17, 5–6.

The apostles said to the Lord, "Increase our faith!" And the Lord said, "If you had faith as a grain of mustard seed, you could say to this sycamine tree, 'Be rooted up, and be planted in the sea,' and it would obey you."

The parable of the good servant
Lk. 17, 7–10.

"Will any one of you, who has a servant ploughing or keeping sheep, say to him when he has come in from the field, 'Come at

239

The village of Jenin photographed from the north-west with a telephoto lens. It was here that Jesus healed the ten lepers.

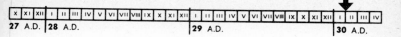
once and sit down at table'? Will he not rather say to him, 'Prepare supper for me, and gird yourself and serve me, till I eat and drink; and afterward you shall eat and drink' Does he thank the servant because he did what was commanded? So you also, when you have done all that is commanded you, say, 'We are unworthy servants; we have only done what was our duty.' "

Jesus heals ten lepers
Lk. 17, 11-19

On the way to Jerusalem he was passing along between Samaria and Galilee. And as he entered a village, he was met by ten lepers, who stood at a distance and lifted up their voices and said, "Jesus, Master, have mercy on us." When he saw them he said to them, "Go and show yourselves to the priests." And as they went they were cleansed. Then one of them, when he saw that he was healed, turned back, praising God with a loud voice; and he fell on his face at Jesus' feet, giving him thanks. Now he was a Samaritan. Then said Jesus, "Were not ten cleansed? Where are the nine? Was no one found to return and give praise to God except this foreigner?" And he said to him, "Rise and go your way; your faith has made you well."

Jesus speaks of his second coming
Lk. 17, 20-37

Being asked by the Pharisees when the kingdom of God was coming, he answered them, "The kingdom of God is not coming with signs to be observed; nor will they say, 'Lo, here it is!' or 'There!' for behold, the kingdom of God is in the midst of you."

And he said to the disciples, "The days

* The kingdom of God is brought into being at two quite distinct times. The first is this present age in which we ourselves live (the Kingdom of God is within us by his Grace); the second will be that of Jesus glorified and visible to all at the end of the world. This second coming will be unexpected, and will be

241

Hand-mill for grinding corn in Jesus' time. A stick inserted in the central hole provided an axis, and one fixed into the hole at the side a handle. As a rule this work was done by women.

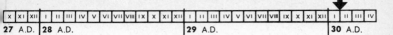

| X | XI | XII | I | II | III | IV | V | VI | VII | VIII | IX | X | XI | XII | I | II | III | IV | V | VI | VII | VIII | IX | X | XI | XII | I | II | III | IV |

27 A.D.　　**28** A.D.　　　　　　　　　　**29** A.D.　　　　　　　　　　**30** A.D.

are coming when you will desire to see one of the days of the Son of man, and you will not see it. And they will say to you, 'Lo, there!' or 'Lo, here!' Do not go, do not follow them. For as the lightning flashes and lights up the sky from one side to the other, so will the Son of man be in his day. But first he must suffer many things and be rejected by this generation. As it was in the days of Noah, so will it be in the days of the Son of man. They ate, they drank, they married, they were given in marriage, until the day when Noah entered the ark, and the flood came and destroyed them all. Likewise as it was in the days of Lot—they ate, they drank, they bought, they sold, they planted, they built, but on the day when Lot went out from Sodom fire and brimstone rained from heaven and destroyed them all — so will it be on the day when the Son of man is revealed. On that day, let him who is on the housetop, with his goods in the house, not come down to take them away; and likewise let him who is in the field not turn back. Remember Lot's wife. Whoever seeks to gain his life will lose it, but whoever loses his life will preserve it. I tell you, in that night there will be two men in one bed; one will be taken and the other left. There will be two women grinding together; one will be taken and the other left." And they said to him, "Where, Lord?" He said to them, "Where the body is, there the eagles will be gathered together."

salvation for the good and catastrophe for the wicked.

Parable of the importunate widow
Lk. 18, 1–8

And he told them a parable, to the effect that they ought always to pray and not lose

* The Apostles ask the Lord where all this will happen, and Jesus answers: 'wherever men are to be found!'

243

| X | XI | XII | I | II | III | IV | V | VI | VII | VIII | IX | X | XI | XII | I | II | III | IV | V | VI | VII | VIII | IX | X | XI | XII | I | II | III | IV |

27 A.D.　28 A.D.　29 A.D.　30 A.D.

heart. He said, "In a certain city there was a judge who neither feared God nor regarded man; and there was a widow in that city who kept coming to him and saying, 'Vindicate me against my adversary.' For a while he refused; but afterward he said to himself, 'Though I neither fear God nor regard man, yet because this widow bothers me, I will vindicate her, or she will wear me out by her continual coming.' " And the Lord said, "Hear what the unrighteous judge says. And will not God vindicate his elect, who cry to Him day and night? Will he delay long over them? I tell you, he will vindicate them speedily. Nevertheless, when the Son of man comes, will he find faith on earth?"

Parable of the Pharisee and the publican
Lk. 18, 9–14

*

He also told this parable to some who trusted in themselves that they were righteous and despised others: "Two men went up into the temple to pray, one a Pharisee and the other a tax collector. The Pharisee stood and prayed thus with himself, 'God, I thank thee that I am not like other men, extortioners, unjust, adulterers, or even like this tax collector. I fast twice a week, I give tithes of all that I get.' But the tax collector, standing far off, would not even lift up his eyes to heaven, but beat his breast, saying, 'God, be merciful to me a sinner!' I tell you, this man went down to his house justified rather than the other; for every one who exalts himself will be humbled, but he who humbles himself will be exalted."

Parable of the labourers
Mt. 20, 1–16

**

"For the kingdom of heaven is like a

* These 'some people' were probably Pharisees who were present during Jesus' discourse and whom he wished to teach that humility is an essential quality in prayer.

** The parable is based on the customs of that time: when an employer wanted labourers he called them from the market-place, where the unemployed used to pass their time, and settled their wages with them. The teaching of the parable is that the goodness and generosity of God surpass the good works that we do: they are a gift rather than a wage.

244

| X | XI | XII | I | II | III | IV | V | VI | VII | VIII | IX | X | XI | XII | I | II | III | IV | V | VI | VII | VIII | IX | X | XI | XII | I | II | III | IV |

27 A.D.   **28** A.D.   **29** A.D.   **30** A.D.

householder who went out early in the morning to hire labourers for his vineyard. After agreeing with the labourers for a denarius a day, he sent them into his vineyard. And going out about the third hour he saw others standing idle in the market place; and to them he said, 'You go into the vineyard too, and whatever is right I will give you.' So they went. Going out again about the sixth hour and the ninth hour, he did the same. And about the eleventh hour he went out and found others standing; and he said to them, 'Why do you stand here idle all day?' They said to him, 'Because no one has hired us.' He said to them, 'You go into the vineyard too.' And when evening came the owner of the vineyard said to his steward, 'Call the labourers and pay them their wages, beginning with the last, up to the first.' And when those hired about the eleventh hour came, each of them received a denarius. Now when the first came, they thought they would receive more; but each of them also received a denarius. And on receiving it they grumbled at the householder, saying, 'These last worked only one hour, and you have made them equal to us who have borne the burden of the day and the scorching heat.' But he replied to one of them, 'Friend, I am doing you no wrong; did you not agree with me for a denarius? Take what belongs to you, and go; I choose to give to this last as I give to you. Am I not allowed to do what I choose with what belongs to me? Or do you begrudge my generosity? 'So the last will be first, and the first last."

Lazarus, Jesus' friend is taken ill and dies
Jn. 11, 1−16

Now a certain man was ill, Lazarus of

Bethany. The present entrance to the tomb of Lazarus, cut out of its back wall. It was from this tomb that Jesus recalled to life the friend who had been dead four days and whose body was already decomposing.

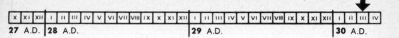

| X | XI | XII | I | II | III | IV | V | VI | VII | VIII | IX | X | XI | XII | I | II | III | IV | V | VI | VII | VIII | IX | X | XI | XII | I | II | III | IV |

27 A.D.   **28** A.D.   **29** A.D.   **30** A.D.

Bethany, the village of Mary and her sister Martha. It was Mary who anointed the Lord with ointment and wiped his feet with her hair, whose brother Lazarus was ill. So the sisters sent to him, saying, "Lord, he whom you love is ill." But when Jesus heard it he said, "This illness is not unto death; it is for the glory of God, so that the Son of God may be glorified by means of it."

Now Jesus loved Martha and her sister and Lazarus. So when he heard that he was ill, he stayed two days longer in the place where he was. Then after this he said to the disciples, "Let us go into Judea again." The disciples said to him, "Rabbi, the Jews were but now seeking to stone you, and are you going there again?" Jesus answered, "Are there not twelve hours in the day? If any one walks in the day, he does not stumble, because he sees the light of this world. But if any one walks in the night, he stumbles, because the light is not in him." Thus he spoke, and then he said to them, "Our friend Lazarus has fallen asleep, but I go to awake him out of sleep." The disciples said to him, "Lord, if he has fallen asleep, he will recover." Now Jesus had spoken of his death, but they thought that he meant taking rest in sleep. Then Jesus told them plainly, "Lazarus is dead; and for your sake I am glad that I was not there, so that you may believe. But let us go to him." Thomas, called the Twin, said to his fellow disciples, "Let us also go, that we may die with him."

Jesus goes to visit Lazarus' tomb
Jn. 11, 17–37

Now when Jesus came, he found that Lazarus had already been in the tomb four days. Bethany was near Jerusalem, about two miles off, and many of the Jews had come to

* Jesus compares his life to a day's journey ('twelve hours'). Since he must still complete what God has entrusted to him, he cannot be in any danger from his enemies. But when he has completed everything then it will be as though night were fallen with all its dangers; then his enemies will be able to do him to death.

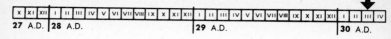

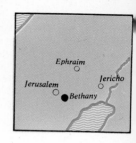

Martha and Mary to console them concerning their brother. When Martha heard that Jesus was coming, she went and met him, while Mary sat in the house. Martha said to Jesus, "Lord, if you had been here, my brother would not have died. And even now I know that whatever you ask from God, God will give you." Jesus said to her, "Your brother will rise again." Martha said to him, "I know that he will rise again in the resurrection at the last day." Jesus said to her, "I am the resurrection and the life; he who believes in me, though he die, yet shall he live, and whoever lives and believes in me shall never die. Do you believe this?" She said to him, "Yes, Lord; I believe that you are the Christ, the Son of God, he who is coming into the world."

When she had said this, she went and called her sister Mary, saying quietly, "The Teacher is here and is calling for you." And when she heard it, she rose quickly and went to him. Now Jesus had not yet come to the village, but was still in the place where Martha had met him. When the Jews who were with her in the house, consoling her, saw Mary rise quickly and go out, they followed her, supposing that she was going to the tomb to weep there. Then Mary, when she came where Jesus was and saw him, fell at his feet, saying to him "Lord, if you had been here, my brother would not have died." When Jesus saw her weeping, and the Jews who came with her also weeping, he was deeply moved in spirit and troubled; and he said, "Where have you laid him?" They said to him, "Lord, come and see." Jesus wept. So the Jews said, "See how he loved him!" But some of them said, "Could not he who opened the eyes of the blind man have kept this man from dying?"

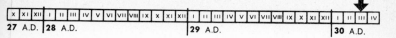

| X | XI | XII | I | II | III | IV | V | VI | VII | VIII | IX | X | XI | XII | I | II | III | IV | V | VI | VII | VIII | IX | X | XI | XII | I | II | III | IV |

27 A.D.   **28** A.D.   **29** A.D.   **30** A.D.

Jesus raises Lazarus from the dead
Jn. 11, 38–44

Then Jesus, deeply moved again, came to the tomb; it was a cave, and a stone lay upon it. Jesus said, "Take away the stone." Martha, the sister of the dead man, said to him, "Lord, by this time there will be an odour, for he has been dead four days." Jesus said to her, "Did I not tell you that if you would believe you would see the glory of God?" So they took away the stone. And Jesus lifted up his eyes and said, "Father, I thank thee that thou hast heard me. I knew that thou hearest me always, but I have said this on account of the people standing by, that they may believe that thou didst send me." When he had said this, he cried with a loud voice, "Lazarus, come out." The dead man came out, his hands and feet bound with bandages, and his face wrapped with a cloth. Jesus said to them, "Unbind him, and let him go."

The Jewish leaders decide to kill Jesus
Jn. 11, 45–53

Many of the Jews therefore, who had come with Mary and had seen what he did, believed in him; but some of them went to the Pharisees and told them what Jesus had done. So the chief priests and the Pharisees gathered the council, and said, "What are we to do? For this man performs many signs. If we let him go on thus, every one will believe in him, and the Romans will come and destroy both our holy place and our nation." But one of them, Caiaphas, who was high priest that year, said to them, "You know nothing at all; you do not understand that it is expedient for you

* The miracle worked by Jesus in order to show his divine mission became for his enemies a motive for deadly hatred. It is this kind of sin which Jesus had said so often is unpardonable; closing the eyes so as not to see.

249

Ephraim, the town north of Bethany, whither Jesus withdrew with his disciples when the Jewish leaders were looking for him.

| X | XI | XII | I | II | III | IV | V | VI | VII | VIII | IX | X | XI | XII | I | II | III | IV | V | VI | VII | VIII | IX | X | XI | XII | I | II | III | IV |

27 A.D.   28 A.D.   29 A.D.   30 A.D.

that one man should die for the people, and that the whole nation should not perish." He did not say this of his own accord, but being high priest that year he prophesied that Jesus should die for the nation, and not for the nation only, but to gather into one the children of God who are scattered abroad. So from that day on they took counsel how to put him to death.

Jesus withdraws to Ephraim
Jn. 11, 54—57

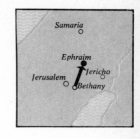

Jesus therefore no longer went about openly among the Jews, but went from there to the country near the wilderness, to a town called Ephraim; and there he stayed with the disciples.

Now the Passover of the Jews was at hand, and many went up from the country to Jerusalem before the Passover, to purify themselves. They were looking for Jesus and saying to one another as they stood in the temple, "What do you think? That he will not come to the feast?" Now the chief priests and the Pharisees had given orders that if any one knew where he was, he should let them know, so that they might arrest him.

Jesus again foretells his passion
Mt. 20, 17—19. Mk. 10, 32—34. Lk. 18, 31—34

And they were on the road, going up to Jerusalem, and Jesus was walking ahead of them; and they were amazed, and those who followed were afraid. And taking the twelve again, he began to tell them what was to happen to him, saying, "Behold, we are going up to Jerusalem; and the Son of man will be delivered to the chief priests and the scribes, and they will condemn him to death, and deliver him to the Gentiles; and they will

* St. John declares that this was a true prophecy, even though the man who uttered it did not understand its real meaning. God can in fact make use even of wicked men to accomplish his wonders.

251

The site of Herodian Jericho, the town which existed in Jesus' time.
It is not to be confused with Ancient Jericho (the town destroyed by
Joshua) nor with present-day Jericho.

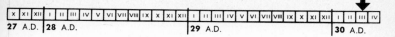

| X | XI | XII | I | II | III | IV | V | VI | VII | VIII | IX | X | XI | XII | I | II | III | IV | V | VI | VII | VIII | IX | X | XI | XII | I | II | III | IV |

27 A.D. | **28** A.D. | **29** A.D. | **30** A.D.

mock him, and spit upon him, and scourge him, and kill him; and after three days he will rise."

Claims of the sons of Zebedee
Mt. 20, 20–23. Mk. 10, 35–40

And James and John, the sons of Zebedee, came forward to him, and said to him, "Teacher, we want you to do for us whatever we ask of you." And he said to them, "What do you want me to do for you?" And they said to him, "Grant us to sit, one at your right hand and one at your left, in your glory." But Jesus said to them, "You do not know what you are asking. Are you able to drink the cup that I drink, or to be baptized with the baptism with which I am baptized?" And they said to him, "We are able." And Jesus said to them, "The cup that I drink you will drink; and with the baptism with which I am baptized, you will be baptized; but to sit at my right hand or at my left is not mine to grant, but it is for those for whom it has been prepared."

* The word 'to baptize' in the Greek language used by the Evangelists means 'to plunge into'; and it was as customary to say 'to be plunged into suffering' then as it is to-day. By this saying Jesus warns the two apostles that they too will have to suffer martyrdom.

Jesus preaches humility
Mt. 20, 24–28. Mk. 10, 41–45

And when the ten heard it, they began to be indignant at James and John. And Jesus called them to him and said to them, "You know that those who are supposed to rule over the Gentiles lord it over them, and their great men exercise authority over them. But it shall not be so among you; but whoever would be great among you must be your servant, and whoever would be first among you must be slave of all. For the Son of man also came not to be served but to serve, and to give his life as a ransom for many."

| X | XI | XII | I | II | III | IV | V | VI | VII | VIII | IX | X | XI | XII | I | II | III | IV | V | VI | VII | VIII | IX | X | XI | XII | I | II | III | IV |

27 A.D. | 28 A.D. | 29 A.D. | 30 A.D.

Jesus cures Bartimaeus, the blind man of Jericho

Mt. 20, 29−34. Mk. 10, 46−52.Lk. 18, 35−43

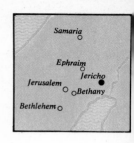

And they came to Jericho; and as he was leaving Jericho with his disciples and a great multitude, Bartimaeus, a blind beggar, the son of Timaeus, was sitting by the roadside. And when he heard that it was Jesus of Nazareth, he began to cry out and say, "Jesus, Son of David, have mercy on me!" And many rebuked him, telling him to be silent; but he cried out all the more, "Son of David, have mercy on me!" And Jesus stopped and said, "Call him." And they called the blind man, saying to him, "Take heart; rise, he is calling you." And throwing off his mantle he sprang up and came to Jesus. And Jesus said to him, "What do you want me to do for you?" And the blind man said to him, "Master, let me receive my sight." And Jesus said to him, "Go your way; your faith has made you well." And immediately he received his sight and followed him on the way.

Jesus converts Zacchaeus, the tax-gatherer

Lk. 19, 1−10

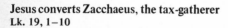

* He entered Jericho and was passing through. And there was a man named Zacchaeus; he was a chief tax collector, and rich. And he sought to see who Jesus was, but could not, on account of the crowd, because he was small of stature. So he ran on ahead and climbed up into a sycamore tree to see him, for he was to pass that way. And when Jesus came to the place, he looked up and said to him, "Zacchaeus, make haste and come down; for I must stay at your house today." So he made haste and came down, and received him joyfully. And when they saw it

* The fact that Zacchaeus was head of the tax-gatherers in a rich town like Jericho makes us understand why all the people murmured about Jesus allowing himself to be invited to his house. But Jesus himself said that he had come on purpose to convert sinners. And in fact Zacchaeus decided to give back all his improper extortions.

254

X	XI	XII	I	II	III	IV	V	VI	VII	VIII	IX	X	XI	XII	I	II	III	IV	V	VI	VII	VIII	IX	X	XI	XII	I	II	III	IV

27 A.D.   **28** A.D.   **29** A.D.   **30** A.D.

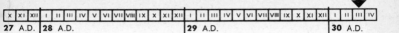

they all murmured, "He has gone in to be the guest of a man who is a sinner." And Zacchaeus stood and said to the Lord, "Behold, Lord, the half of my goods I give to the poor; and if I have defrauded any one of anything, I restore it fourfold." And Jesus said to him, "Today salvation has come to this house, since he also is a son of Abraham. For the Son of man came to seek and to save the lost."

Parable of the pounds
Lk. 19, 11–27

As they heard these things, he proceeded to tell a parable, because he was near to Jerusalem, and because they supposed that the kingdom of God was to appear immediately. He said therefore, "A nobleman went into a far country to receive kingly power and then return. Calling ten of his servants, he gave them ten pounds, and said to them, 'Trade with these till I come.' But his citizens hated him and sent an embassy after him, saying, 'We do not want this man to reign over us.' When he returned, having received the kingly power, he commanded these servants, to whom he had given the money, to be called to him, that he might know what they had gained by trading. The first came before him, saying, 'Lord, your pound has made ten pounds more.' And he said to him, 'Well done, good servant! Because you have been faithful in a very little, you shall have authority over ten cities.' And the second came, saying, 'Lord, your pound has made five pounds.' And he said to him, 'And you are to be over five cities.' Then another came, saying, 'Lord, here is your pound, which I kept laid away in a napkin; for I was afraid of you, because you are a severe man; you take up what you did

* The 'pound' was not a coin, but a certain weight of silver.

255

Phials of irridescent glass of the time of Jesus found at Bethany. Precious ointments were kept in similar phials.

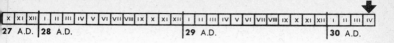

| X | XI | XII | I | II | III | IV | V | VI | VII | VIII | IX | X | XI | XII | I | II | III | IV | V | VI | VII | VIII | IX | X | XI | XII | I | II | III | IV |
27 A.D. | 28 A.D. | 29 A.D. | 30 A.D.

not lay down, and reap what you did not sow.' He said to him, 'I will condemn you out of your own mouth, you wicked servant! You knew that I was a severe man, taking up what I did not lay down and reaping what I did not sow? Why then did you not put my money into the bank, and at my coming I should have collected it with interest? And he said to those who stood by, 'Take the pound from him, and give it to him who has the ten pounds.' (And they said to him, 'Lord, he has ten pounds!') 'I tell you, that to every one who has will more be given; but from him who has not, even what he has will be taken away. But as for these enemies of mine, who did not want me to reign over them, bring them here and slay them before me.' "

Jesus goes to a banquet in the house of Simon the Leper at Bethany
Mt. 26, 6–13. Mk. 14, 3–9. Jn. 12, 1–11

Six days before the Passover, Jesus came to Bethany, where Lazarus was, whom Jesus had raised from the dead. There they made him a supper; Martha served, and Lazarus was one of those at table with him. Mary took a pound of costly ointment of pure nard and annointed the feet of Jesus and wiped his feet with her hair; and the house was filled with the fragrance of the ointment. But Judas Iscariot, one of his disciples (he who was to betray him), said, "Why was this ointment not sold for three hundred denarii and given to the poor?" This he said, not that he cared for the poor but because he was a thief, and as he had the money box he used to take what was put into it. Jesus said, "Let her alone, let her keep it for the day of my burial. The poor you

* St. Mark tells us that this incident took place in the house of a certain Simon called 'the Leper' (perhaps because he had been cured of leprosy). Nard was a perfume extracted from an aromatic plant and the best quality was imported from India. The quality and quantity of the perfume used by Mary caused Judas to set its value at 300 denarii (and the denarius was an average day's pay).

** Burial among the Jews was preceded by a kind of embalming of the body, for which many precious perfumes were used.

257

always have with you, but you do not always have me."

When the great crowd of the Jews learned that he was there, they came, not only on account of Jesus but also to see Lazarus, whom he had raised from the dead. So the chief priests planned to put Lazarus also to death, because on account of him many of the Jews were going away and believing in Jesus.

III
THE PASSION AND DEATH
OF JESUS

Bethphage, the little village between Bethany and Jerusalem, whence Jesus told the disciples to fetch the donkey and colt.

Palm Sunday

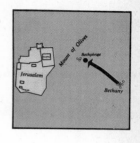

The triumph of Jesus as Messiah King
Mt. 21, 1–9. Mk. 11, 1–10. Lk. 19, (29–38)
39–40. Jn. 12, 12–19

And when they drew near to Jerusalem and came to Bethphage, to the Mount of Olives, then Jesus sent two disciples, saying to them, "Go into the village opposite you, and immediately you will find an ass tied, and a colt with her; untie them and bring them to me. If any one says anything to you, you shall say, 'The Lord has need of them,' and he will send them immediately." This took place to fulfil what was spoken by the prophet, saying,

"Tell the daughter of Zion,
Behold, your king is coming to you,
humble, and mounted on an ass,
and on a colt, the foal of an ass."

The disciples went and did as Jesus had directed them; they brought the ass and the colt, and put their garments on them, and he sat thereon. Most of the crowd spread their garments on the road, and others cut branches from the trees and spread them on the road. And the crowds that went before him and that followed him shouted, "Hosanna to the Son of David! Blessed is he who comes in the name of the Lord! Hosanna in the highest!"

➤ And some of the Pharisees in the multitude said to him, "Teacher, rebuke your disciples." He answered, "I tell you, if these were silent, the very stones would cry out."

* They are the words of the prophet Zechariah who lived about 500 years before the coming of Jesus. He was announcing to the people the Messiah as King and Liberator (see Zec. 9,9). With this action Jesus applied the prophecy to himself.

** The acclamations of the crowd show us that it had at last recognized in Jesus the Messiah: 'Son of David' was precisely one of the titles of the Messiah.

261

Jerusalem seen from inside the Church built over the place where Jesus wept, on the Mount of Olives.

Near Jerusalem, Jesus weeps
Lk. 19, 41–44

And when he drew near and saw the city he wept over it, saying, "Would that even today you knew the things that make for peace! But now they are hid from your eyes. For the days shall come upon you, when your enemies will cast up a bank about you and surround you, and hem you in on every side, and dash you to the ground, you and your children within you; and they will not leave one stone upon another in you; because you did not know the time of your visitation."

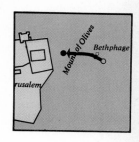

Jesus enters Jerusalem
Mt. 21, 10–12; 21, 14–16

And when he entered Jerusalem, all the city was stirred, saying, "Who is this?" And the crowds said, "This is the prophet Jesus from Nazareth of Galilee."

And the blind and the lame came to him in the temple, and he healed them. But when the chief priests and the scribes saw the wonderful things that he did, and the children crying out in the temple, "Hosanna to the Son of David!" they were indignant; and they said to him, "Do you hear what these are saying?" And Jesus said to them, "Yes; have you never read'

'Out of the mouth of babes and sucklings thou hast brought perfect praise'?"

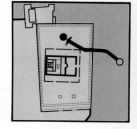

Jesus returns to Bethany
Mt. 21, 17. Mk. 11, 11

And leaving them he went out of the city to Bethany and lodged there.

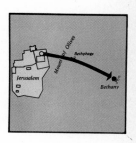

263

Monday

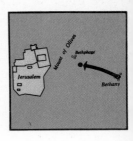

Jesus curses the fig-tree
Mt. 21, 18–19. Mk. 11, 12–14

*   On the following day, when they came from Bethany, he was hungry. And seeing in the distance a fig tree in leaf, he went to see if he could find anything on it. When he came to it, he found nothing but leaves, for it was not the season for figs. And he said to it, "May no one ever eat fruit from you again." And his disciples heard it.

The people listen to Jesus' teaching
Lk. 21, 37–38

And every day he was teaching in the temple, but at night he went out and lodged on the mount called Olivet. And early in the morning all the people came to him in the temple to hear him.

Jesus explains why he must die
Jn. 12, 20–36

Now among those who went up to worship at the feast were some Greeks. So these came to Philip, who was from Beth-saida in Galilee, and said to him, "Sir, we wish to see Jesus." Philip went and told Andrew; Andrew went with Philip and they told Jesus. And
** Jesus answered them, "The hour has come for the Son of man to be glorified. Truly, truly, I say to you, unless a grain of wheat falls into the earth and dies, it remains alone; but if it

*   The cursing of the fig-tree is a 'symbolic action', that is, a parable which is acted as well as spoken. With it Jesus wishes to show the severity with which those who do no good works will be judged.

** The 'hour of glorification' is the hour of Jesus' death. Indeed only if a grain of wheat die can bear much fruit.

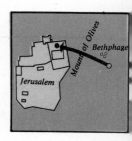

dies, it bears much fruit. He who loves his life loses it, and he who hates his life in this world will keep it for eternal life. If any one serves me, he must follow me; and where I am, there shall my servant be also; if any one serves me, the Father will honour him.

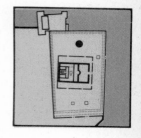

"Now is my soul troubled. And what shall I say? 'Father, save me from this hour'? No, for this purpose I have come to this hour. Father, glorify thy name." Then a voice came from heaven, "I have glorified it, and I will glorify it again." The crowd standing by heard it and said that it had thundered. Others said, "An angel has spoken to him." Jesus answered, "This voice has come for your sake, not for mine. Now is the judgment of this world, now shall the ruler of this world be cast out; and I, when I am lifted up from the earth will draw all men to myself." He said this to show by what death he was to die. The crowd answered him, "We have heard from the law that the Christ remains for ever. How can you say that the Son of man must be lifted up? Who is this Son of man?" Jesus said to them, "The light is with you for a little longer. Walk while you have the light, lest the darkness overtake you; he who walks in the darkness does not know where he goes. While you have the light believe in the light, that you may become sons of light."

When Jesus had said this, he departed and hid himself from them.

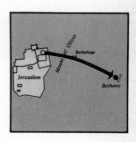

The picturesque road from Bethany to Jerusalem.

Tuesday

'Have faith in God'
Mt. 21, 20–22. Mk. 11, 20–26

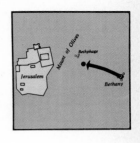

As they passed by in the morning, they saw the fig tree withered away to its roots. And Peter remembered and said to him, "Master, look! The fig tree which you cursed has withered." And Jesus answered them, "Have faith in God. Truly, I say to you, whoever says to this mountain, 'Be taken up and cast into the sea,' and does not doubt in his heart, but believes that what he says will come to pass, it will be done for him. Therefore I tell you, whatever you ask in prayer, believe that you receive it, and you will. And whenever you stand praying, forgive, if you have anything against any one; so that your Father also who is in heaven may forgive you your trespasses."

'By what authority are you doing these things?'
Mt. 21, 23–27. **Mk. 11, 27–33.** Lk. 20, 1–8

And they came again to Jerusalem. And as he was walking in the temple, the chief priests and the scribes and the elders came to him, and they said to him, "By what authority are you doing these things, or who gave you this authority to do them?" Jesus said to them, "I will ask you a question; answer me, and I will tell you by what authority I do these things. Was the baptism of John from heaven or from men? Answer me." And they argued with one another, "If we say, 'From heaven,' he will say, 'Why then did you not believe him?' But shall we say, 'From men'?"—they were afraid of the people, for all held that John was a real

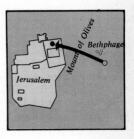

prophet. So they answered Jesus, "We do not know." And Jesus said to them, "Neither will I tell you by what authority I do these things."

Parable of the two sons sent to work
Mt. 21, 28–32

"What do you think? A man had two sons; and he went to the first and said, 'Son, go and work in the vineyard today.' And he answered, "I will not'; but afterwards he repented and went. And he went to the second and said the same; and he answered, 'I go, sir,' but did not go. Which of the two did the will of his father?" They said, "The first." Jesus said to them, "Truly, I say to you, the tax collectors and the harlots go into the kingdom of God before you. For John came to you in the way of righteousness, and you did not believe him, but the tax collectors and the harlots believed him; and even when you saw it, you did not afterward repent and believe him.

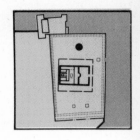

The parable of the murderous vine-dressers
Mt. 21, 33–46. Mk. 12, 1–12. Lk. 20, 9–19

* "Hear another parable. There was a householder who planted a vineyard, and set a hedge around it, and dug a wine press in it, and built a tower, and let it out to tenants, and went into another country. When the season of fruit drew near, he sent his servants to the tenants, to get his fruit; and the tenants took his servants and beat one, killed another, and stoned another. Again he sent other servants, more than the first; and they did the same to them. Afterward he sent his son to them, saying ' 'They will respect my son.' But when the tenants saw the son, they said to them-

* The same simile of the vine was used by the prophet Isaiah (5, 1–7) to illustrate, though in different circumstances, the same situation: the love of God for his people and, by contrast, the lack of response to it. In the parable Jesus, in adddition to condemning the wickedness and bad faith of the religious leaders (see v.45), explicitly declares himself to be Son of God (v.37).

Saturday 1	Sunday 2	Monday 3	Tuesday 4	Wednesday 5	Thursday 6	Friday 7	Saturday 8

April, **30** · A.D.

selves, 'This is the heir; come, let us kill him and have his inheritance.' And they took him and cast him out of the vineyard, and killed him. When therefore the owner of the vineyard comes, what will he do to those tenants?" They said to him, "He will put those wretches to a miserable death, and let out the vineyard to other tenants who will give him the fruits in their seasons."

Jesus said to them, "Have you never read in the scriptures:

'The very stone which the builders rejected has become the head of the corner;
this was the Lord's doing,
and it is marvellous in our eyes?'

Therefore I tell you, the kingdom of God will be taken away from you and given to a nation producing the fruits of it. And he who falls on this stone will be broken to pieces; but when it falls on any one, it will crush him."

When the chief priests and the Pharisees heard his parables, they perceived that he was speaking about them. But when they tried to arrest him, they feared the multitudes, because they held him to be a prophet.

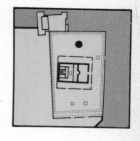

* Quotation from Ps. 117, 22-23. The keystone rejected by the Jews is Jesus himself.

Parable of the wedding feast
Mt. 22, 1—14

And again Jesus spoke to them in parables, saying, "The kingdom of heaven may be compared to a king who gave a marriage feast for his son, and sent his servants to call those who were invited to the marriage feast; but they would not come. Again he sent other servants, saying, 'Tell those who are invited, Behold I have made ready my dinner, my oxen and my fat calves are killed, and everything is ready; come to the marriage feast.'

** The meaning of this parable is similar to that of the one before it: the guests (the Jews) invited to the wedding of the king's son (the Kingdom of God) have refused to come (i.e. they have not believed in Jesus) and have also killed the king's servants (the prophets). Therefore their place will be given to others (all other peoples).

269

'Whose likeness and inscription is this?' 'Caesar's'. This is the silver 'denarius' bearing the likeness and name of Tiberius Caesar Augustus.

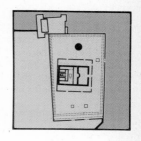

But they made light of it and went off, one to
his farm, another to his business, while the
rest seized his servants, treated them shame-
fully, and killed them. The king was angry,
and he sent his troops and destroyed those
murderers and burned their city. Then he said
to his servants, 'The wedding is ready, but
those invited were not worthy. Go therefore
to the thoroughfares, and invite to the
marriage feast as many as you find.' And those
servants went out into the streets and
gathered all whom they found, both bad and
good; so the wedding hall was filled with
guests.

"But when the king came in to look at
the guests, he saw there a man who had no
wedding garment; and he said to him, 'Friend,
how did you get in here without a wedding
garment?' And he was speechless. Then the
king said to the attendants, 'Bind him hand
and foot, and cast him into the outer darkness; there men will weep and gnash their
teeth.' For many are called, but few are
chosen."

Render to Caesar the things that are Caesar's and to God the things that are God's
Mt. 22, 15–22. Mk. 12, 13–17. Lk. 20, 20–26

Then the Pharisees went and took
counsel how to entangle him in his talk. And
they sent their disciples to him, along with the
Herodians, saying, "Teacher, we know that
you are true, and teach the way of God
truthfully, and care for no man; for you do
not regard the position of men. Tell us, then,
what you think. Is it lawful to pay taxes to
Caesar, or not?" But Jesus, aware of their
malice, said, "Why put me to the test, you
hypocrites? Show me the money for the tax."

* This second part of
the parable is meant to
teach that anyone who
wishes to enter the King-
dom of God must keep
to its rules.

271

And they brought him a coin. And Jesus said to them, "Whose likeness and inscription is this?" They said, "Caesar's." Then he said to them, "Render therefore to Caesar the things that are Caesar's, and to God the things that are God's." When they heard it, they marvelled; and they left him and went away.

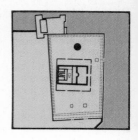

Jesus explains what we shall be like after the resurrection
Mt. 22, 23–33. Mk. 12, 18–27. Lk. 20, 27–40

* The same day Sadducees came to him, who say that there is no resurrection; and they asked him a question, saying, "Teacher, Moses said, 'If a man dies, having no children, his brother must marry the widow, and raise up children for his brother.' Now there were seven brothers among us; the first married, and died, and having no children left his wife to his brother. So too the second and third, down to the seventh. After them all, the women died. In the resurrection, therefore, to which of the seven will she be wife? For they all had her."

But Jesus answered them, "You are wrong, because you know neither the scriptures nor the power of God. For in the resurrection they neither marry nor are given ** in marriage, but are like angels in heaven. And as for the resurrection of the dead, have you not read what was said to you by God, 'I am the God of Abraham, and the God of Isaac, and the God of Jacob'? He is not God of the dead, but of the living." And when the crowd heard it, they were astonished at his teaching.

Jesus teaches the greatest commandment
Mt. 22, 34–40. Mk. 12, 28–34

And one of the scribes came up and

* Moses gave the levirate law (see Deut 38, 8) which was designed to secure the continuance of the family and the stability of family possessions. This law laid down that if a married man died without male issue, his brother must marry his widow, and any sons born of this union must bear the name and inherit the possessions of the first husband.

** See Exod.3, 6. God speaking to Moses from the Bush which burns without being burnt up says: 'I am the God of Abraham, the God of Isaac and the God of Jacob.' Therefore, Jesus concludes, he means that these men are alive and their bodies are destined for the resurrection.

272

heard them disputing with one another, and seeing that he answered them well, asked him, "Which commandment is the first of all?" Jesus answered. "The first is, 'Hear, O Israel: The Lord our God, the Lord is one; and you shall love the Lord your God with all your heart, and with all your soul, and with all your mind, and with all your strength.' The second is this, 'You shall love your neighbour as yourself.' There is no other commandment greater than these." And the scribe said to him, "Your are right, Teacher; you have truly said that he is one, and there is no other but he; and to love him with all the heart, and with all the understanding, and with all the strength, and to love one's neighbour as oneself, is much more than all whole burnt offerings and sacrifices." And when Jesus saw that he answered wisely, he said to him, "You are not far from the kingdom of God." And after that no one dared to ask him any question.

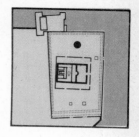

Christ is David's Lord
Mt. 22, 41–46. Mk. 12, 35–37. Lk. 20, 41–44

Now while the Pharisees were gathered together, Jesus asked them a question, saying, "What do you think of the Christ? Whose son is he?" They said to him, "The son of David." He said to them, "How is it then that David, inspired by the Spirit, calls him Lord, saying,

'The Lord said to my Lord,

Sit at my right hand,

till I put thy enemies under thy feet'?

If David thus calls him Lord, how is he his son?" And no one was able to answer him a word, nor from that day did any one dare to ask him any more questions.

* The first commandment is quoted by Jesus from Deut. 6,5. and the second from Lv.19, 18. Jesus puts them forward as the most important and declares that they are one single commandment. St John in his first epistle (4, 20) states this precisely: 'If anyone says: "I love God" and hates his brother he is a liar.'

** Jesus quotes Ps.110, 1 and argues that therefore the Messiah is superior even to David.

273

A Jewish father teaches his little son to pray. The picture is by Krestin and clearly shows the 'phylacteries' (pouches containing passages from the Law) bound to the forehead and left arm of the old man, and the 'tassels', long tufts hanging from the shawl of the child.

Jesus denounces the conduct of the scribes and Pharisees

Mt. 23, 1–12. Mk. 12, 38. Lk. 20, 45–47

Then said Jesus to the crowds and to his disciples, "The scribes and the Pharisees sit on Moses' seat; so practise and observe whatever they tell you, but not what they do; for they preach, but do not practise. They bind heavy burdens, hard to bear, and lay them on men's shoulders; but they themselves will not move them with their finger. They do all their deeds to be seen by men; for they make their phylacteries broad and their fringes long, and they love the place of honour at feasts and the best seats in the synagogues, and salutations in the market places, and being called rabbi by men. But you are not to be called rabbi, for you have one teacher, and you are all brethren. And call no man your father on earth, for you have one Father, who is in heaven. Neither be called masters, for you have one master, the Christ. He who is greatest among you shall be your servant; whoever exalts himself will be humbled, and whoever humbles himself will be exalted."

'Woe to you, hypocrites'

Mt. 23, 13–33. Mk. 12, 38–40. Lk. 20, 45–47

"But woe to you, scribes and Pharisees, hypocrites! because you shut the kingdom of heaven against men; for you neither enter yourselves, nor allow those who would enter to go in. Woe to you, scribes and Pharisees, hypocrites! for you traverse sea and land to make a single proselyte, and when he becomes a proselyte, you make him twice as much a child of hell as yourselves.

"Woe to you, blind guides, who say, 'If any one swears by the temple, it is nothing;

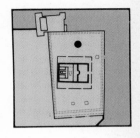

* The Mosaic Law (see Deut. 6, 8) says of its own words: 'You shall bind them as a sign on your hand and they shall be as frontlets between your eyes,' by which God meant: 'You must never forget them'. Instead, in Jesus' time the usual interpretation of these words was literal, so that the Jews, even at prayers, wore small leather pouches (the 'phylacteries') containing little rolls of parchment on which passages of the Bible were written, and which they fixed on their foreheads or bound on their left arms. Jesus reproached the Pharisees for enlarging such objects in order to attract attention. The same reproof was directed against the ostentatious length of the tassels or tufts ordered

275

'Woe to you, Pharisees, hypocrites, for you . . . adorn the monuments of the righteous . . . ' (Mt. 23,29). This is the very beautiful tomb said to be Absalom's, which was already in existence in the Vale of Kedron in Jesus' time.

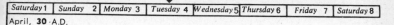
but if any one swears by the gold of the temple, he is bound by his oath.' You blind fools! For which is greater, the gold or the temple that has made the gold sacred? And you say, 'If any one swears by the altar, it is nothing; but if any one swears by the gift that is on the altar, he is bound by his oath.' You blind men! For which is greater, the gift or the altar that makes the gift sacred? So he who swears by the altar, swears by it and by everything on it; and he who swears by the temple, swears by it and by him who dwells in it; and he who swears by heaven, swears by the throne of God and by him who sits upon it.

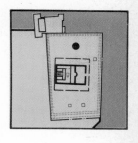

by the Law (Num.15, 37–41), to be worn at the four corners of garments.

"Woe to you, scribes and Pharisees, hypocrites! for you tithe mint and dill and cummin, and have neglected the weightier matters of the law, justice and mercy and faith; these you ought to have done, without neglecting the others. You blind guides, straining out a gnat and swallowing a camel!

"Woe to you, scribes and Pharisees, hypocrites! for you cleanse the outside of the cup and of the plate, but inside they are full of extortion and rapacity. You blind Pharisee! first cleanse the inside of the cup and of the plate, that the outside also may be clean.

"Woe to you, scribes and Pharisees, hypocrites! for you are like whitewashed tombs, which outwardly appear beautiful, but within they are full of dead men's bones and all uncleanness. So you also outwardly appear righteous to men, but within you are full of hypocrisy and iniquity.

"Woe to you, scribes and Pharisees, hypocrites! for you build the tombs of the prophets and adorn the monuments of the righteous, saying, 'If we had lived in the days of our fathers, we would not have taken part

with them in shedding the blood of the
prophets.' Thus you witness against yourselves, that you are sons of those who murdered the prophets. Fill up, then, the measure
of your fathers. You serpents, you brood of
vipers, how are you to escape being sentenced
to hell?"

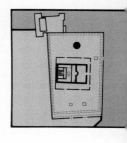

Jesus grieves at his rejection by Jerusalem
Mt. 23, 37–39. Lk. 13, 34–35

"O Jerusalem, Jerusalem, killing the
prophets and stoning those who are sent to
you? How often would I have gathered your
children together as a hen gathers her brood
under her wings, and you would not! Behold,
your house is forsaken and desolate. For I tell
you, you will not see me again, until you say,
'Blessed is he who comes in the name of the
Lord.'"

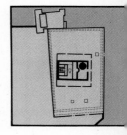

Jesus extols the widow's alms
Mk. 12, 41–44. Lk. 21, 1–4

And he sat down opposite the treasury,
and watched the multitude putting money
into the treasury. Many rich people put in
large sums. And a poor widow came, and put
in two copper coins, which make a penny.
And he called his disciples to him, and said to
them, "Truly, I say to you, this poor widow
has put in more than all those who are
contributing to the treasury. For they all
contributed out of their abundance; but she
out of her poverty has put in everything she
had, her whole living."

278

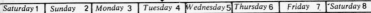
The Eschatological Discourse

Jesus foretells the ruin of the Temple
Mt. 24, 1–3. Mk. 13, 1–4. Lk. 21, 5–7

And as he came out of the temple, one of his disciples said to him, "Look, Teacher, what wonderful stones and what wonderful buildings!" And Jesus said to him, "Do you see these great buildings? There will not be left here one stone upon another, that will not be thrown down."

And as he sat on the Mount of Olives opposite the temple, Peter and James and John and Andrew asked him privately, "Tell us, when will this be, and what will be the sign when these things are all to be accomplished?"

Jesus tells of the warning signs
Mt. 24, 4–14. Mk. 13, 5–10. Lk. 21, 12–19

And Jesus began to say to them, "Take heed that no one leads you astray. Many will come in my name, saying, 'I am he!' and they will lead many astray. And when you hear of wars and rumours of wars, do not be alarmed; this must take place, but the end is not yet. For nation will rise against nation, and kingdom against kingdom; there will be earthquakes in various places, there will be famines; this is but the beginning of the sufferings.

But take heed to yourselves; for they will deliver you up to councils; and you will be beaten in synagogues; and you will stand before governors and kings for my sake, to bear testimony before them. And the gospel must first be preached to all nations.

▶ But before all this they will lay their hands on you and persecute you, delivering you up

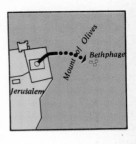

* When they had arrived on the Mount of Olives, the disciples, distrubed by the prophecy Jesus had uttered, ask him to explain it. The Mount rises to a height of about 50 metres above Jerusalem and the view of the city obtained from it is truly moving even to-day. In Jesus' time it must have been even more impressive as one looked at the Temple with its domes covered with gold plating.

** Jesus, starting from the approaching destruction of Jerusalem (which would happen 40 years later) enlarged his prophecy to include the end of the world too. But these warning signs which can be related equally to either event were not to be taken to mean that the end itself was near.

279

Jerusalem. The 'Wailing Wall', remains of the Herodian walls on the western side of the esplanade. Jesus' expression: 'Not one stone upon another' (Mk. 13,2) is evidently not to be taken literally but indicates total destruction.

to the synagogues and prisons, and you will be brought before kings and governors for my name's sake. This will be a time for you to bear testimony. Settle it therefore in your minds, not to meditate beforehand how to answer; for I will give you a mouth and wisdom, which none of your adversaries will be able to withstand or contradict. You will be delivered up even by parents and brothers and kinsmen and friends, and some of you they will put to death; you will be hated by all for my name's sake. But not a hair of your head will perish. By your endurance you will gain your lives."

The end of the Temple at Jerusalem
Mt. 24, 15−25. Mk. 13, **14−23**. Lk. 21, 20−24

"But when you see the desolating sacrilege set up where it ought not to be (let the reader understand), then let those who are in Judea flee to the mountains; let him who is on the housetop not go down, nor enter his house, to take anything away; and let him who is in the field not turn back to take his mantle. And alas for those who are with child and for those who give suck in those days! Pray that it may not happen in winter. For in those days there will be such tribulation as has not been from the beginning of the creation which God created until now, and never will be. And if the Lord had not shortened the days, no human being would be saved; but for the sake of the elect, whom he chose, he shortened the days. And then if any one says to you, 'Look, here is the Christ!' or 'Look, there he is!' do not believe it. False Christs and false prophets will arise and show signs and wonders, to lead astray, if possible, the elect. But take heed; I have told you all things beforehand."

* Jesus makes a veiled allusion to the profanation of the holy place (i.e. the Temple) to show the imminence of its destruction. In those circumstances it will still be possible to escape. It is in fact not of the end of the world that he speaks but of the destruction of Jerusalem brought about by the Roman legions in 70 A.D. after a long and terrible siege.

** He goes on to speak of the final tribulation which, like the first, will be troubled by the presence of false Messiahs.

Tiles showing the name of the Roman 10th Legion and with its symbol, the wild boar, discovered at Jerusalem. The 10th Legion was one of those under the command of Titus which destroyed Jerusalem in 70 A.D.

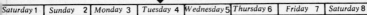
The day of the Son of Man
Mt. 24, 26–28

So, if they say to you, "Lo, he is in the wilderness,' do not go out; if they say, 'Lo, he is in the inner rooms,' do not believe it. For as the lightning comes from the east and shines as far as the west, so will be the coming of the Son of man. Wherever the body is, there the eagles will be gathered together."

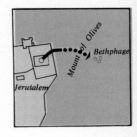

The end of the world
Mt. 24, 29–31. Mk. 13, 24–27. Lk. 21, 25–28

"Immediately after the tribulation of those days the sun will darkened, and the moon will not give its light, and the stars will fall from heaven, and the powers of the heavens will be shaken; then will appear the sign of the Son of man in heaven, and then all the tribes of the earth will mourn, and they will see the Son of man coming on the clouds of heaven with power and great glory; and he will send out his angels with a loud trumpet call, and they will gather his elect from the four winds, from one end of heaven to the other."

* The date of the return of Jesus cannot be forecast. Jesus uses the proverbial expression of that time: here it means that everyone will hasten towards the Lord when he returns as Judge at the end of the world.

The date of the end of Jerusalem
Mt. 24, 32–35. Mk. 13, 28–31. Lk. 21, 29–33

"From the fig tree learn its lesson: as soon as its branch becomes tender and puts forth its leaves, you know that summer is near. So also, when you see these things taking place, you know that he is near, at the very gates. Truly, I say to you, this generation will not pass away before all these things take place. Heaven and earth will pass away, but my words will not pass away."

** The date of the end of Jerusalem can be forecast: it will be during the course of one generation.

283

Another view showing the enormous size of Herod's Temple. Here we are at the base of the Pinnacle: the man's height is compared with the enormous cut stones of Herod's day at his left.

Saturday 1	Sunday 2	Monday 3	Tuesday 4	Wednesday 5	Thursday 6	Friday 7	Saturday 8

April, **30** ·A.D.

The coming of the end of the world
Mt. 24, 36–42. Mk. 13, 32

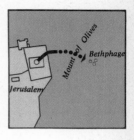

"But of that day and hour no one knows, not even the angels of heaven, nor the Son, but the Father only. As were the days of Noah, so will be the coming of the Son of man. For as in those days before the flood they were eating and drinking, marrying and giving in marriage, until the day when Noah entered the ark, and they did not know until the flood came and swept them all away, so will be the coming of the Son of man. Then two men will be in the field; one is taken and one is left. Two women will be grinding at the mill; one is taken and one is left. Watch therefore, for you do not know on what day your Lord is coming.

Jesus urges watchfulness
Lk. 21, 34–36

"But take heed to yourselves lest your hearts be weighed down with dissipation and drunkenness and cares of this life, and that day come upon you suddenly like a snare; for it will come upon all who dwell upon the face of the whole earth. But watch at all times, praying that you may have strength to escape all these things that will take place, and to stand before the Son of man."

Parable of the thief at night
Mt. 24, 43–44

"But know this, that if the householder had known in what part of the night the thief was coming, he would have watched and would not have let his house be broken into. Therefore you also must be ready; for the Son of man is coming at an hour you do not expect."

* On the other hand when the world will end has not been revealed. Jesus with his divine knowledge evidently knew when it would happen, but it was no part of his mission to reveal it to men. About the story of Noah see Gen. 6.

** In the five parables which follow the prophecy Jesus wishes to urge his faithful to watchfulness since no one can know when he will return as judge. They refer either to what Jesus has predicted or to the death of each person which is also unforseeable and represents the coming of Jesus to individuals.

285

Small jars for oil, lantern (centre) and lamps of Jesus' time. The lamps of the ten virgins were not however of this last type but real candelabra in the shape of torches, fed with oil.

Parable of the conscientious steward
Mt. 24, 45–51. Mk. 13, 33–37

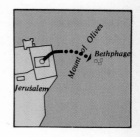

"Who then is the faithful and wise servant, whom his master has set over his household, to give them their food at the proper time? Blessed is that servant whom his master when he comes will find so doing. Truly, I say to you, he will set him over all his possessions. But if that wicked servant says to himself, 'My master is delayed,' and begins to beat his fellow servants, and eats and drinks with the drunken, the master of that servant will come on a day when he does not expect him and at an hour he does not know, and will punish him, and put him with the hypocrites; there men will weep and gnash their teeth."

Parable of the ten virgins
Mt. 25, 1–13

"Then the kingdom of heaven shall be compared to ten maidens who took their lamps and went to meet the bridegroom. Five of them were foolish, and five were wise. For when the foolish took their lamps, they took no oil with them; but the wise took flasks of oil with their lamps. As the bridegroom was delayed, they all slumbered and slept. But at midnight there was a cry, 'Behold, the bridegroom! Come out to meet him.' Then all those maidens rose and trimmed their lamps. And the foolish said to the wise, 'Give us some of your oil, for our lamps are going out.' But the wise replied, 'Perhaps there will not be enough for us and for you; go rather to the dealers and buy for yourselves. And while they went to buy, the bridegroom came, and those who were ready went in with him to the marriage

* Jesus gets his idea for the parable from contemporary Jewish customs connected with the last stage of a wedding. These included accompanying the bride to the bridegroom's house. Towards evening she, with her friends, awaited the arrival of the bridegroom's party. Then, together, they all went into the house where the bridal feast had already been prepared. The point of the parable is the alert expectation in which the faithful must always live, since the Lord (the bridegroom) will come when he is least expected.

287

feast: and the door was shut. Afterward the other maidens came also saying, 'Lord, lord, open to us.' But he replied, 'Truly, I say to you, I do not know you. Watch therefore, for you know neither the day nor the hour'.

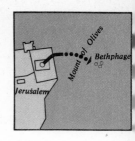

Parable of the talents
Mt. 25, 14—30

*   "For it will be as when a man going on journey called his servants and entrusted to them his property; to one he gave five talents, to another two, to another one, to each according to his ability. Then he went away. He who had received the five talents went at once and traded with them; and he made five talents more. So also, he who had the two talents made two talents more. But he who had received the one talent went and dug in the ground and hid his master's money. Now after a long time the master of those servants came and settled accounts with them. And he who had received the five talents; came toward, bringing five talents more, saying, 'Master you delivered to me five talents; here I have made five talents more.' His master said to him, 'Well done, good and faithful servant; you have been faithful over a little, I will set you over much; enter into the joy of your master.' And he also who had the two talents came forward, saying, 'Master, you delivered to me two talents; here I have made two talents more.' His master said to him, 'Well done, good and faithful servant; you have been faithful over a little, I will set you over much; enter into the joy of your master.' He also who had received the one talent came forward, saying, 'Master, I knew you to be a

*   The meaning of the parable is that we must always use and develop as much as possible the gifts that God has given us, so that we may be ready to present them to him whenever he calls us (the master returning). Failure to use God's gifts is considered a sin worthy of punishment.

288

hard man, reaping where you did not sow, and gathering where you did not winnow; so I was afraid, and I went and hid your talent in the ground. Here you have what is yours.' But his master answered him, 'You wicked and slothful servant! You knew that I reap where I have not sowed, and gather where I have not winnowed? Then you ought to have invested my money with the bankers, and at my coming I should have received what was my own with interest. So take the talent from him, and give it to him who has the ten talents. For to every one who has will more be given, and he will have abundance; but from him who has not, even what he has will be taken away. And cast the worthless servant into the outer darkness; there men will weep and gnash their teeth.'

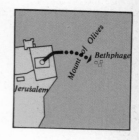

Jesus describes the Last Judgment
Mt. 25, 31–46

"When the Son of man comes in his glory, and all the angels with him, then he will sit on his glorious throne. Before him will be gathered all the nations, and he will separate them one from another as a shepherd separates the sheep from the goats, and he will place the sheep at his right hand, but the goats at the left. Then the King will say to those at his right hand, 'Come, O blessed of my Father, inherit the kingdom prepared for you from the foundation of the world; for I was hungry and you gave me food, I was thirsty and you gave me drink, I was a stranger and you welcomed me, I was naked and you clothed me, I was sick and you visited me, I was in prison and you came to me.' Then the righteous will answer him, 'Lord, when did we see thee hungry and feed thee, or thirsty and

* The Lord, after having, by means of the parables we have just read, urged vigilant expectancy of his unheralded return, ends by speaking openly about the Last Judgment which awaits every one at the end of the world. From this almost poetic description of the universal judgment which the Lord gives us we see clearly how his judgment will ultimately be based on the degree of charity with which we have loved our neighbour.

289

View of the Pinnacle of the Temple from below.

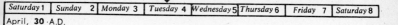

Saturday 1	Sunday 2	Monday 3	Tuesday 4	Wednesday 5	Thursday 6	Friday 7	Saturday 8

April, **30** ·A.D.

give thee drink? And when did we see thee a stranger and welcome thee, or naked and clothe thee? And when did we see thee sick or in prison and visit thee? And the King will answer them, 'Truly I say to you, as you did it to one of the least of these my brethren, you did it to me.' Then he will say to those at his left hand, 'Depart from me, you cursed, into the eternal fire prepared for the devil and his angels; for I was hungry and you gave me no food, I was thirsty and you gave me no drink, I was a stranger and you did not welcome me, naked and you did not clothe me, sick and in prison and you did not visit me.' Then they also will answer, 'Lord, when did we see thee hungry or thirsty or a stranger or naked or sick or in prison, and did not minister to thee?' Then he will answer them, 'Truly, I say to you, as you did it not to one of the least of these, you did it not to me.' And they will go away into eternal punishment, but the righteous into eternal life."

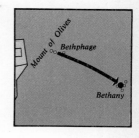

Silver half-shekel minted at Tyre. Most probably the silver coins for which Judas bargained, as St. Matthew tells us (26,15 & 17,3), were of this kind.

Wednesday

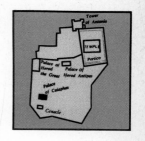

The Sanhedrim conspires against Jesus
Mt. 26, 1–5. Mk. 14, 1–2. Lk. 22, 1–2

When Jesus had finished all these sayings, he said to his disciples, "You know that after two days the Passover is coming, and the Son of man will be delivered up to be crucified."

Then the chief priests and the elders of the people gathered in the palace of the high priest, who was called Caiaphas, and took counsel together in order to arrest Jesus by stealth and kill him. But they said, "Not during the feast, lest there be a tumult among the people."

Judas betrays Jesus
Mt. 26, 14–16. Mk. 14, 10–11. Lk. 22, 3–6

Then one of the twelve, who was called Judas Iscariot, went to the chief priests and said, "What will you give me if I deliver him to you?" And they paid him thirty pieces of silver. And from that moment he sought an opportunity to betray him.

The mystery of unbelief
Jn. 12, 37–50

Though he had done so many signs before them, yet they did not believe in him; it was that the word spoken by the prophet Isaiah might be fulfilled:

"Lord, who has believed our report,
 and to whom has the arm of the Lord been revealed?"

* This sum is the equivalent of the price of a slave. Indeed the Mosaic Law (see Exod. 21, 32) sentences anyone who has accidentally killed a slave to pay such a sum.

293

Therefore they could not believe. For Isaiah again said,

"He has blinded their eyes and hardened their heart,
lest they should see with their eyes and perceive with their heart,
and turn for me to heal them."

Isaiah said this because he saw his glory and spoke of him. Nevertheless many even of the authorities believed in him, but for fear of the Pharisees they did not confess it, lest they should be put out of the synagogue: for they loved the praise of men more than the praise of God.

*   And Jesus cried out and said, "He who believes in me believes not in me, but in him who sent me. And he who sees me sees him who sent me. I have come as light into the world, that whoever believes in me may not remain in darkness. If any one hears my sayings and does not keep them, I do not judge him; for I did not come to judge the world but to save the world. He who rejects me and does not receive my sayings has a judge; the word that I have spoken will be his judge on the last day. For I have not spoken on my own authority; the Father who sent me has himself given me commandment what to say and what to speak. And I know that his commandment is eternal life. What I say, therefore, I say as the Father has bidden me."

*   As this was the last discourse which Jesus gave to the crowds, St John makes a special point of recording that he 'cried out'. Our Lord wishes for the last time to assert his divine messianic mission in the face of the unbelievers and the waverers.

Maundy Thursday

Jesus arranges the preparation of the Passover supper
Mt. 26, 17–19. Mk. 14, 12–16. **Lk. 22, 7–13.**

Then came the day of Unleavened Bread, on which the passover lamb had to be sacrificed. So Jesus sent Peter and John, saying, "Go and prepare the passover for us, that we may eat it." They said to him, "Where will you have us prepare it?" He said to them, "Behold, when you have entered the city, a man carrying a jar of water will meet you; follow him into the house, which he enters, and tell the householder, "The Teacher says to you, Where is the guest room, where I am to eat the passover with my disciples?' And he will show you a large upper room furnished; there make ready." And they went, and found it as he had told them; and they prepared the passover.

Jesus and the apostles at the Passover supper
Mt. 26, 20; 26, 29. Mk. 14, 17; 14, 25.
Lk. 22, 14–18

And when the hour came, he sat at table, and the apostles with him. And he said to them, "I have earnestly desired to eat this passover with you before I suffer; for I tell you I shall not eat it until it is fulfilled in the kingdom of God. And he took a cup, and when he had given thanks he said, "Take this, and divide it among yourselves; for I tell you that from now on I shall not drink of the fruit of the vine until the kingdom of God comes."

* The Days of Unleavened Bread so called because the Mosaic Law ordained that during those days only bread without leaven was to be used.

** These words refer to the first blessing of the Paschal meal. Jesus knows that he is spending his last hours with his Apostles. The long and moving discourse which he addresses to them has the aim of preparing them for the

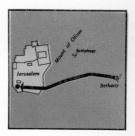

Jerusalem seen from the south with the Church of Dormition built on the site of the Assumption of our Lady. The smaller dome to the right is over the site of the Upper Room.

About	1	2	3	4	5	6	7	8	9	10	11	12	1	2	3	4	5	6	7	8	9	10	11	12	o'clock

Thursday, **6** April, **30** A.D.   a.m. | p.m.

Jesus teaches humility
Lk. 22, 24–30

A dispute also arose among them, which of them was to be regarded as the greatest. And he said to them, "The kings of the Gentiles exercise lordship over them; and those in authority over them are called benefactors. But not so with you; rather let the greatest among you become as the youngest, and the leader as one who serves. For which is the greater, one who sits at table, or one who serves? Is it not the one who sits at table? But I am among you as one who serves.

"You are those who have continued with me in my trials; as my Father appointed a kingdom for me, so do I appoint for you that you may eat and drink at my table in my kingdom, and sit on thrones judging the twelve tribes of Israel."

'scandal' of his Passion and at the same time is as it were his spiritual testament.

Jesus washes the disciples' feet
Jn. 13, 1–17

Now before the feast of the Passover, when Jesus knew that his hour had come to depart out of this world to the Father, having loved his own who were in the world, he loved them to the end. And during supper, when the devil had already put it into the heart of Judas Iscariot, Simon's son, to betray him, Jesus knowing that the Father had given all things into his hands, and that he had come from God and was going to God, rose from supper, laid aside his garments, and girded himself with a towel. Then he poured water into a basin, and began to wash the disciples' feet, and to wipe them with the towel with which he was girded. He came to Simon Peter; and Peter said to him, "Lord, do you wash my

* From the way in which St John's Gospel speaks here and elsewhere, and from other indications, it seems that Jesus may have anticipated the Paschal Supper the day before (Thursday evening instead of Friday evening), probably following the calendar of some other Jewish sect. We have historical evidence of such a difference in calendars.

297

Jerusalem. Exterior of the Upper Room.

feet?" Jesus answered him, "What I am doing you do not know now, but afterward you will understand." Peter said to him, "You shall never wash my feet." Jesus answered him, "If I do not wash you, you have no part in me." Simon Peter said to him, "Lord, not my feet only but also my hands and my head!" Jesus said to him, "He who has bathed does not need to wash, except for his feet, but he is clean all over; and you are clean, but not all of you." For he knew who was to betray him; that was why he said, "You are not all clean."

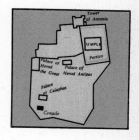

When he had washed their feet, and taken his garments, and resumed his place, he said to them, "Do you know what I have done to you? You call me Teacher and Lord; and you are right, for so I am. If I then, your Lord and Teacher have washed your feet, you also ought to wash one another's feet. For I have given you an example, that you also should do as I have done to you. Truly, truly, I say to you, a servant is not greater than his master; nor is he who is sent greater than he who sent him. If you know these things, blessed are you if you do them.

Jesus tells who will betray him
Mk. 14, 18–21. Lk. 22, 21–23. Jn. 13, 18–21
Mt. 26, 22–24. Jn. 13, 22–30

I am not speaking of you all; I know whom I have chosen; it is that the scripture may be * fulfilled, 'He who ate my bread has lifted his heel against me.' I tell you this now, before it takes place, that when it does take place you may believe that I am he. Truly, truly, I say to you, he who receives any one whom I send receives me; and he who receives me receives him who sent me."

When Jesus had thus spoken, he was

* In our Lord's day people did not 'sit' at table, but reclined on divans with their feet away from the table. It was usual then for slaves to approach and wash the feet of the guests before the meal. On this occasion Jesus, so as to teach humility, performed a function normally left to slaves; thus it is easy to understand St Peter's reaction.

** From Ps. 39, 10; it means: my most intimate friend (he who has eaten my bread) has betrayed me (has rebelled against me).

299

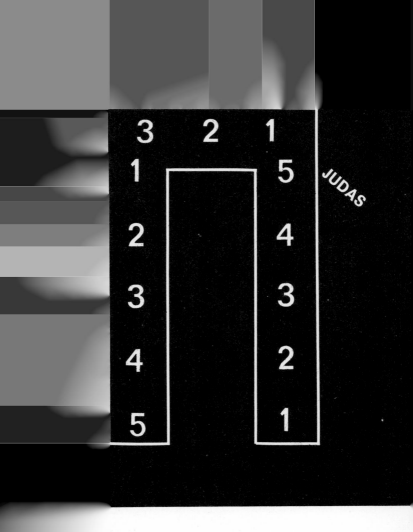

3   2   1

1   5   JUDAS

2   4

3   3

4   2

5   1

tions of those present at Jesus' Last Passover Supper. The
clining on divans with their left elbows on the table.

About	1	2	3	4	5	6	7	8	9	10	11	12	1	2	3	4	5	6	7	8	9	10	11	12	o'clock

Thursday, **6** April, **30** A.D.   a.m. | p.m.

troubled in spirit, and testified "Truly, truly, I say to you, one of you will betray me."

And they were very sorrowful, and began to say to him one after another, "Is it I, Lord?" He answered, "He who has dipped his hand in the dish with me, will betray me. The Son of man goes as it is written of him, but woe to that man by whom the Son of man is betrayed! It would have been better for that man if he had not been born."

The disciples looked at one another, uncertain of whom he spoke. One of his disciples, whom Jesus loved, was lying close to the breast of Jesus; so Simon Peter beckoned to him and said, "Tell us who it is of whom he speaks." So lying thus, close to the breast of Jesus, he said to him, "Lord, who is it?" Jesus answered, "It is he to whom I shall give this morsel when I have dipped it." So when he had dipped the morsel, he gave it to Judas, the son of Simon Iscariot. Then after the morsel, Satan entered into him. Jesus said to him, "What you are going to do, do quickly." Now no one at the table knew why he said this to him. Some thought that, because Judas had the money box, Jesus was telling him, "Buy what we need for the feast"; or, that he should give something to the poor. So, after receiving the morsel, he immediately went out; and it was night

Jesus institutes the Eucharist
Mt. 26, 26–28. Mk. 14, 22–24. Lk. 22, 19–20

Now as they were eating, Jesus took bread, and blessed, and broke it, and gave it to the disciples and said, "Take, eat; this is my body." And he took a cup, and when he had given thanks he gave it to them, saying, "Drink of it, all of you; for this is my blood of

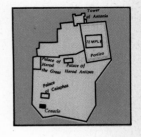

* As the guests were reclining, leaning on their left elbows, John was not at the side of but in front of Jesus with his back to him. Peter was at the corner of another divan so that he was able to catch John's eye. Judas was very close to Jesus, on his left (behind him) or on another divan, but also using the common table which was arranged between the divans.

** The act of offering a piece of bread dipped in the dish was a courteous gesture like ours of pouring wine for an honoured guest. But the courteous gesture to Judas was of no avail.

*** The breaking of bread was the gesture of almost ritual significance with which every

301

Jerusalem. Interior of the upper floor of the Holy cenacle, traditional site of the room in which Jesus instituted the Eucharist and gave his last messages to his apostles.

About																								o'clock
	1	2	3	4	5	6	7	8	9	10	11	12	1	2	3	4	5	6	7	8	9	10	11	12	

Thursday, **6** April, **30** A.D.   a.m.   p.m.

the covenant, which is poured out for many for the forgiveness of sins.

'I give you a new commandment'
Jn. 13, 31–35

When Judas had gone out, Jesus said, "Now is the Son of man glorified; and in him God is glorified; if God is glorified in him, God will also glorify him in himself, and glorify him at once. Little children, yet a little while I am with you. You will seek me; and as I said to the Jews so now I say to you, 'Where I am going you cannot come.' A new commandment I give to you, that you love one another; even as I have loved you, that you also love one another. By this all men will know that you are my disciples, if you have love for one another."

Jesus foretells Peter's denial
Mk. 14, 27–31. Jn. 13, 36–38. Mt. 26, 31–34. Lk. 22, 31–38

Simon Peter said to him, "Lord, where are you going?" Jesus answered, "Where I am going you cannot follow me now; but you shall follow afterward." Peter said to him, "Lord, why cannot I follow you now? I will lay down my life for you." Jesus answered, "Will you lay down your life for me? Truly, truly, I say to you, the cock will not crow, till you have denied me three times."

You will all fall away because of me this night; for it is written, 'I will strike the shepherd, and the sheep of the flock will be scattered." But after I am raised up, I will go before you to Galilee." Peter declared to him, "Though they all fall away because of you, I will never fall away." Jesus said to him,

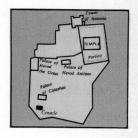

feast began. The first Christian communities used the expression 'breaking of the bread' to mean the Eucharistic meal. The cup 'after supper' was that over which the prayer of thanksgiving (blessing) was pronounced. Jesus used it for the institution of the Eucharist.

* God gave his law to the Hebrews on Mount Sinai as a treaty of alliance (a covenant) between him and his people; Jesus now means: henceforward the covenant between God and his people is based on my body and blood (that is, on his sacrificial death).

** The prophecy which Jesus makes to St Peter at this time alludes to the sort of martyrdom

303

| About | 1 | 2 | 3 | 4 | 5 | 6 | 7 | 8 | 9 | 10 | 11 | 12 | 1 | 2 | 3 | 4 | 5 | 6 | 7 | 8 | 9 | 10 | 11 | 12 | o'clock |

Thursday, **6** April, **30** A.D.   a.m. | p.m.

"Truly, I say to you, this very night, before the cock crows, you will deny me three times.

Lk "Simon, Simon, behold, Satan demanded to have you, that he might sift you like wheat,
* but I have prayed for you that your faith may not fail; and when you have turned again, strengthen your brethren." And he said to him, "Lord I am ready to go with you to prison and death." He said, "I tell you, Peter, the cock will not crow this day, until you three times deny that you know me."

And he said to them, "When I sent you out with no purse or bag or sandals, did you lack anything?" They said, "Nothing." He said to them, "But now, let him who has a
** purse take it, and likewise a bag. And let him who has no sword sell his mantle and buy one. For I tell you that this scripture must be fulfilled in me, 'And he was reckoned with transgressors'; for what is written about me has its fulfilment." And they said, "Look, Lord, here are two swords." And he said to them, "It is enough."

Jesus consoles the disciples
Jn. 14, 1–4

"Let not your hearts be troubled; believe in God, believe also in me. In my Father's house are many rooms; if it were not so, would I have told you that I go to prepare a place for you? And when I go and prepare a place for you, I will come again and will take you to myself, that where I am you may be also. And you know the way where I am going."

'I am the way and the truth and the life
Jn. 14, 5–11

Thomas said to him, "Lord, we do not

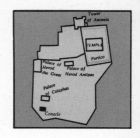

with which the Apostle would follow Jesus' example 37 years later. St Peter too died on a cross.

* See Zech. 13, 7. In all this passage Jesus is concerned to prepare the Apostles for the difficult trial to which their faith will be subjected when they see him condemned and crucified. The Lord gives St Peter the task of sustaining the faith of the others.

** The image of the sword which Jesus uses is intended to show the strength of the defences with which they must be armed against the trial to which Satan will subject them (see v.31 above). The quotation is from Isaiah the prophet who in 53, 12 speaks of the sufferings and humiliations which the Messiah will have to undergo.

| About | 1 | 2 | 3 | 4 | 5 | 6 | 7 | 8 | 9 | 10 | 11 | 12 | 1 | 2 | 3 | 4 | 5 | 6 | 7 | 8 | 9 | 10 | 11 | 12 | o'clock |

Thursday, **6** April, **30** A.D.   a.m. | p.m.

know where you are going; how can we know
* the way?" Jesus said to him, "I am the way,
and the truth, and the life; no one comes to
the Father, but by me. If you had known me,
you would have known my Father also;
henceforth you know him and have seen
him."

Philip said to him, "Lord, show us the
Father, and we shall be satisfied." Jesus said
to him, "Have I been with you so long, and yet
you do not know me, Philip? He who has seen
me has seen the Father; how can you say,
'Show us the Father'? Do you not believe
that I am in the Father and the Father in me?
The words that I say to you I do not speak on
my own authority; but the Father who dwells
in me does his works. Believe me that I am in
the Father and the Father in me; or else
believe me for the sake of the works themselves."

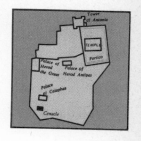

'He who believes in me. . .'
Jn. 14, 12–14

"Truly, truly, I say to you, he who
believes in me will also do the works that I do;
and greater works than these will he do,
because I go to the Father. Whatever you ask
in my name, I will do it, that the Father may
be glorified in the Son; if you ask anything in
my name, I will do it."

Jesus promises the Holy Spirit
Jn. 14, 15–17

"If you love me, you will keep my
commandments. And I will pray the Father,
and he will give you another Counsellor, to be
with you for ever, even the Spirit of truth,
whom the world cannot receive, because it
neither sees him nor knows him; you know
him, for he dwells with you, and will be in
you."

* Jesus asserts that he
himself is the only path
('way') by which it is
possible to reach God,
the personification of
'truth' and our spiritual
'life', that is the life of
grace.

** This is the promise of
the coming of the Holy
Spirit. The Greek word
'Paraclete' which we
often find in St John
means 'Comforter' and
also 'advocate', 'help',
'defender' and 'protec-
tor'.

305

Jerusalem. Present entrance (made out of an old window) of the Upper Room of the Holy Cenacle.

About	1	2	3	4	5	6	7	8	9	10	11	12	1	2	3	4	5	6	7	8	9	10	11	12	o'clock

Thursday, **6** April, **30** A.D.   a.m. | p.m.

'I will not leave you desolate'
Jn. 14, 18–24

"I will not leave you desolate; I will come to you. Yet a little while, and the world will see me no more, but you will see me; because I live, you will live also. In that day you will know that I am in my Father, and you in me, and I in you. He who has my commandments and keeps them, he it is who loves me; and he who loves me will be loved by my Father, and I will love him and manifest myself to him." Judas (not Iscariot) said to him, "Lord, how is it that you will manifest yourself to us, and not to the world?" Jesus answered him, "If a man loves me, he will keep my word, and my Father will love him, and we will come to him and make our home with him. He who does not love me does not keep my words; and the word which you hear is not mine but the Father's who sent me."

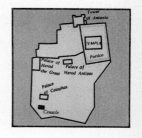

Jesus again promises the Holy Spirit
Mt. 26, 30. Mk. 14, 26. Jn. 14, 25–31

"These things I have spoken to you, while I am still with you. But the Counsellor, the Holy Spirit, whom the Father will send in my name, he will teach you all things, and bring to your remembrance all that I have said to you. Peace I leave with you; my peace I give to you; not as the world gives do I give to you. Let not your hearts be troubled, neither let them be afraid. You heard me say to you, 'I go away, and I will come to you.' If you loved me, you would have rejoiced, because I go to the Father; for the Father is greater than I. And now I have told you before it takes place, so that when it does take place, you may believe. I will no longer talk much with you, for the ruler of

* The Lord's answer means: I will show myself to you because you love me and believe in what I say and so, believing in me, believe in God.

** Jesus sometimes declares himself to be equal with the Father and at other times (as in this passage) to be inferior to him. The contradiction is however only in appearance since he was God and man; that is man like us (as in apart from sin) and therefore inferior to God, and at the same time truly God like the Father and so equal to him.

307

'I am the vine, you are the branches' (Jn. 15,5). This Jewish Christian tomb of the second century A.D., situated to the west of Nazareth, already displays the symbolism of the vine and the branches used by Jesus to teach us the mystery of our incorporation in the Godhead.

About	1	2	3	4	5	6	7	8	9	10	11	12	1	2	3	4	5	6	7	8	9	10	11	12	o'clock

Thursday, **6** April, **30** A.D.   a.m. | p.m.

this world is coming. He has no power over me; but I do as the Father has commanded me, so that the world may know that I love the Father. Rise, let us go hence."

'I am the vine, you are the branches'
Jn. 15, 1—11

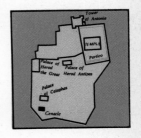

"I am the true vine, and my Father is the vinedresser. Every branch of mine that bears no fruit, he takes away, and every branch that does bear fruit he prunes that it may bear more fruit. You are already made clean by the word which I have spoken to you. Abide in me, and I in you. As the branch cannot bear fruit by itself, unless it abides in the vine, neither can you, unless you abide in me. I am the vine, you are the branches. He who abides in me, and I in him, he it is that bears much fruit, for apart from me you can do nothing. If a man does not abide in me, he is cast forth as a branch and withers; and the branches are gathered, thrown into the fire and burned. If you abide in me, and my words abide in you, ask whatever you will, and it shall be done for you. By this my Father is glorified, that you bear much fruit, and so prove to be my disciples. As the Father has loved me, so have I loved you; abide in my love. If you keep my commandments, you will abide in my love, just as I have kept my Father's commandments and abide in his love. These things I have spoken to you, that my joy may be in you, and that your joy may be full."

'This is my commandment, that you love one another. . .'
Jn. 15, 12—17

"This is my commandment, that you love one another as I have loved you. Greater

* This image of the vine is very apt as explaining the life of Grace which is the active entering into the 'mystical' (mysterious) body of Jesus, i.e. into living his own life, so that anyone who is cut off from him dies to the divine life just like branches cut off from the vine. This also explains the meaning of the sentence (see v.5) 'apart from me you can do nothing'.

309

'If they persecuted me, they will persecute you' (Jn. 15,20). The garden at the bottom of the Vale of Kedron (foreground in the photograph) is the traditional site of the martyrdom of St. Stephen, the first Christian martyr.

About	1	2	3	4	5	6	7	8	9	10	11	12	1	2	3	4	5	6	7	8	9	10	11	12	o'clock

Thursday, **6** April, **30** A.D.   a.m. | p.m.

love has no man than this, that a man lay down his life for his friends. You are my friends if you do what I command you. No longer do I call you servants, for the servant does not know what his master is doing; but I have called you friends, for all that I have heard from my Father I have made known to you. You did not choose me, but I chose you and appointed you that you should go and bear fruit and that your fruit should abide; so that whatever you ask the Father in my name, he may give it to you. This I command you, to love one another."

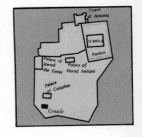

'If they persecuted me, they will persecute you'

Jn. 15, 18–27; 16, 1–4

"If the world hates you, know that it has hated me before it hated you. If you were of the world, the world would love its own; but because you are not of the world, but I chose you out of the world, therefore the world hates you. Remember the word that I said to you, 'A servant is not greater than his master.' If they persecuted me, they will persecute you; if they kept my word, they will keep yours also. But all this they will do to you on my account, because they do not know him who sent me. If I had not come and spoken to them, they would not have sin; but now they have no excuse for their sin. He who hates me hates my Father also. If I had not done among them the works which no one else did, they would not have sin; but now they have seen and hated both me and my Father. It is to fulfil the word that is written in their law, 'They hated me without a cause.' But when the Counsellor comes, whom I shall send to you from the Father, even the Spirit of truth,

* In Psalm 69 the psalmist describes figuratively the agonies of the Saviour in his passion, the outrages of 'those who hate him without cause'. (v. 4).

** These words express very clearly the doctrine of the Holy Trinity. Jesus who comes from the Father, will, when he returns to the Father, send 'from the Father' the Holy Spirit who 'issues from' the Father and also issues from the Son since he is sent by him and 'takes' from him the truth which he is to reveal.

311

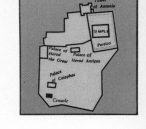

who proceeds from the Father, he will bear witness to me; and you also are witnesses, because you have been with me from the beginning. I have said all this to you to keep you from falling away. They will put you out of the synagogues; indeed, the hour is coming when whoever kills you will think he is offering service to God. And they will do this because they have not known the Father, nor me."

Jesus explains the work of the Holy Spirit
Jn. 16, 4–15

"But I have said these things to you, that when their hour comes you may remember that I told you of them. "I did not say these things to you from the beginning, because I was with you. But now I am going to him who sent me; yet none of you asks me, 'Where are you going?' But because I have said these things to you, sorrow has filled your hearts. Nevertheless I tell you the truth: it is to your advantage that I go away, for if I do not go away, the Counsellor will not come to you; but if I go, I will send him to you. And when he comes, he will convince the world of sin and of righteousness and of judgment: of sin, because they do not believe in me; of righteousness, because I go to the Father, and you will see me no more; of judgment, because the ruler of this world is judged.

"I have yet many things to say to you, but you cannot bear them now. When the Spirit of truth comes, he will guide you into all the truth; for he will not speak on his own authority, but whatever he hears he will speak, and he will declare to you the things that are to come. He will glorify me, for he will take what is mine and declare it to you.

312

| About | 1 | 2 | 3 | 4 | 5 | 6 | 7 | 8 | 9 | 10 | 11 | 12 | 1 | 2 | 3 | 4 | 5 | 6 | 7 | 8 | 9 | 10 | 11 | 12 | o'clock |

Thursday, 6 April, 30 A.D.   a.m. | p.m.

All that the Father has is mine; therefore I said that he will take what is mine and declare it to you."

'Again a little while and you will see me'
Jn. 16, 16–24

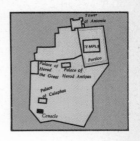

"A little while, and you will see me no more; again a little while, and you will see me." Some of his disciples said to one another, "What is this that he says to us, 'A little while, and you will not see me, and again a little while, and you will see me'; and, 'because I go to the Father'?" They said, "What does he mean by 'a little while'? We do not know what he means." Jesus knew that they wanted to ask him; so he said to them, "Is this what you are asking yourselves, what I meant by saying, 'A little while, and you will not see me, and again a little while, and you will see me'? Truly truly, I say to you, you will weep and lament, but the world will rejoice; you will be sorrowful but your sorrow will turn into joy. When a woman is in travail she has sorrow, because her hour has come; but when she is delivered of the child, she no longer remembers the anguish, for joy that a child is born into the world. So you have sorrow now, but I will see you again and your hearts will rejoice, and no one will take your joy from you. In that day you will ask nothing of me. Truly, truly, I say to you, if you ask anything of the Father, he will give it to you in my name. Hitherto you have asked nothing in my name; ask, and you will receive, that your joy may be full."

'Be brave: I have conquered the world'
Jn. 16, 25–33

"I have said this to you in figures; the

* The meaning of this and the following expressions is to be found in his approaching Passion and Death ('a little while and you will see me no more'); while the 'again a little while and you will see me' refers to his appearances after the resurrection and also to the sight of him which the Apostles will have again in the life to come.

313

| About | 1 | 2 | 3 | 4 | 5 | 6 | 7 | 8 | 9 | 10 | 11 | 12 | 1 | 2 | 3 | 4 | 5 | 6 | 7 | 8 | 9 | 10 | 11 | 12 | o'clock |

Thursday, **6** April, **30** A.D.   a.m. | p.m.

hour is coming when I shall no longer speak to you in figures but tell you plainly of the Father. In that day you will ask in my name; and I do not say to you that I shall pray the
* Father for you; for the Father himself loves you, because you have loved me and have believed that I came from the Father. I came from the Father and have come into the world; again, I am leaving the world and going to the Father."

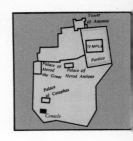

His disciples said, "Ah, now you are speaking plainly, not in any figure! Now we know that you know all things, and need none to question you; by this we believe that you came from God." Jesus answered them, "Do you now believe? The hour is coming, indeed it has come, when you will be scattered, every man to his home, and will leave me alone; yet I am not alone, for the Father is with me. I have said this to you, that in me you may have peace. In the world you have tribulation; but be of good cheer, I have overcome the world."

Jesus prays for himself
Jn. 17, 1–5

** When Jesus had spoken these words, he lifted up his eyes to heaven and said, "Father, the hour has come; glorify thy Son that the Son may glorify thee, since thou hast given him power over all flesh, to give eternal life to all whom thou hast given him. And this is eternal life, that they know thee the only true God, and Jesus Christ whom thou hast sent. I glorified thee on earth, having accomplished the work which thou gavest me to do; and now, Father, glorify thou me in thy own presence with the glory which I had with thee before the world was made.

* The meaning of this saying is not that the disciples will no longer need Jesus, but that they will be united to him in such a way that it will be unnecessary for him to intercede for them because the Father himself will love his Son in them; in other words Jesus will be the perfect Mediator between God and his Christians.

** The final prayer with which Jesus ended the Last Supper and his long discourse is called the 'high priestly prayer of Jesus', and is one of the most beautiful passages in the Gospel. It is the longest outpouring of the Son to the Father, and at the same time the loftiest revelation of himself given by Jesus.

314

About	1	2	3	4	5	6	7	8	9	10	11	12	1	2	3	4	5	6	7	8	9	10	11	12	o'clock

Thursday, 6 April, 30 A.D.   a.m. | p.m.

Jesus prays for his disciples
Jn. 17, 6—19

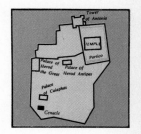

"I have manifested thy name to the men whom thou gavest me out of the world; thine they were, and thou gavest them to me, and they have kept thy word. Now they know that everything that thou hast given me is from thee; for I have given them the words which thou gavest me, and they have received them and know in truth that I came from thee; and they have believed that thou didst send me. I am praying for them; I am not praying for the world but for those whom thou hast given me, for they are thine; all mine are thine, and thine are mine, and I am glorified in them. And now I am no more in the world, but they are in the world, and I am coming to thee. Holy Father, keep them in thy name, which thou hast given me, that they may be one, even as we are one. While I was with them, I kept them in thy name, which thou hast given me; I have guarded them, and none of them is lost but the son of perdition, that the scripture might be fulfilled. But now I am coming to thee; and these things I speak in the world, that they may have my joy fulfilled in themselves. I have given them thy word; and the world has hated them because they are not of the world, even as I am not of the world. I do not pray that thou shouldst take them out of the world, but that thou shouldst keep them from the evil one. They are not of the world, even as I am not of the world. Sanctify them in the truth; thy word is truth. As thou didst send me into the world, so I have sent them into the world. And for their sake I consecrate myself, that they also may be consecrated in truth."

* This refers to Judas Iscariot who betrayed him. The phrase has not quite the sense of fatality which we associate with the word 'perdition' by which it is sometimes translated. The reference to Holy Scripture is to Psalm 41, 9.

315

Jerusalem. Ancient pathway with steps which descends from the neighbourhood of the Cenacle to the Pool of Siloam and thence to the Kedron. This was in all probability the road which Jesus followed on the night of Maundy Thursday.

Jesus prays for the Church
Jn. 17, 20—26

"I do not pray for these only, but also for those who believe in me through their word, that they may all be one; even as thou, Father, art in me, and I in thee, that they also may be in us, so that the world may believe that thou hast sent me. The glory which thou hast given me I have given to them, that they may be one even as we are one, I in them and thou in me, that they may become perfectly one, so that the world may know that thou hast sent me and hast loved them even as thou hast loved me. Father, I desire that they also, whom thou hast given me, may be with me where I am, to behold my glory which thou hast given me in thy love for me before the foundation of the world. O righteous Father, the world has not known thee, but I have known thee; and these know that thou hast sent me. I made known to them thy name, and I will make it known, that the love with which thou hast loved me may be in them, and I in them."

Jesus sets out for Gethsemane
Mt. 26, 36. Mk. 14, 32. Lk. 22, 39—40
Jn. 18, 1

* When Jesus had spoken these words, he went forth with his disciples across the Kidron valley, where there was a garden, which he and his disciples entered.

At Gethsemane Jesus prays and enters upon his agony
Mt. 26, **37—44**. Mk. 14, 33—40. Lk. 22, 43—44
Mt. 26, 45—46

And he said to his disciples, "Sit here, while I go yonder and pray." And taking with

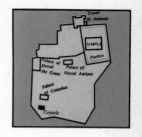

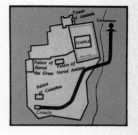

* The last petition of Jesus' prayer is that all those who believe in him (the Christians) may for ever remain deeply united in the love of God. For this reason this last section is generally called the 'prayer for unity'.

** From the account which St. Luke gives of it in his Gospel it follows that the place was familiar to them. The Hebrew name Gethsemane means 'oil-

317

Jerusalem. View of the Vale of Kedron from the Garden of Gethsemane.

| About | 1 | 2 | 3 | 4 | 5 | 6 | 7 | 8 | 9 | 10 | 11 | 12 | 1 | 2 | 3 | 4 | 5 | 6 | 7 | 8 | 9 | 10 | 11 | 12 | o'clock |

Thursday, **6** April, **30** A.D.   a.m. | p.m.

him Peter and the two sons of Zebedee, he began to be sorrowful and troubled. Then he said to them, "My soul is very sorrowful, even to death; remain here, and watch with me." And going a little farther he fell on his face and prayed, "My Father, if it be possible, let this cup pass from me; nevertheless, not as I will, but as thou wilt." And he came to the disciples and found them sleeping; and he said to Peter, "So, could you not watch with me one hour? Watch and pray that you may not enter into temptation; the spirit indeed is willing, but the flesh is weak." Again, for the second time, he went away and prayed, "My Father, if this cannot pass unless I drink it, thy will be done." And again he came and found them sleeping, for their eyes were heavy. So, leaving them again, he went away and prayed for the third time, saying the same words.

And there appeared to him an angel from heaven, strengthening him. And being in an agony he prayed more earnestly; and his sweat became like great drops of blood falling down upon the ground.

Then he came to the disciples and said to them, "Are you still sleeping and taking your rest? Behold, the hour is at hand, and the Son of man is betrayed into the hands of sinners. Rise, let us be going; see, my betrayer is at hand."

The kiss of Judas

Mt. 26, 47–50. Mk. 14, 41–45. Lk. 22, 45–48 Jn. 18, 4–9

While he was still speaking, Judas came, one of the twelve, and with him a great crowd with swords and clubs, from the chief priests and the elders of the people. Now the betrayer had given them a sign, saying, "The one I shall kiss is the man; seize him." And he came up to

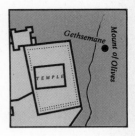

press'; it must therefore have been an olive-grove (the whole mountain was itself called Mt. of Olives) with a press for making oil on the site.

* The 'great crowd' which Judas led to arrest Jesus was made up of officers and soldiers of the Temple guard, who could be detailed for duty by the Sanhedrim to which they were attached. Among them there were Roman soldiers who reinforced the operation without having direct responsibility for it.

319

Jerusalem. Garden of Gethsemane. Basilica built on the site of the Agony.

| About | 1 | 2 | 3 | 4 | 5 | 6 | 7 | 8 | 9 | 10 | 11 | 12 | 1 | 2 | 3 | 4 | 5 | 6 | 7 | 8 | 9 | 10 | 11 | 12 | o'clock |

Thursday, **6** April, **30** A.D.   a.m. | p.m.

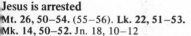

Jesus at once and said, "Hail, Master!" And he kissed him. Jesus said to him, "Friend, why are you here?"

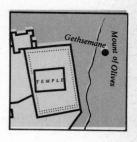

Then Jesus, knowing all that was to befall him, came forward and said to them, "Whom do you seek?" They answered him, "Jesus of Nazareth." Jesus said to them, "I am he." Judas, who betrayed him, was standing with them. When he said to them, "I am he," they drew back and fell to the ground. Again he asked them, 'Whom do you seek?" And they said, "Jesus of Nazareth." Jesus answered, "I told you that I am he; so, if you seek me, let these men go." This was to fulfil the word which he had spoken, "Of those whom thou gavest me I lost not one."

Jesus is arrested
Mt. 26, 50–54. (55–56). Lk. 22, 51–53.
Mk. 14, 50–52. Jn. 18, 10–12

Then came up and laid hands on Jesus and seized him. And behold, one of those who were with Jesus stretched out his hand and drew his sword, and struck the slave of the high priest, and cut off his ear. Then Jesus said to him, "Put your sword back into its place; for all who take the sword will perish by the sword. Do you think that I cannot appeal to my Father, and he will at once send me more than twelve legions of angels? But how then should the scriptures be fulfilled, that it must be so?"

➤ And he touched his ear and healed him. Then Jesus said to the chief priests and captains of the temple and elders, who had come out against him, "Have you come out as against a robber, with swords and clubs? When I was with you day after day in the temple, you did not lay hands on me. But

* This is a reference to a sentence in the high priestly prayer which Jesus had uttered a short while before.

321

About	1	2	3	4	5	6	7	8	9	10	11	12	1	2	3	4	5	6	7	8	9	10	11	12	o'clock

Thursday, **6** April, **30** A.D.   a.m. | p.m.

this is your hour, and the power of darkness." And they all forsook him, and fled.

Mk⟩ And a young man followed him, with nothing but a linen cloth about his body, and they seized him, but he left the linen * cloth and ran away naked.

* This incident, mentioned by St Mark alone, suggests a personal memory: the evangelist may have been this very boy.

Aerial view of Jerusalem showing the principal sites of the Passion.

322

About	1	2	3	4	5	6	7	8	9	10	11	12	1	2	3	4	5	6	7	8	9	10	11	12	o'clock

Friday, 7 April, 30 A.D.   a.m. | p.m.

Good Friday

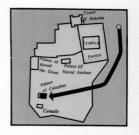

Jesus before Annas the Priest
Mt. 26, 57. Lk. 22, 54. Jn. 18, 12–24

So the band of soldiers and their captain and the officers of the Jews seized Jesus and bound him. First they led him to Annas; for he was the father-in-law of Caiaphas, who was high priest that year. It was Caiaphas who had given counsel to the Jews that it was expedient that one man should die for the people.

The high priest then questioned Jesus about his disciples and his teaching. Jesus answered him, "I have spoken openly to the world; I have always taught in synagogues and in the temple, where all Jews come together; I have said nothing secretly. Why do you ask me? Ask those who have heard me, what I said to them; they know what I said." When he had said this, one of the officers standing by struck Jesus with his hand, saying, "Is that how you answer the high priest?" Jesus answered him, "If I have spoken wrongly, bear witness to the wrong; but if I have spoken rightly why do you strike me?" Annas then sent him bound to Caiaphas the high priest.

Jesus before Caiaphas and the Sanhedrim
Mt. 26, 59–66. Mk. 14, 53–64

Now the chief priests and the whole council sought false testimony against Jesus that they might put him to death, but they found none, though many false witnesses came forward. At last two came forward and said, "This fellow said, 'I am able to destroy

* Annas (i.e. Ananias) had been high priest from A.D. 6 to 15. He was then deposed by the Roman procurator Valerius Gratus but continued to enjoy great prestige as though he were still in office as of right. In addition to his son-in-law Caiaphas five of his sons held the office in succession. He was the instigator of the struggle against Jesus, so it is understandable that the prisoner was first subjected to an interrogation by him.

** Joseph Caiaphas was High Priest from 18 to 36. It was his duty to preside over the Sanhedrim (a late Hebrew word which means Assembly), which was the Jewish High Court and was made up of 71 judges, heads of priestly families, elders of noble birth and a certain num-

323

Jerusalem. West wall of the old city. On the extreme left is the site of the Palace of the elder Herod (called the Great). Tradition is that Annas' house was situated on the bastion on the right.

About	1	2	3	4	5	6	7	8	9	10	11	12	1	2	3	4	5	6	7	8	9	10	11	12	o'clock

Friday, 7 April, 30 A.D.   a.m.   p.m.

the temple of God, and to build it in three days.' "" And the high priest stood up and said, "Have you no answer to make? What is it that these men testify against you?" But Jesus was silent. And the high priest said to him, "I adjure you by the living God, tell us if you are the Christ, the Son of God." Jesus said to him, "You have said so. But I tell you, hereafter you will see the Son of man seated at the right hand of Power, and coming on the clouds of heaven." Then the high priest tore his robes, and said, "He has uttered blasphemy. Why do we still need witnesses? You have now heard his blasphemy. What is your judgment?" They answered, "He deserves death."

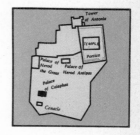

ber of expert lawyers (scribes). The Sandehrim or a deputation from it is here seen to have met in Caiaphas' house.

* To evidence which is false and prepared beforehand, Jesus makes no reply. But when Caiaphas questions him in his capacity of High Priest, Jesus does answer, and his reply is the official proclamation of his Messianic and divine status before the official representative at that time of the whole Old Testament. All the sacred history of the Jewish people begins and ends in this question. It is here that the Jewish authority officially rejects the Messiah, and so itself loses the privileges reserved for the chosen people.

Jesus is insulted and struck
Mt. 26, 67–68. Mk. 14, 66–68. Lk. 22, 55–57. Jn. 18, 15–17

Then they spat in his face, and struck him; and some slapped him, saying, "Prophesy to us, you Christ! Who is it that struck you?"

Peter denies Jesus thrice
Mt. 26, 58; 26, 69–75. Mk. 14, 66–72. **Jn. 18, 15–27.** Lk. 22, 61–62

Simon Peter followed Jesus, and so did another disciple. As this disciple was known to the high priest, he entered the court of the high priest along with Jesus, while Peter stood outside at the door. So the other disciple, who was known to the high priest, went out and spoke to the maid who kept the door and brought Peter in. The maid who kept the door said to Peter, "Are not you also one of this man's disciples?" He said, "I am not." Now the servants and officers had made a charcoal fire, because it was cold, and they were

Jerusalem. The Church of St. Peter in Gallicantu, which commemorates Peter's tears.

| About | 1 | 2 | 3 | 4 | 5 | 6 | 7 | 8 | 9 | 10 | 11 | 12 | 1 | 2 | 3 | 4 | 5 | 6 | 7 | 8 | 9 | 10 | 11 | 12 | o'clock |

Friday, 7 April, 30 A.D.   a.m. | p.m.

standing and warming themselves; Peter also was with them, standing and warming himself. They said to him, "Are not you also one of his disciples?" He denied it and said, "I am not." One of the servants of the high priest, a kinsman of the man whose ear Peter had cut off, asked, "Did I not see you in the garden with him?" Peter again denied it; and at once the cock crowed.

▷ And the Lord turned and looked at Peter. And Peter remembered the word of the Lord, how he had said to him, "Before the cock crows today, you will deny me three times." And he went out and wept bitterly.

Second meeting of the Sanhedrim
Lk. 22, 66–71. Mt. 27, 2. Mk. 15, 1

When day came, the assembly of the elders of the people gathered together, both chief priests and scribes; and they led him away to their council, and they said, "If you are the Christ, tell us." But he said to them, "If I tell you, you will not believe; and if I ask you, you will not answer. But from now on the Son of man shall be seated at the right hand of the power of God." And they all said, "Are you the Son of God, then?" And he said to them, "You say that I am." And they said, "What further testimony do we need? We have heard it ourselves from his own lips."

▷ And they bound him and led him away and delivered him to Pilate the governor.

Judas' suicide
Mt. 27, 3–10.

When Judas, his betrayer, saw that he was condemned, he repented and brought back

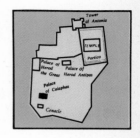

* The Lord as he leaves the hall where he has been questioned, turns his gaze on his apostle Peter as he passes him. Peter, when he meets that gaze, understands the Lord's silent reproach.

** After the first examination in the High Priest's house, the full Sanhedrim meets, to give an official character to the sentence already pronounced in Caiaphas' house. On this occasion too Jesus' affirmation of his divinity has an official character. It is uncertain whether this meeting took place in the Hall of the Sanhedrim near the western wall of the Temple area.

*** The Roman authorities had taken away from the Sanhedrim the right of inflicting capital punishment.

327

Jerusalem. The site of Aceldama or the 'Field of Blood' in the Valley of Gehenna to the southwest of the city, bought by the Priests with Judas' wage and intended for the burial of pilgrims.

| About | 1 | 2 | 3 | 4 | 5 | 6 | 7 | 8 | 9 | 10 | 11 | 12 | 1 | 2 | 3 | 4 | 5 | 6 | 7 | 8 | 9 | 10 | 11 | 12 | o'clock |

Friday, 7 April, 30 A.D.   a.m.   p.m.

the thirty pieces of silver to the chief priests and the elders, saying, "I have sinned in betraying innocent blood." They said, "What is that to us? See to it yourself." And throwing down the pieces of silver in the temple, he departed; and he went and hanged himself. But the chief priests, taking the pieces of silver, said, "It is not lawful to put them into the treasury, since they are blood money." So they took counsel, and brought with them the potter's field, to bury strangers in. Therefore that field has been called the Field of Blood to this day. Then was fulfilled what had been spoken by the prophet Jeremiah, saying, "And they took the thirty pieces of silver, the price of him on whom a price had been set by some of the sons of Israel, and they gave them for the potter's field, as the Lord directed me."

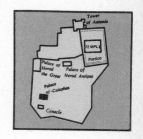

Jesus before Pilate

Mt. 27, 11. Jn. 18, 28–32. Lk. 23, 2

Then they led Jesus from the house of Caiaphas to the praetorium. It was early. They themselves did not enter the praetorium, so that they might not be defiled, but might eat the passover. So Pilate went out to them and said, "What accusation do you bring against this man?" They answered him, "If this man were not an evildoer, we would not have handed him over." Pilate said to them, "Take him yourselves and judge him by your own law." The Jews said to him, "It is not lawful for us to put any man to death." This was to fulfil the word which Jesus had spoken to show by what death he was to die.

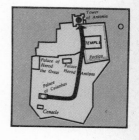

And they began to accuse him, saying, "We found this man perverting our nation, and forbidding us to give tribute to Caesar, and saying that he himself is Christ a king."

* That Friday (Parasceue) being the eve of the Passover, the Jews did not enter Pilate's house as he was not a Jew. In fact contacts with pagans were legal defilements which, among other things, prevented them from being legally clean for the celebration of the Passover.

329

Jerusalem. The citadel built on the foundations of the palace of Herod the Great, with a section of the western walls. According to some this was the site of the Praetorium in which Pilate lived when he came to Jerusalem. It is however more probable that for the Paschal festival Pilate established the Praetorium in the Tower of Antonia.

| About | 1 | 2 | 3 | 4 | 5 | 6 | 7 | 8 | 9 | 10 | 11 | 12 | 1 | 2 | 3 | 4 | 5 | 6 | 7 | 8 | 9 | 10 | 11 | 12 | o'clock |

Friday, 7 April, 30 A.D.   a.m. | p.m.

Pilate questions Jesus privately
Mt. 27, 11. Mk. 15, 2. Lk. 23, 3.
Jn. 18, 33–38

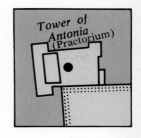

Tower of Antonia (Praetorium)

Pilate entered the praetorium again and called Jesus, and said to him, "Are you the King of the Jews?" Jesus answered, "Do you say this of your own accord, or did others say it to you about me?" Pilate answered, "Am I a Jew? Your own nation and the chief priests have handed you over to me; what have you done?" Jesus answered, "My kingship is not of this world; if my kingship were of this world, my servants would fight, that I might not be handed over to the Jews; but my kingship is not from the world." Pilate said to him, "So you are a king?" Jesus answered, "You say that I am a king. For this I was born, and for this I have come into the world, to bear witness to the truth. Every one who is of the truth hears my voice." Pilate said to him, "What is truth?"

New charges by the Sanhedrim
Mt. 27, 12–14. Mk. 15, 3–5. Lk. 23, 4–7.
Jn. 18, 38

And the chief priests accused him of many things. And Pilate again asked him, "Have you no answer to make? See how many charges they bring against you." But Jesus made no further answer, so that Pilate wondered.

And Pilate said the chief priests and the multitudes, "I find no crime in this man." But they were urgent, saying, "He stirs up the people, teaching throughout all Judaea, from Galilee even to this place."

▶ When Pilate heard this, he asked whether the man was a Galilean. And when he learned that he belonged to Herod's jurisdiction, he sent him over to Herod who was himself in Jerusalem at that time.

* Whereas the real reason for the Sanhedrim's sentence of death on Jesus was his claim to be the Son of God, before Pilate – who would not have been able to understand the gravity which such a 'blasphemy' had in their eyes – the reason was given a political slant. Pilate realized that the charge they brought was not the real one and tried to find out what that was. So, to the surprise of the priests, the charge was found difficult to press and they tried the ultimate indictment: Jesus has claimed to be king.

331

Jerusalem. Site of the Tower of Antonia where Pilate set up his Praetorium, seen from the esplanade of the Temple.

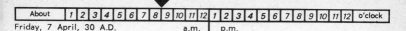

| About | 1 | 2 | 3 | 4 | 5 | 6 | 7 | 8 | 9 | 10 | 11 | 12 | 1 | 2 | 3 | 4 | 5 | 6 | 7 | 8 | 9 | 10 | 11 | 12 | o'clock |

Friday, 7 April, 30 A.D.　　　　　a.m.　│　p.m.

Jesus before Herod Antipas
Lk. 23, 8–12

When Herod saw Jesus, he was very glad, for he had long desired to see him, because he had heard about him, and he was hoping to see some sign done by him. So he questioned him at some length; but he made no answer. The chief priests and the scribes stood by, vehemently accusing him. And Herod with his soldiers treated him with contempt and mocked him; then, arraying him in gorgeous apparel, he sent him back to Pilate. And Herod and Pilate became friends with each other that very day, for before this they had been at enmity with each other.

'I will chastise him and release him'
Lk. 23, 13–16

Pilate then called together the chief priests and the rulers and the people, and said to them, "You brought me this man as one who was perverting the people; and after examining him before you, behold, I did not find this man guilty of any of your charges against him; neither did Herod, for he sent him back to us. Behold, nothing deserving death has been done by him; I will therefore chastise him and release him."

Barabbas is preferred to Jesus
Mt. 27, 15–23. Mk. 15, 6–15. Lk. 23, 17–25. Jn. 18, 39–40

Now at the feast the governor was accustomed to release for the crowd any one prisoner whom they wanted. And they had then a notorious prisoner, called Barabbas. So when they had gathered, Pilate said to them, "Whom do you want me to release for you, Barabbas or Jesus who is called Christ?" For

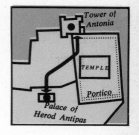

* This is the tetrarch Herod Antipas, son of Herod the Great. On the death of the father the kingdom was divided among his sons. To Herod Antipas fell the quarter which included Galilee, where Jesus had been brought up. Herod was in Jerusalem to keep the Passover as he wished to seem a practising Jew.

** From this moment of the trial Pilate, by now convinced of the innocence of Jesus, makes a series of attempts to find a way of freeing him. The aim of these is to influence the people who had been incited by the Jewish leaders. Thus he wishes to achieve justice by devious ways without meeting the difficulties and the unpopularity which justice often brings.

333

Jerusalem. Interior of the Church of the Flagellation, built by the Franciscans in the neighbourhood of the actual site.

About	1	2	3	4	5	6	7	8	9	10	11	12	1	2	3	4	5	6	7	8	9	10	11	12	o'clock

Friday, 7 April, 30 A.D.   a.m.   p.m.

he knew that it was out of envy that they had delivered him up. Besides, while he was sitting on the judgment seat, his wife sent word to him, "Have nothing to do with that righteous man, for I have suffered much over him today in a dream." Now the chief priests and the elders persuaded the people to ask for Barabbas and destroy Jesus. The governor again said to them, "Which of the two do you want me to release for you?" And they said, "Barabbas." Pilate said to them, "Then what shall I do with Jesus who is called Christ?" They all said, "Let him be crucified." And he said, "Why, what evil has he done?" But they shouted all the more, "Let him be crucified."

Jesus is scourged
Mt. 27, 26. Mk. 15, 15. **Jn. 19, 1**

Then Pilate took Jesus and scourged him.

Jesus is crowned with thorns
Mt. 27, 27–30. Mk. 15, 16–19. Jn. 19, 2–3

Then the soldiers of the governor took Jesus into the praetorium, and they gathered the whole battalion before him. And they stripped him and put a scarlet robe upon him, and plaiting a crown of thorns they put it on his head, and put a reed in his right hand. And kneeling before him they mocked him, saying, "Hail, King of the Jews!" And they spat upon him, and took the reed and struck him on the head.

'Here is the man!'
Jn. 19, 4–7

Pilate went out again, and said to them "Behold, I am bringing him out to you, that you may know that I find no crime in him." So Jesus came out, wearing the crown of

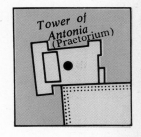

* Pilate's first attempt is to suggest to the people a choice between releasing either a 'notorious' prisoner or Jesus.

** The second attempt is the scourging and crowning with thorns. The 'scourge' was a club having attached to one end leather thongs ending in little metal chains with lead pellets or hooks. The scourging had to be inflicted in public and must therefore have taken place in the courtyard of the Praetorium. The crowning with thorns was not ordered by Pilate, but the soldiers thought of it when they heard that the victim was accused of wishing to make himself king. The thorns were taken from the faggots which the soldiers kept for lighting fires with which to keep themselves warm during the night watches.

335

Jerusalem. The so-called Arch of the 'Ecce Homo'. It is very near to the site of the Gospel incident, but the Roman arch is a century later.

thorns and the purple robe. Pilate said to them, "Here is the man!" When the chief priests and the officers saw him, they cried out, "Crucify him, crucify him!" Pilate said to them, "Take him yourselves and crucify him, for I find no crime in him." The Jews answered him, "We have a law, and by that law he ought to die, because he has made himself the Son of God."

The responsibility of Pilate and of the Jews
Jn. 19, 8–11

When Pilate heard these words, he was the more afraid; he entered the praetorium again and said to Jesus, "Where are you from?" But Jesus gave no answer. Pilate therefore said to him, "You will not speak to me? Do you not know that I have power to release you, and power to crucify you?" Jesus answered him, "You would have no power over me unless it had been given you from above; therefore he who delivered me to you has the greater sin."

Pilate's last attempts to release Jesus
Jn. 19, 12–15

Upon this Pilate sought to release him, but the Jews cried out, "If you release this man, you are not Caesar's friend; every one who makes himself a king sets himself against Caesar." When Pilate heard these words, he brought Jesus out and sat down on the judgment seat at a place called The Pavement, and in Hebrew, Gabbatha. Now it was the day of Preparation of the Passover; it was about the sixth hour. He said to the Jews, "Here is your King!" They cried out, "Away with him, away with him, crucify him!" Pilate said to them, "Shall I crucify your King?" The chief

Tower of Antonia

* Pilate, a pagan and, though superstitious, a sceptic, cannot have understood the sentence in the full meaning which we ascribe to it. But all the same these words instil in him a vague sense of fear.

** Pilate's attempts to free Jesus are now more direct, not only because of his sense of justice but also because of the fear with which this man affected him. On their side the Jews resort to another threat which faces him with a dilemma: either to betray justice or to incur the emperor's displeasure. Washing his hands publicly (see next incident) does not absolve him of his responsibility.

337

A section of the 'Pavement', the stone terrace on the west side of the Tower of Antonia. The big stone in the middle of the picture has cut into it the so-called 'King's Game', much played by Roman soldiers.

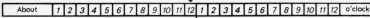

About	1	2	3	4	5	6	7	8	9	10	11	12	1	2	3	4	5	6	7	8	9	10	11	12	o'clock

Friday, 7 April, 30 A.D.   a.m. p.m.

priests answered, "We have no king but Caesar."

The death sentence
Mt. 27, 24—26. Mk. 15, 15. Lk. 23, 25. Jn. 19, 16—17

So when Pilate saw that he was gaining nothing, but rather that a riot was beginning, he took water and washed his hands before the crowd, saying, "I am innocent of this righteous man's blood; see to it yourselves." And all the people answered, "His blood be on us and on our children!" Then he released for them Barabbas, and having scourged Jesus, delivered him to be crucified.

Simon of Cyrene is forced to help Jesus
Mt. 27, 31—32. Mk. 15, 20—21. Lk. 23, 26. Jn. 19, 17

And when they had mocked him, they stripped him of the robe, and put his own clothes on him, and led him away to crucify him.

As they were marching out, they came upon a man of Cyrene, Simon by name; this man they compelled to carry his cross.

The women of Jerusalem weep for Jesus
Lk. 23, 27—32

And there followed him a great multitude of the people, and of women who bewailed and lamented him. But Jesus turning to them said, "Daughters of Jerusalem, do not weep for me, but weep for yourselves and for your children. For behold, the days are coming when they will say, 'Blessed are the barren, and the wombs that never bore, and the breasts that never gave suck!' Then they will begin to say to the mountains, 'Fall on

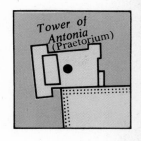

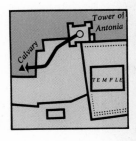

* Probably, in accordance with Roman practice, the 'cross' carried by Jesus was only the 'gallows', that is the crossbar, whereas the vertical post had been prepared beforehand at the place of execution. Simon was a repatriate from Cyrene where there was a fairly large community of Jews.

339

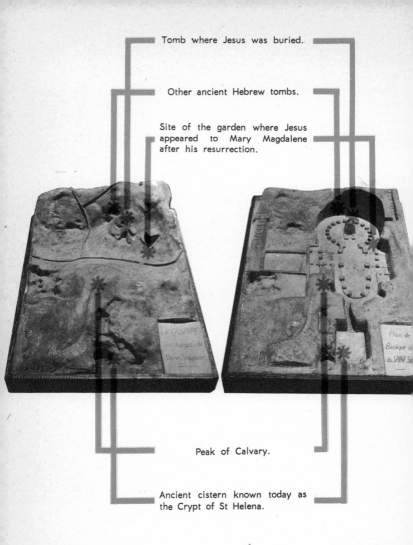

Tomb where Jesus was buried.

Other ancient Hebrew tombs.

Site of the garden where Jesus appeared to Mary Magdalene after his resurrection.

Peak of Calvary.

Ancient cistern known today as the Crypt of St Helena.

Models of the neighbourhood of Calvary in the time of Jesus and in our own day. Their juxtaposition allows us easily to pick out the whereabouts of the holy places not incorporated in the Basilica of the Holy Sepulchre.

| About | 1 | 2 | 3 | 4 | 5 | 6 | 7 | 8 | 9 | 10 | 11 | 12 | 1 | 2 | 3 | 4 | 5 | 6 | 7 | 8 | 9 | 10 | 11 | 12 | o'clock |

Friday, 7 April, 30 A.D.   a.m. | p.m.

us'; and to the hills, 'Cover us.' For if they do this when the wood is green, what will happen when it is dry?"

Two others also, who were criminals, were led away to be put to death with him.

At Golgotha: the Crucifixion
Mt. 27, 33–34; (27, 38). Mk. 15, 22–25.
Lk. 23, (33) **34. Mk. 15, 27–28.** Jn. 19, 18

And they brought him to the place called Golgotha (which means the place of a skull). And they offered him wine mingled with myrrh; but he did not take it. And they crucified him, and divided his garments among them, casting lots for them, to decide what each should take. And it was the third hour, when they crucified him.

▷ And Jesus said, "Father forgive them; for they know not what they do."

▷ And with him they crucified two robbers one on his right and one on his left. And the scripture was fulfilled which says, "He was reckoned with the transgressors."

The inscription on the Cross
Mt. 27, 37. Mk. 15, 26. Lk. 23, 38
Jn. 19, 19–22

Pilate also wrote a title and put it on the cross; it read, "Jesus of Nazareth, the King of the Jews." Many of the Jews read this title, for the place where Jesus was crucified was near the city; and it was written in Hebrew, in Latin, and in Greek. The chief priests of the Jews then said to Pilate, "Do not write, 'The King of the Jews,' but, 'This man said, I am King of the Jews,' " Pilate answered, "What I have written I have written."

* The distance from Praetorium, where Jesus was sentenced, to Golgotha, where he was to be crucified, was about 600 metres. Golgotha in Aramaic means skull; the name was certainly derived from the shape of the craggy little hill. It lay just outside the walls of the city and was reached by way of the Gate of Ephraim. The crucifixion took place at the end of the third hour, that is towards noon. The wine mixed with myrrh was given to daze the victim so that, being in a semiconscious state, he might feel less pain. The prophecy quoted in verse 28 is from Isa. 53, 12.

** It was usual at that time to put an inscription near to a condemened man (in this

341

Hebrew tombs cut out of the rock of the rotunda of the Basilica of the Holy Sepulchre, which show that there was a burial place there.

About	1	2	3	4	5	6	7	8	9	10	11	12	1	2	3	4	5	6	7	8	9	10	11	12	o'clock

Friday, 7 April, 30 A.D.   a.m. | p.m.

The soldiers cast lots for Jesus' clothes
Mt. 27, 35. Mk. 15, 24. Lk. 23, 34.
Jn. 19, 23—24

When the soldiers had crucified Jesus they took his garments and made four parts, one for each soldier; also his tunic. But the tunic was without seam, woven from top to bottom; so they said to one another, "Let us not tear it, but cast lots for it to see whose it shall be." This was to fulfil the scripture,

"They parted my garments among them, and for my clothing they cast lots."

Then they sat down and kept watch over him there.

case on the Cross) giving the reason for his sentence.

Jesus is mocked as he is dying
Mt. 27, 36; 39—44. Mk. 15, 29—32
Lk. 23, 35—37

And those who passed by derided him, wagging their heads and saying, "You who would destroy the temple and build it in three days, save yourself! If you are the Son of God, come down from the cross." So also the chief priests, with the scribes and elders, mocked him, saying, "He saved others; he cannot save himself. He is the King of Israel; let him come down now from the cross, and we will believe in him. He trusts in God; let God deliver him now, if he desires him; for he said, 'I am the Son of God.' And the robbers who were crucified with him also reviled him in the same way.

One of the two thieves puts his trust in Jesus
Lk. 23, 39—43

One of the criminals who were hanged railed at him, saying, "Are you not the Christ? Save yourself and us!" But the other rebuked him saying, "Do you not fear God, since you

* The quotation is from Ps. 22, 18.

343

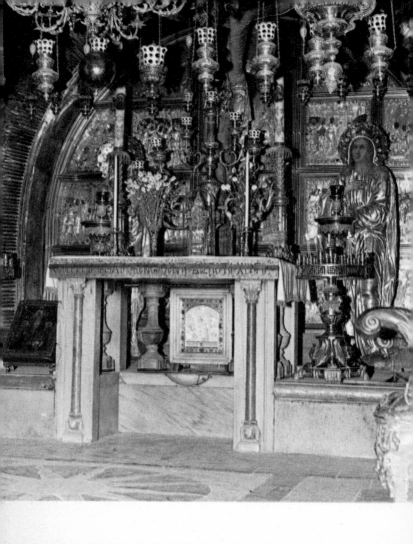

Jerusalem. Basilica of the Holy Sepulchre. Altar built on the top of Calvary. Through the hole in the paving under the altar it is possible to touch the naked rock.

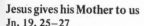

| About | 1 | 2 | 3 | 4 | 5 | 6 | 7 | 8 | 9 | 10 | 11 | 12 | 1 | 2 | 3 | 4 | 5 | 6 | 7 | 8 | 9 | 10 | 11 | 12 | o'clock |

Friday, 7 April, 30 A.D. a.m. | p.m.

are under the same sentence of condemnation? And we indeed justly; for we are receiving the due reward of our deeds; but this man has done nothing wrong." And he said, "Jesus, remember me when you come in your kingly power." And he said to him, "Truly, I say to you, today you will be with me in Paradise."

Jesus gives his Mother to us
Jn. 19, 25—27

But standing by the cross of Jesus were his mother, and his mother's sister, Mary the wife of Clopas, and Mary Magdalene. When Jesus saw his mother, and the disciple whom he loved standing near, he said to his mother, "Woman, behold, your son!" Then he said to the disciple, "Behold, your mother!" And from that hour the disciple took her to his own home.

'My God, my God'
Mt. 27, 45—47. Mk. 15, 33—35

Now from the sixth hour there was darkness over all the land until the ninth hour. And about the ninth hour Jesus cried with a loud voice, "Eli, Eli, lama sabach-thani?" that is, "My God, my God, why hast thou forsaken me?" And some of the bystanders hearing it said, "This man is calling Elijah."

Jesus dies on the Cross
Mt. 27, 48—50. Mk. 15, 36—38. Jn. 19, 28—30. Lk. 23, 46

After this Jesus, knowing that all was now finished, said (to fulfil the scripture), "I thirst." A bowl full of vinegar stood there; so they put a sponge full of the vinegar on hyssop

* The sentence which Jesus uttered at this moment (in Aramaic) is the beginning of Psalm 22 in which the Psalmist, interpreting prophetically the state of mind of the Messiah at the time of trial, expresses immense suffering under various images. Jesus quoting the first of them claims that the whole Psalm refers to himself. It is not therefore a cry of despair, but another implicit affirmation that the Prophets spoke of him.

** The mention of Holy Scripture refers to Ps.22,15 and Ps.69,21.

Jerusalem. Basilica of the Holy Sepulchre.

and held it to his mouth. When Jesus had received the vinegar, he said, "It is finished." ▶ Then Jesus, crying with a loud voice, said, "Father into thy hands I commit my spirit!" And having said this he breathed his last.

Events after Jesus' death

Mt. 27, 51—56. Mk. 15, 38—41.
Lk. 23, 45—49

* And behold, the curtain of the temple was torn in two, from top to bottom; and the earth shook, and the rocks were split; the tombs also were opened, and many bodies of the saints who had fallen asleep were raised, and coming out of the tombs after his resurection they went into the holy city and appeared to many. When the centurion and those who were with him, keeping watch over Jesus, saw the earthquake and what took place, they were filled with awe, and said, "Truly this was the Son of God!"

There were also many women there, looking on from afar, who had followed Jesus from Galilee, ministering to him; among whom were Mary Magdalene, and Mary the mother of James and Joseph, and the mother of the sons of Zebedee.

His heart is pierced

Jn. 19, 31—37

Since it was the day of Preparation, in order to prevent the bodies from remaining on the cross on the sabbath (for that sabbath was a high day), the Jews asked Pilate that their legs might be broken, and that they might be taken away. So the soldiers came and broke the legs of the first, and of the other who had been crucified with him; but when they came

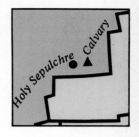

Holy Sepulchre ● Calvary ▲

* These miraculous events have a significant role which it is important to notice: Death is conquered by the death of Christ (the dead who rise again) and the ancient covenant (the Old Testament) is dissolved (the veil of the temple is torn) because the new covenant is now inaugurated.

** John emphasizes this incident because it shows that Jesus really died and shed all his blood for us. The two passages from Scripture are found in Exod.12, 46 (cf. Nu. 9, 12 and Zech. 12, 10). From the former passage it is seen that at the same time as Jesus died on the Cross the lambs to be used that evening for the Paschal supper were being killed in the Temple. John uses the

347

Jerusalem. Basilica of the Holy Sepulchre. Exterior of the shrine built over the Tomb of Jesus. The woman who can be seen inside it is kissing the stone which covers the rock on which the Body of Jesus was laid.

Saturday 1	Sunday 2	Monday 3	Tuesday 4	Wednesday 5	Thursday 6	Friday 7	Saturday 8

April, **30** ·A.D.

to Jesus and saw that he was already dead, they did not break his legs. But one of the soldiers pierced his side with a spear, and at once there came out blood and water. He who saw it has borne witness—his testimony is true, and he knows that he tells the truth—that you also may believe. For these things took place that the scripture might be fulfilled, "Not a bone of him shall be broken." And again another scripture says, "They shall look on him whom they have pierced."

Jesus is buried
Mt. 27, 57—61. Mk. 15, 42—45. Jn. 19, 39. Mk. 15, 46. Lk. 23, 55—56

And when evening had come, since it was the day of Preparation, that is, the day before the sabbath, Joseph of Arimathea, a respected member of the council, who was also himself looking for the kingdom of God, took courage and went to Pilate, and asked for the body of Jesus. And Pilate wondered if he were already dead; and summoning the centurion, he asked him whether he was already dead. And when he learned from the centurion that he was dead, he granted the body to Joseph.

Nicodemus also, who had at first come to him by night, came bringing a mixture of myrrh and aloes, about a hundred pounds' weight.

And he brought a linen shroud, and taking him down, wrapped him in the linen shroud, and laid him in a tomb which had been hewn out of the rock; and he rolled a stone against the door of the tomb.

The women who had come with him from Galilee followed, and saw the tomb, and

Paschal Lamb as a symbol of Jesus crucified and notes that, as it was laid down that the bones of the Paschal Lamb should not be broken, so it was with Jesus.

* The preoccupation of the Priests, that the bodies of the crucified should not remain hanging on the crosses was shared by his disciples though for different reasons. The 'Preparation' was the vigil of the sabbath, and that particular

349

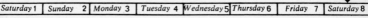
how his body was laid; and then they returned, and prepared spices and ointments.

On the sabbath they rested according to the commandment.

The chief priests put a guard on the tomb
Mt. 27, 62–66

Next day, that is, after the day of Preparation, the chief priests and the Pharisees gathered before Pilate and said, "Sir, we remember how that impostor said, while he was still alive, 'After three days I will rise again.' Therefore order the sepulchre to be made secure until the third day, lest his disciples go and steal him away, and tell the people, 'He has risen from the dead,' and the last fraud will be worse than the first." Pilate said to them, "You have a guard of soldiers; go, make it as secure as you can." So they went and made the sepulchre secure by sealing the stone and setting a guard.

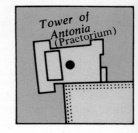

sabbath was specially festive because it coincided with the Passover. The obligation to rest was one of the most binding and began with the appearance of the first stars of the vigil (see verse 56).

350

IV

THE RESURRECTION
AND APPEARANCES
OF JESUS

Entrance of Herod's tomb which is of the time of Jesus and has, in the manner of that time, the great stone which, by rolling into slots conveniently cut into the rock, closed its entrance.

The stone is rolled away!

Mt. 28, 1–4. Mk. 16, 1–4. Lk. 24, 1–2. Jn. 20, 2

Now after the sabbath, toward the dawn of the first day of the week, Mary Magdalene and the other Mary went to see the sepulchre. And behold, there was a great earthquake; for an angel of the Lord descended from heaven and came rolled back the stone, and sat upon it. His appearance was like lightning, and his raiment white as snow. And for fear of him the guards trembled and became like dead men.

And Mary Magdalene, and Mary the mother of James, and Salome, bought spices so that they might go and anoint him. And very early on the first day of the week they went to the tomb when the sun had risen. And they were saying to one another, "Who will roll away the stone for us from the door of the tomb?" And looking up they saw the stone was rolled back; for it was very large.

So Mary Magdalene went to Simon Peter and the other disciple, the one whom Jesus loved, and said to them, "They have taken the Lord out of the tomb, and we do not know where they have laid him."

'He has risen!'

Mt. 28, 5–7. Mk. 16, 5–8. Lk. 24, 3–8

And entering the tomb, they saw a young man sitting on the right side, dressed in a white robe; and they were amazed. And he said to them, "Do not be amazed; you seek Jesus of Nazareth, who was crucified. He has risen, he is not here; see the place where they laid him. But go, tell his disciples and Peter that he is going before you to Galilee; there you will see him, as he told you." And they went out and fled from the tomb; for tremb-

* The first day of the week, in memory of Jesus' resurrection, was named by Christians 'the Lord's Day', and the obligation of keeping it as a holy day was transferred to it from the sabbath. The women intended to complete the hurried embalming of Friday evening.

353

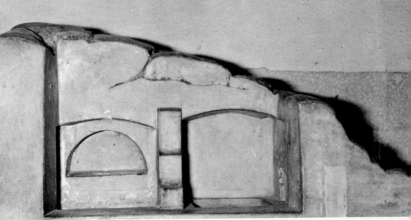

Model of a Jewish tomb seen from the front and, in section, from the side.

ling and astonishment had come upon them; and they said nothing to any one, for they were afraid.

Peter and John run to the tomb
Jn. 20, 3–10

Peter then came out with the other disciple, and they went toward the tomb. They both ran, but the other disciple outran Peter and reached the tomb first; and stooping to look in, he saw the linen cloths lying there, but he did not go in. Then Simon Peter came, following him, and went into the tomb; he saw the linen cloths lying, and the napkin, which had been on his head, not lying with the linen cloths but rolled up in a place by itself. Then the other disciple, who reached the tomb first, also went in, and he saw and believed; for as yet they did not know the scripture, that he must rise from the dead. Then the disciples went back to their homes.

Jesus appears to Mary Magdalene
Mk. 16, 9–11. Jn. 20, 11–18

But Mary stood weeping outside the tomb, and as she wept she stooped to look into the tomb; and she saw two angels in white, sitting where the body of Jesus had lain, one at the head and one at the feet. They said to her, "Woman, why are you weeping?" She said to them, "Because they have taken away my Lord, and I do not know where they have laid him." Saying this, she turned round and saw Jesus standing, but she did not know that it was Jesus. Jesus said to her, "Woman, why are you weeping? Whom do you seek?" Supposing him to be the gardener, she said to him, "Sir, if you have carried him away, tell me where you have laid him,

* The other disciple is St. John the Evangelist who never refers to himself by name in his Gospel but makes use of some turn of phrase like this. From this incident it is also clear that John was much younger than Peter.

** The words 'linen cloths' mean the winding sheets and other pieces of linen which were generally used for the burial of dead persons of a certain standing (the shroud was a large kerchief). The covering of cloths remained in its place but the dead body was no longer inside it: from this St. John draws the conclusion that the body could not have been taken away.

355

The hills of Emmaus at dusk.

and I will take him away." Jesus said to her, "Mary." She turned and said to him in Hebrew, "Rab-Boni!" Jesus said to her, "Do not hold me, for I have not yet ascended to the Father; but go to my brethren and say to them, I am ascending to my Father and your Father, to my God and your God." Mary Magdalene went and said to the disciples, "I have seen the Lord"; and she told them that he had said these things to her.

* Possibly Matthew writes 'women' in a general way, but is alluding to the Magdalene. In that case this is the story of the same appearance as that which St. John describes more precisely.

Jesus appears to the women
Mt. 28, 9–10

And behold, Jesus met the women and said, "Hail!" And they came up and took hold of his feet and worshipped him. Then Jesus said to them, "Do not be afraid; go and tell my brethren to go to Galilee, and there they will see me."

** A propos these false rumours the comment that St. Augustine made about them remains valid: if they were asleep how did they see his disciples take away the Lord's body.

False rumours
Mt. 28, 11–15

While they were going, behold, some of the guard went into the city and told the chief priests all that had taken place. And when they had assembled with the elders and taken counsel, they gave a sum of money to the soldiers and said, "Tell people, "His disciples came by night and stole him away while we were asleep." And if this comes to the governor's ears, we will satisfy him and keep you out of trouble." So they took the money and did as they were directed; and this story has been spread among the Jews to this day.

Jesus appears to two disciples on the road to Emmaus
Lk. 24, 13–35

* That very day two of them were going to a village named Emmaus, about seven miles from Jerusalem, and talking with each other about all these things that had happened. While they were talking and discussing together, Jesus himself drew near and went with them. But their eyes were kept from recognizing him. And he said to them, "What is this conversation which you are holding with each other as you walk?" And they stood still, looking sad. Then one of them, named Cleopas, answered him, "Are you the only visitor to Jerusalem who does not know the things that have happened there in these days?" And he said to them, "What things?" And they said to him, "Concerning Jesus of Nazareth, who was a prophet mighty in deed and word before God and all the people, and how our chief priests and rulers delivered him up to be condemned to death, and crucified him. But we had hoped that he was the one to redeem Israel. Yes, and besides all this, it is now the third day since this happened. Moreover, some women of our company amazed us. They were at the tomb early in the morning and did not find his body; and they came back saying that they had even seen a vision of angels, who said that he was alive. Some of those who were with us went to the tomb, and found it just as the women had said; but him they did not see." And he said to them, "O foolish men, and slow of heart to believe all that the prophets have spoken! Was it not necessary that the Christ should suffer these things and enter into his glory?" And beginning with Moses and all the prophets, he

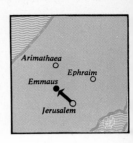

* The Greek text has 'sixty stadia'. The Roman stadium, also used by the Jews in the time of our Lord as a unit of distance, was the equivalent of about 185 metres, so 60 stadia were about 11 km.

358

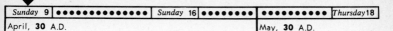
interpreted to them in all the scriptures the things concerning himself.

So they drew near to the village to which they were going. He appeared to be going further, but they constrained him, saying, "Stay with us, for it is toward evening and the day is now far spent." So he went in to stay with them. When he was at table with them, he took the bread and blessed, and broke it, and gave it to them. And their eyes were opened and they recognized him; and he vanished out of their sight. They said to each other, "Did not our hearts burn within us while he talked to us on the road while he opened to us the scriptures?" And they rose that same hour and returned to Jerusalem; and they found the eleven gathered together and those who were with them, who said, "The Lord has risen indeed, and has appeared to Simon!" Then they told what had happened on the road, and how he was known to them in the breaking of the bread.

Jesus appears to the Apostles in the Upper Room. . .
Lk. 24, 36–43. Jn. 20, 19–20

As they were saying this, Jesus himself stood among them, and said to them "Peace to you!" But they were startled and frightened, and supposed that they saw a spirit. And he said to them, "Why are you troubled, and why do questionings rise in your hearts? See my hands and my feet, that it is I myself; handle me, and see; for a spirit has not flesh and bones as you see that I have." And when he had said this, he showed them his hands and his feet. And while they still disbelieved for joy, and wondered, he said to them, "Have you anything here to eat?" They gave him a

* The appearances of the Lord were intended to show the Apostles the truth of his resurrection. In fact they were to provide authentic testimonies of this fact to all men. On the occasion of this appearance he confers on them the power to remit sins in his name and so institutes the sacrament of Penance.

359

A poetic view of the Lake of Gennesaret or Sea of Tiberias (Jn. 21, 1) where the risen Jesus appeared to the apostles.

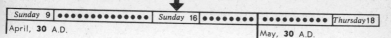
piece of broiled fish, and he took it and ate before them.

...and gives them the power to remit sins
Jn. 20, 21–23

Jesus said to them again, "Peace be with you. As the Father has sent me, even so I send you." And when he had said this, he breathed on them, and said to them, "Receive the Holy Spirit. If you forgive the sins of any, they are forgiven; if you retain the sins of any, they are retained."

Jesus appears again to the Apostles in the Upper Room
Jn. 20, 24–29

Now Thomas, one of the twelve, called the Twin, was not with them when Jesus came. So the other disciples told him, "We have seen the Lord." But he said to them, "Unless I see in his hands the print of the nails, and place my finger in the mark of the nails, and place my hand in his side, I will not believe."

Eight days later, his disciples were again in the house, and Thomas was with them. The doors were shut, but Jesus came and stood among them, and said, "Peace be with you." Then he said to Thomas, "Put your finger here, and see my hands; and put out your hand, and place it in my side; do not be faithless, but believing." Thomas answered him, "My Lord and my God!" Jesus said to him, "Have you believed because you have seen me? Blessed are those who have not seen and yet believe."

* This appearance of Jesus to his people, with which St. John ends his Gospel, makes one of the liveliest and most beautiful pages in the Gospel.

Jesus appears to the disciples near the lake of Galilee
Jn. 21, 1–14

After this Jesus revealed himself again to

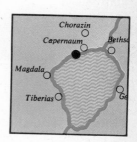

Lake of Gennesaret. The place where Jesus conferred on St. Peter the primacy over the other apostles. The Chapel partially seen on the left is built on the foundations of very old churches which guarantee the authenticity of the site.

the disciples by the Sea of Tiberias; and he revealed himself in this way. Simon Peter, Thomas called the Twin, Nathanael of Cana in Galilee, the sons of Zebedee, and two others of his disciples were together. Simon Peter said to them, "I am going fishing." They said to him, "We will go with you." They went out and got into the boat; but that night they caught nothing.

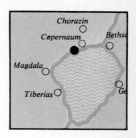

Just as day was breaking, Jesus stood on the beach; yet the disciples did not know that it was Jesus. Jesus said to them, "Children, have you any fish?" They answered him, "No." He said to them, "Cast the net on the right side of the boat, and you will find some." So they cast it, and now they were not able to haul it in, for the quantity of fish. That disciple whom Jesus loved said to Peter, "It is the Lord!" When Simon Peter heard that it was the Lord, he put on his clothes, for he was stripped for work, and sprang into the sea. But the other disciples came in the boat, dragging the net full of fish, for they were not far from the land, but about a hundred yards off.

When they got out on land, they saw a charcoal fire there, with fish lying on it, and bread. Jesus said to them, "Bring some of the fish that you have just caught." So Simon Peter went aboard and hauled the net ashore, full of large fish, a hundred and fifty-three of them; and although there were so many, the net was not torn. Jesus said to them, "Come and have breakfast." Now none of the disciples dared ask him, "Who are you?" They knew it was the Lord. Jesus came and took the bread and gave it to them, and so with the fish. This was now the third time that Jesus was revealed to the disciples after he was raised from the dead.

*   St. John says 200 cubits, and as a cubit is the equivalent of about 46 cm, the boat was about 100 metres from the shore.

. . . and confers the primacy on Peter
Jn. 21, 15–23

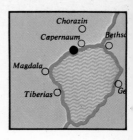

When they had finished breakfast, Jesus said to Simon Peter, "Simon, son of John, do you love me more than these?" He said to him, "Yes, Lord; you know that I love you." He said to him, "Feed my lambs." A second time he said to him, "Simon, son of John, do you love me?'' He said to him, "Yes, Lord; you know that I love you." He said to him, "Tend my sheep." He said to him the third time, "Simon, son of
* John, do you love me?" Peter was grieved because he said to him the third time, "Do you love me?" And he said to him, "Lord, you know everything; you know that I love you." Jesus said to him, "Feed my sheep. Truly, truly, I say to you, when you were young, you girded yourself and walked where you would;
** but when you are old, you will stretch out your hands, and another will gird you and carry you where you do not wish to go." (This he said to show by what death he was to glorify God.) And after this he said to him, "Follow me."

Peter turned and saw following them the disciple whom Jesus loved, who had lain close to his breast at the supper and had said, "Lord, who is it that is going to betray you?" When Peter saw him, he said to Jesus, "Lord, what about this man?" Jesus said to him, "If it is my will that he remain until I come, what is that to you? Follow me!" The saying spread abroad among the brethren that this disciple was not to die; yet Jesus did not say to him that he was not to die, but, "If it is my will that he remain until I come, what is that to you?"

* This question which Jesus put three times to Peter about his love for him forcibly recalls to our minds St Peter's three-fold denial during the Passion. At the same time, when St. Peter makes his three-fold protestation of love, Jesus confers on him the primacy over the whole Church. That is to say, he makes him the first Pope.

** In fact St. Peter suffered martyrdom in Rome during the persecution of the emperor Nero in 67 A.D. In consequence of this incident the rumour spread that St. John (the disciple 'whom Jesus loved') would not die but would survive.

364

Jesus appears to the disciples on a hill in Galilee . . .

Mt. 28, 16–17

Now the eleven disciples went to Galilee, to the mountain to which Jesus had directed them. And when they saw him they worshipped him; but some doubted.

. . . and gives them their apostolic commission

Mt. 28, 18–20. Mk. 16, 15–18

And Jesus came and said to them, "All authority in heaven and on earth has been given to me. Go therefore and make disciples of all nations, baptizing them in the name of the Father and of the Son and of the Holy Spirit, teaching them to observe all that I have commanded you; and lo, I am with you always, to the close of the age."

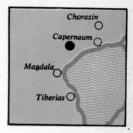

* Jesus institutes the sacrament of baptism and affirms it to be indispensable for reaching eternal salvation.

** In the Old Testament there are several passages which speak of the suffering and Passion of the Messiah, but in Jesus' time the Jews preferred to read the pages concerned with his glory. This helps us to understand the insistence with which our Lord taught his Apostles about so fundamental an element in his revelation.

The Ascension

At Jerusalem, Jesus gives his last messages

Lk. 24, 44–49

Then he said to them, "These are my words which I spoke to you, while I was still with you, that everything written about me in the law of Moses and the prophets and the psalms must be fulfilled." Then he opened their minds to understand the scriptures, and said to them, "Thus it is written, that the
* Christ should suffer and on the third day rise from the dead, and that repentance and for-

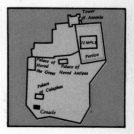

Jerusalem. Mount of Olives. Place of the Ascension.

giveness of sins should be preached in his name to all nations, beginning from Jerusalem. You are witnesses of these things. And behold, I send the promise of my Father upon you; but stay in the city, until you are clothed with power from on high."

On the Mount of Olives, Jesus ascends to heaven
Mk. 16, 19–20. Lk. 24, 50–53

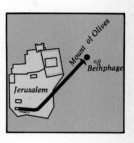

Then he led them out as far as Bethany, and lifting up his hands he blessed them. While he blessed them, he parted from them, and was carried up into heaven. And they worshipped him, and returned to Jerusalem with great joy, and were continually in the temple blessing God.

Epilogue by St. John the Evangelist
Jn. 20, 30–31

Now Jesus did many other signs in the presence of the disciples, which are not written in this book; but these are written that you may believe that Jesus is the Christ, the Son of God, and that believing you may have life in his name.

Epilogue by the disciples of John the Evangelist
Jn. 21, 24–25

This is the disciple who is bearing witness to these things, and who has written these things; and we know that his testimony is true.

But there are also many other things which Jesus did; were every one of them to be written, I suppose that the world itself could not contain the books that would be written.

INDEX

1. THE INFANCY AND THE HIDDEN LIFE OF JESUS

2. THE PUBLIC MINISTRY OF JESUS

BEGINNING OF THE MINISTRY IN GALILEE

FIVE ENCOUNTERS WITH THE PHARISEES

THE SERMON ON THE MOUNT

CONTINUATION OF THE MINISTRY IN GALILEE

THE PARABLES OF THE KINGDOM OF GOD

MIRACLES IN GALILEE AND FAILURE AT NAZARETH

THE JOURNEY TO JERUSALEM

AT JERUSALEM FOR THE FEAST OF TABERNACLES

MINISTRY IN PERAEA

THE RAISING OF LAZARUS AND PALM SUNDAY

3. THE PASSION AND DEATH OF JESUS

4. THE RESURRECTION AND APPEARANCES OF JESUS

Printed in Italy
Scuola Grafica Istituto San Gaetano
Vicenza